W9-CZM-374

CO-OPERATIVE
DEMOCRACY

OTHER BOOKS ON COOPERATION
BY J. P. WARBASSE

WHAT IS COOPERATION—Vanguard Press, 1927

THE DOCTOR AND THE PUBLIC—Harper & Brothers, 1935

COOPERATION A WAY OF PEACE—Harper & Brothers, 1939, 1947

PROBLEMS OF COOPERATION—Cooperative League, U.S.A., 1942

THE COOPERATIVE WAY—A METHOD OF WORLD RECONSTRUCTION—Barnes & Noble, 1946

PAMPHLETS

WHAT IS CONSUMERS COOPERATION

COOPERATIVE EDUCATION

COOPERATIVE MEDICINE

THE SURE WAY IS THE QUICK WAY

ORGANIZATION AND MANAGEMENT OF COOPERATIVE ASSOCIATIONS

ORGANIZATION AND MANAGEMENT OF CONSUMERS COOPERATIVE HOUSING ASSOCIATIONS

THE SOCIALISTIC TREND

A SHORT HISTORY OF THE COOPERATIVE LEAGUE

NATION-WIDE ORGANIZATION OF CONSUMER COOPERATION IN THE UNITED STATES

A NATIONAL COOPERATIVE COLLEGE

THE MEANING OF CONSUMER COOPERATION

THE SMALL COMMUNITY—THE HOPE OF CIVILIZATION

THE FOOD STORE, A HEALTH CENTER

THE ACQUISITIVE STRUGGLE

WHO OWNS THE COOPERATIVE SURPLUS SAVINGS

GASOLINE REFINERY, built in 1940 at Phillipsburg, Kansas. This is one of the ten gasoline refineries owned and operated by the consumer co-operatives of the United States. These refineries have a capacity of 70,000 barrels a day. The oil from which they produce gasoline comes from 489 consumer-owned oil wells. It is carried through 1,664 miles of consumer-owned pipe-lines. The gasoline is distributed at cost to the members of these cooperatives.

CO-OPERATIVE DEMOCRACY

THROUGH VOLUNTARY ASSOCIATION
OF THE PEOPLE AS CONSUMERS

*A Discussion of the Co-operative Movement,
Its Philosophy, Methods, Accomplishments,
and Possibilities, and Its Relation to the
State, to Science, Art, and Commerce, and
to Other Systems of Economic Organization*

by JAMES PETER WARBASSE

President Emeritus,
The Co-operative League of the U. S. A.

FIFTH EDITION

30130

HARPER & BROTHERS PUBLISHERS

NEW YORK AND LONDON

I. M. HODGES LIBRARY
WHARTON COUNTY JUNIOR COLLEGE
WHARTON, TEXAS

CO-OPERATIVE DEMOCRACY

FIFTH EDITION

Copyright, 1936, 1942, 1947, by Harper & Brothers

Printed in the United States of America

*All rights in this book are reserved.
No part of the book may be reproduced in any
manner whatsoever without written permission
except in the case of brief quotations embodied
in critical articles and reviews. For information
address Harper & Brothers*

I-W

DEDICATED
TO
THE CONSUMERS

Who are everybody
And who are learning to supply their needs co-
operatively, with the view of ultimately creating
a co-operative democracy, through which to
control and administer for their mutual service
their social economic functions, independent of
the political state

334
W197co

- 30130

CONTENTS

v

PREFACE

IN this book co-operation is discussed as a practical, working method, which is organizing society upon a voluntary, nonpolitical basis. It is seen building within the present economic system something fundamentally different. It is giving man another attitude toward industry and toward his fellow men. This it is doing by slow and evolutionary steps.

Co-operation is not found to be a palliative for smoothing the path of the poor, nor a scheme for softening the conflict between capital and labor. While it does, to a degree, ameliorate present ills, it is not a method of reform for patching up the existing order of society.

To bear witness to these assertions, I have invoked the organized co-operators in some sixty countries who even now seem to be building, quietly and without ostentation, this different kind of civilization.

The main purpose of this book is to discover a way, through the voluntary association of neighbors, by which the individual may save himself from being enveloped and dominated by centralized power, and by which he may preserve his personal freedom without relinquishing personal responsibility.

Other schemes of social reorganization aim to make conversion and rapid change of social structure; examination of co-operation shows that it is deliberate, constant, and evolutionary.

Great social changes that are permanent are those brought about by means which are similar in character to the end sought. Co-operation exemplifies this. By applying certain methods, in a series of smaller co-operative societies, a great co-operative society, employing these very methods, is ultimately attained.

I have tried to show that, if a co-operative democracy is to be reached, it will come about, not by voting, not by sabotage, not by the general strike, not by taxing, nor through revolution or the class struggle, but by putting into operation co-operative democracy—first on a small scale, and then ever increasing and expanding. Like results come from like causes. Desirable ends are reached by desirable means. Co-operative democracy may thus be attained by building co-operation here and now. Voting may bring a political change; sabotage may drive capitalist owners from industry; the general strike may cause industrial upheaval; taxing may equalize wealth; but not one of these brings a permanent economic change. Permanent results come by evolution.

In the co-operative movement a structure is seen in process of building which holds a promise of efficiency for the future. People are traveling the road, training themselves on the way by doing precisely the things that will be done in a different, and maybe better, society to come.

The student of co-operation, if he is not already familiar with the facts, will discover with some amazement its actual extent. This revelation is bound to interest anyone who is seeking a tested method for the reorganization of society. In many of the twenty-three different countries in which I have observed co-operation in action, I have for months at a time lived and traveled among co-operative societies, where I have seen many thousands of co-operators—occupying their co-operative houses, supplied by their own stores, working in their own industries, financed through their own banks, entertained in their own theaters. I have seen children sporting in their own playgrounds. And I have realized that I was in actual contact with a demonstration of that very society for which utopian theorists hope as a remote possibility and strive to attain by some means other than by building it.

It is a source of surprise that this movement is not better known and understood. There is not only a noteworthy lack of public information of the accomplishments of co-operation, but a lack of understanding of its theory and philosophy among many teachers and students of economic and social problems.

The events of the world at the present time constitute a doleful picture. People are dejected and discouraged. The news in the papers is depressing. A collapse of every relic of civilization seems imminent. The leadership in world affairs is inept, confused, and often vicious. This can be attributed to the influence of the price and profit economy that dominates the situation. Bad news, impending calamities, and disaster sell papers and make money for periodicals and books. The political systems, as well as the economic system, are ineffective and outmoded.

Despite all this, there are noble ideas, there are honest and capable people, and there are splendid and constructive events taking place every day and hour. But these are not in the political field nor are they newsy occurrences. The constructive things going on everywhere in the world are quiet events. They lack dramatic or tragic appeal. They are not at the hands of the captains of industry, the diplomats, the politicians, the admirals, and the generals. They are events created by the common people. Constructive events are changing the picture of the world before our very eyes, and yet are scarcely seen. Not only are intelligent plans for world betterment proposed and formulated, but they are being put into operation. Not only are lofty ideals expressed, but they are in action. Not only are brotherhood, mutual aid, and self-help advocated, but they are to be seen in organized and practically promoted form in every country in the world. While injustices and the promotion of suffering are conspicuous, and their knowledge is in every mind, quiet and constructive virtues are scarcely noticed or even known. These significant but unostentatious events are described in this book.

The reader is asked to bear in mind that the material here presented is taken from a movement developing so rapidly that many of its facts and figures are out of date by the time the book is published. These facts, it should be understood, are presented here mainly for the purpose of explaining the philosophy of co-operation. Exact data should be sought in the co-operative yearbooks, reports, and current periodicals. The First Edition of this book was published in 1923. The Second Edition appeared in 1927. The Third Edition was published in 1936, and the Fourth Edition in 1942. The book has been translated into German, Japanese, Bulgarian, Chinese, Yugoslav, Turkish, French, Portuguese, and Spanish.

This present edition is brought out at the close of World War II. The effect of this war upon the co-operatives cannot yet be fully determined.

Attention is called to the fact that this book discusses the possibilities of co-operation. This means that in many situations the maximum or optimum of accomplishment is presented. Otherwise the ultimate possibilities could not be made clear. Unless this is understood, the reader may, in places, get the idea of a personal bias which is not intended. Where examples are needed to show the potentialities of the co-operative method, an average example might be given; but this would fall short of illustrating the attainable. I have attempted to compensate for this by introducing a chapter on the "Deficiencies of Co-operation" and by references to shortcomings and difficulties. But the purpose in view is to present co-operation in the light of its workability and, indeed, of its desirability as an economic method.

For the convenience of readers, the history and achievements of co-operation are placed together in the first part of the book. The conclusions which have been drawn are based on the facts here presented. Co-operation differs from other social theories; its philosophy grows out of its accomplishments.

I pay homage, for their illuminating discussions of this subject, to Dr. William King, Prof. Charles Gide, and the several other authors whose works are referred to in the appended Bibliography, who have contributed constructive thinking and added points of view which have opened the field to larger vision. To Agnes Dyer Warbasse, my wife, my obligation for advice, information, and inspiration transcends the possibilities of homage or public acknowledgment.

I have dealt with co-operation as a factor, moving toward a different society of the future, and as an element in a social complex. I have attempted not to isolate it, but to discuss it in its relation to existing conditions.

JAMES PETER WARBASSE

Gladheim
Woods Hole, Massachusetts
15 June, 1947

Part I
PRINCIPLES, METHODS, AND
ACCOMPLISHMENTS OF CO-OPERATION

Chapter I

THE MEANING AND METHODS OF CO-OPERATION

SERVICE, NOT PROFITS

OUR ancestors, some thousands of years ago, manufactured nothing. They lived by what nature produced. They reaped, but they did not sow. Then through long ages they learned to make things. They learned also to make events happen. The user made the thing he used. The consumer made his bow and arrows, he wove his fish nets, he braided his rope, he fashioned his garments from the skins of animals. While he worked, he was thinking of the efficiency of the thing he was creating.

The motive was not to make something that looked as though it would serve the purpose, but to make something that would truly give the best results to the user. With this motive, the product could contain nothing false. The maker's life depended upon its quality. There was no reason to do poor work; there was every reason to do good work. The man, while he toiled, thought of the use to which the object would be put. His thoughts ran ahead of his work. He had joy in the task itself, joy in inventing better ways of making better things, and above all, joy in the play of his imagination. This was long ago. The intellectual development of the human race was making progress then. Our ancestor who sat at the edge of a grove before his hut and fashioned a mortar in which to grind his corn was occupied in an intellectual and elevating pursuit. He was making something for use. His hand was working with his brain.

Generations came and passed. Handicraft, and that means mindcraft, reached a stage at which men could make more things than they needed for themselves. Experts and specialists developed. Still the simple and primitive motive of producing things for use remained supreme. A principle so salutary and natural is long-lived. To think of the use to which the article is to be put, to think of its service to the user, had become a tradition which would not die. And so down through the Middle Ages came this

3

idea, to hallow the toil of the worker. Animated by it, the artisan pursued his work upon an intellectual plane that made a better man of him every day he labored.

The guild workmen of the thirteenth century, although they were producing things which they sold to other people, were still near enough to that primitive motive of direct service to be inspired by it. The speculative profit-thought had not yet wholly possessed the minds of the guildsmen. The artisan and artist were still thinking of the finished article and of the user in his enjoyment of it. Work was joined with a great ethical principle. Men found joy in their tasks. They created good things and beautiful things. They sang at their labor. The products of their labor sang. Stradivarius made violins.

Until the early part of the nineteenth century, the influence of the old craft ideals was felt throughout industry. The thought persisted. It would not perish. Much of the reason that inspired production was the creation of things that were beautiful and useful.

Then this idea began to wane. Industry ceased to produce things because they were useful and beautiful, and proceeded to produce because somebody could be induced to buy them for more than they cost. A new motive entered upon the scene.

The steam engine, the power loom, and the iron industry begot the discovery that profits could be made by owning machines and hiring other people to run them. This made it possible to secure income and livelihood, not by the performance of service but by the ownership of property. What was still more potent for change of thought and action was the fact that the motive of production, not for use but for profit, became the dominant purpose of industry.

The economic life of society has now become largely organized on this profit basis. Workers have lost interest in the social value of the things they are doing. People who are performing the services of the world are working for profit. "How much money can be made out of the job? How much will the consumer pay?" These are the questions now. The man who owns the machinery asks, "How little can I pay labor? How cheaply can the thing be made? How much can I get from the consumer?" The worker asks, "How much money can I get for the least labor?" These facts may be verified by attending a meeting of a merchants' association, a manufacturers' association, a marketing association, or a trade-union. The consumer's business has been neglected. People have organized to get wages, with little regard to making for themselves or getting direct access to the things they need to give them life. Life has been neglected in the interest of wages and profits.

The chief interest is in trade. It consists in buying commodities or labor at the lowest possible price and selling at the highest practicable price. Among the things that are produced and distributed are things that the people must have in order to live; but their real value is a secondary matter. That is true, whether people are buying goods to sell to customers; or buying land, fertilizer, and seeds to sell as grain, cabbages, or pigs; or buying food to put into their bodies to sell as labor. "How much can I make—how much difference between my costs and my selling price can I get?"—this has become the great question.

As a result of the profit motive, society is permeated with the idea that work is really an object of life. The people who own the machinery of production and distribution are animated by the same idea as the slaveowner. They glorify work. Work is cried up as the great virtue. The lazy are objects of reproach. The ceaseless turning out of profits depends upon the perpetuation of this idea. The workers, the schools, and the press teach that labor is the exalted occupation of man. But the work they exalt is not work to satisfy human wants; it is for a different purpose.

The business man comes home tired after a day's work. At what has he been working? He has been competing with other businessmen, who are trafficking in people's needs. This he has been doing, not to supply the wants of those who needed the eggs, clothing, cigarettes, bonds, patent medicine, or machinery that he sold, but to win for himself the difference between the cost and selling price. Service has become a by-product of the main purpose.

This profit urge is by no means the peculiar possession of any one class. The workingman, as well as the capitalist, is animated by it. The capitalistic motive of production for profit is cherished by the workers who will fight and die for it. Working for wages or profit, as the great aim, with scant regard to the service value of the function, is the level to which humanity has come in these past one hundred and fifty years.

People are giving their energy and using their most valuable time each day, not in living, not in doing the things that would make life most worth while, but in striving to earn the money with which to do these things. And the money that most earn scarcely provides the bare necessities of life.

While the average man is working on his job, his mind is at work on the side. He has flitting thoughts of life. He is thinking of the life to which he may buy access with the wages he obtains for his labor. Food, clothes, housing, music, drama, education, art, self-expression, love, rest—these are the things he wants. His great satisfactions are in his life as a consumer.

If nature produced everything ready-made, if bread and shoes grew by the wayside, the consuming function would be supreme. That day will never come; but the day may come when the worker will make bread which is to be for a fellow worker who is making shoes for him, and when both are mutually bound by common interests as consumers. The consuming function is the main source of joy. Eating the bread and wearing the shoes will always be greater satisfactions than making them.

In the present society, work is not life. When the worker has created wealth with his labor, and has received money in exchange, what will the money buy? That is the question. The worker has not been paid until he spends his wages. When he exchanges his money for life, only then does he know how much his labor has won for him. Not labor but life, and life in greater abundance, is the human need.

I hope that no one will impute to me a disbelief in the worth of work. The work which is here questioned is that done not directly for the sake of the task and its value to the worker or to the consumer, but done for the sake of the money to be got from the consumer. Such work for profit alone will naturally be shirked and slighted. But we have also to reckon with the creative instinct and the hunger for expression which have grown up as necessary results of the hunger to consume. Who consumes what others make, and who does not himself perform service for others, according to his ability, is a thief, and sooner or later suffers the moral and physical consequences of his pilfering.

Finally, there is the physiological value of action. The muscular and nervous systems are built for work. Man is a working animal. He eats by the sweat of his brow. Wherever nature or his fellow man constantly produces for him, he decays. And wherever he constantly serves his fellow man, who does not serve him, he decays.

THE CO-OPERATIVE WAY

Never again in modern society can man go back to the primitive method of personally producing for himself, except in a small way. Specialists, the machine, and commerce have made it possible to get better and cheaper production outside of himself. But he can approach the ancient and natural method by uniting with his neighbors to own and control the machinery that produces for them, and themselves working together with that machinery.

There is in society a way which is adapting the old principle of service to the present economic system. It is the co-operative way. It is making for the evolution of a society in which service is the dominant motive of industry. It is seen in action in associations of consumers, called co-operative societies.

A consumer co-operative society is a voluntary association in which the people organize democratically to supply their needs through mutual action, and in which the motive of production and distribution is service, not profit. In the co-operative way the continuous tendency is toward the creation of a social structure capable of supplanting, to a large degree, both profit-making industry and the compulsory political state. It begins with the people as consumers and represents the individual as an absorber and user of the things that have been produced. This means that its first concern is for the human being in the use and enjoyment of things. It begins with the home and the family. The primary hypothesis of co-operation is that the consumers are everybody, and that all the machinery of industry and the organization of society should be for them. When this supremacy of interest is brought to pass, it is found that the consumers have become the producers and that the interests of producer and consumer are one.

Beginning with the consumer, sex distinctions are not in evidence. Co-operation is concerned for all women as well as for all men. Recognizing the family especially, it begins with that existing organization in which the man and the woman are nearest to equality and in which the interest of children is a matter of supreme concern. Not as workers or voters, but as homemakers, husband and wife, father and mother, hungry for the joys of life, co-operation organizes them as consumers. It makes use of the simple and primitive impulse of mutual aid, by which species and races have survived and the social qualities have been developed and preserved.

Out of this is seen growing a different form of society within the structure of the old. The co-operative method is creating a social organization, which is becoming integrated throughout the world, and which, when developed into a great co-operative society, constitutes a co-operative democracy. In this book, by co-operative democracy will be understood the organization of the social fabric upon a co-operative basis. We may speak of it also as co-operative society.

Co-operation builds gradually as it goes. The people first organize, plan, and work together to supply their wants. In the development of co-operative democracy, meeting new needs, performing more and larger functions, the transference of the control of industry from the hands of the few to the hands of the many goes on without social disturbance. Obvious benefits follow as it proceeds. It is the orderly merging of one system into another. Although its end is the very end which economic revolutionists seek, its method is free from violence and cataclysm. It is the peaceful revolution in action. Like the steady coral deposit, it builds up the new structure; and like the constant drop, it wears away the old. As co-operative democracy advances, the people who were engaged in profit business, and who are capable of making the transfer, go over into the field of co-operation and find their occupation there.

The co-operative movement has not an uncontested field. As profit business melts away, under the influence of its own inherent tendencies making for its decay, the rise of co-operation encounters another opposing force. There stands the socializing state, bent upon performing service, aiming to carry on the industries and to supply the needs of the people which formerly had been supplied by profit business. As co-operation expands, the functions of the state decline. The tendency toward the vanishing state and the vanishing profit method in industry may each be seen in the presence of an expanding co-operative movement.

Since the first half of the nineteenth century, distributive societies have been organized in practically every country in the world, according to certain definite co-operative principles. In some forty countries the distributive societies conducting stores have united to organize national federations or wholesales. Most of these have engaged in importing and manufacturing. In some instances the co-operative wholesale societies have become the largest mercantile business in the land. These societies are now engaged in practically every business which supplies human needs.

Before 1939, in a dozen European countries fully a third of the population was connected with the co-operative societies. Half the families in Denmark, Great Britain, and northern Switzerland belonged to these co-operative consumer organizations.

In hundreds of towns and villages in Europe the number of members of co-operative societies exceeded the number of families. This steady growth since 1844 may be interpreted as a movement toward co-operative democracy. In Europe the growth has been faster than the increase in population.

This co-operative way since its beginning has been steadily moving on toward production, after distribution is first mastered. It has never experienced a setback which was not overcome in time. Its increase in membership and business is in an unreceding upward curve.

THE MANNER OF DEVELOPMENT OF CO-OPERATIVE SOCIETY

Consumer co-operative societies are usually formed by people who live in the same community or have similar interests. They organize a society to run a store, laundry, bank, or other business. This is to supply some need which they think they themselves can better supply. Usually the business is incorporated to limit the liability of the individuals. The members elect a board of directors and often other committees such as a committee for auditing, recreations, education, etc. The directors appoint a manager and other employees. Usually directors give their time gratuitously. Some societies pay them for the meetings they attend. In large societies an executive board is salaried and the members give all their time to the business of the society. The meetings of the members observe the parliamentary principles that make for democracy of control and administration. They are usually held quarterly, although some societies hold only an annual members' meeting, while others meet as often as once a month. The directors and committees meet frequently. Most societies publish or receive a co-operative paper or magazine through which the members are kept informed. Many have bulletins in their places of business for purposes of information. Lectures and educational work are a part of the usual program of these organizations. Unless the society is formed for a single special purpose, it aims to expand and increase the functions it performs.

It would be difficult to mention any useful business or service that is not undertaken by co-operative societies. Naturally the most common business is the distributive retail store. These stores are found handling all the things the people want, from pins to automobiles. The total amount of service performed and of goods handled is large. In some countries the co-operators own and administer many of the largest existing stores, warehouses, and factories.

As an example of the undertakings into which co-operative societies enter, the society of Leeds, England, may be cited. It is not the oldest nor the largest in England, but is typical. The city of Leeds has 430,000 population. The Leeds Cooperative Society has over 110,000 members representing more than half the families in the city. The society has over 250 branches.[1]

[1] These consisted in 1936 of 98 grocery stores, 77 butcher shops, 19 dry goods stores, 19 shoe stores, 16 coalyards, 6 men's furnishing stores, 5 fish and vegetable markets, and 6 farms in the suburbs. Besides these, it has a shoe factory, a furniture factory, a brush factory, a musical instrument factory, a jewelry factory, a flour mill, a paper bag factory, a laundry, a carpet cleaning and dye works, a leather goods factory, a cake and cracker bakery, a ham, bacon, and lard factory, a clothing factory, a hosiery factory, and other industries. It produces 20,000 tons of flour a year. The bread bakery produces 1,000,000 loaves a year. The shoe factory makes 70,000 pairs of shoes yearly, and repairs 130,000 a year. It owns many horses, wagons, carts, vans, automobiles, 183 railroad cars, 27 barges for coal and grain, and 1 steamboat. It has over 3,000 employees.

It distributes about $20,000,000 worth of goods a year and produces $2,500,000 worth of these in its own factories. The British Co-operative Wholesale, owned by the consumer societies, supplies it with an equal amount. Its surplus-savings ("profits") over expenses amount to $2,700,000 a year. This business is done on a share capital of $7,500,000. Shares are $5 each. Each member is required to take five shares, which may be paid for by allowing the savings-returns to accumulate. No member may hold more than forty shares. Its life insurance department pays over 1,000 claims a year, amounting to $250,000. The insurance is given free to all members. Its general banking business has over 50,000 depositors, and its "Penny Bank" has 10,000 depositors. Besides its commercial activities, the society has recreational houses; libraries; meeting halls; restaurants; a printing plant; schools; touring clubs; and clubs for nature study, literature, music, and art. It spends over $35,000 a year on educational work. It adds about 2,500 new members a year. Its Women's Guild has over twenty branch locals. These figures are for 1936. This society was organized by a small number of workingmen. Its buildings are among the finest and most substantial structures in the city.

The beautiful city of Basel, Switzerland, has 215,000 population in 70,000 families. The Basel Cooperative Society has 65,000 member families representing 92 per cent of the population. The society provides most of the people's food. It has a large department store, 193 grocery stores, 44 meat shops, 12 shoe stores, bakeries, banks, and dwelling houses. Supplying the members with goods at market prices, it gives them back a savings-return of 8½ per cent. Pictures comparable to this can be seen in hundreds of European towns.

When enough societies exist, in any country, and the consuming or purchasing power of the members becomes great enough, they federate to form a national organization. There are two forms of national organization: (1) a union or federation for purposes of education, propaganda, research, protection, and advice; and (2) a union for commercial purposes and manufacturing, commonly called a "wholesale." In many countries, as in Sweden, the two are combined in the same national organization. In this event, the wholesale is either a department of the union or the two departments are carried on in close connection. In general, the unions and wholesales are conducted in much the same manner as the local societies. The Rochdale principles are observed. The membership of unions and wholesales consists of societies instead of individuals; and the member societies control them just as do the individuals the local societies. Delegates are elected by the latter to represent them in the affairs of the unions.

The unions and wholesales are administered by boards of directors elected by the constituent societies. These directors in the case of the large wholesales are full-time salaried officials. They elect a president and other officers and appoint superintendents, managers, and experts, and are required to report to the membership and to meetings of the delegates of the constituent societies. Officers and delegates are elected for short terms.

The national wholesale in the course of time finds that it is buying so much from manufacturers and is importing so much that it takes the next natural step and organizes factories and importing agencies. The factories likewise develop the need of so much raw material that land is acquired for its production. Thus co-operative wholesales are found owning forests for the production of lumber and of wood for their furniture, box, and match factories, farm lands for the production of food, coal mines, and fishing fleets on the seas. All this proceeds gradually and in the course of economic evolution. Production is in proportion to the known needs of groups of consumers who own and control the industries.

In this way has come about the development of manufacturing industries as well as the steadily increasing ownership of sources of raw material for the productive purposes of the consumer owners.

Retail societies usually begin with the distribution of the common personal and household things; but the less common needs also are provided for by the co-operative method. Co-operative housing societies are performing an important function in creating homes for the people. Co-operative banking and credit societies are conducted on the nonprofit basis, giving all the advantages of the service to the patrons—the depositors and the borrowers.

Housing societies and banking societies, the same as distributive societies, federate into national organizations.

The question may be asked: Is it possible for a democratic mass of people to organize, finance, control, and administer great and complicated industries involving large-scale production, employment of labor, the intricate problems of securing raw material, distribution of products, and the questions of finance, surrounded as they are by the powerfully organized and dominant competitive system of industry? The answer is that it is being done, and, in most cases, more successfully, more economically, and more efficiently than profit business is carried on. The mistake often made by the inquirer is to assume that the democratic mass *run* the business. They do not. They *control* the business. As we have seen, they elect a board of directors and the directors employ executives as experts to *run* the business. The elected representatives of the people perform a supervisory function, or make themselves administrative experts in their particular field.

Co-operation is a method whereby the democratically organized mass call to their service experts to serve the people. This is the essence of the movement. One is impressed by this fact as he goes through co-operative industries and finds employed there the high grades of talent. He sees chemists with their well-equipped laboratories in the factories and warehouses. The employment of managers, accountants, clerks, and heads of departments is a matter of securing for the people the executives best fitted to serve them in these capacities. Physicians, surgeons, nurses, bacteriologists, apothecaries, machinists, editors, authors, architects, and technicians in all fields are employed by co-operative societies. The national unions and wholesales naturally have a still larger scope for experts. They are found employing all the above classes, and in addition skilled artisans of every trade.

Theoretical critics of co-operation suggest that individual members of the co-operative societies might be found "running to the factory, the warehouse, the laboratory, or the store and giving instructions to the employees." The stockholders in profit corporations do not do such meddlesome things; neither do co-operators.

The members of the co-operative society do something the stockholders of the profit corporation do not do. They have their membership meetings to discuss the details of the business from the standpoint of its service to them. The membership meeting of the co-operative society, whether local or national, is the nearest approach to the democratic control of industry in the interest of the consumers that has yet been devised. At these meetings any representative or employee of the members may be called before the people to report and to be subjected to questions. Through their elected representatives the control of the whole co-operative fabric comes back to these meetings of the members.

Co-operation is based upon the principle of centralized administration, in the interest of efficiency, and decentralized control, in the interest of democracy; whereas profit business practices centralized administration and centralized control in the interest of economic autocracy.

It is true there is much indifference; sometimes only a minority of the membership of local societies feel responsibility for the business. This deficiency is inherent in human character. But the people possess the power, and they are found exercising it when critical questions require their attention. There is something engendered by this form of organization that is characteristic: it is the co-operative spirit. These people have a realization that they are engaged in a beneficial social enterprise. They also are aware that the ownership and responsibility are theirs.

A feature of the co-operative organization is that it trains people to take the initiative in organizing, to assume the responsibility in administering and directing, and to create experts from their own ranks to carry on enterprises in their own interests. This is a matter of profound importance. There are ills inherent in the social psychology of today which are due to the spirit of profit-making. Possibly this will gradually fade away as education and participation in consumer co-operation progress and as new generations with a new psychology appear.

A significant result of the co-operative method is that it teaches people to administer their own affairs. That in itself proves useful. When the workingman buys at a private store, the private merchant gets the experience in the administration of a distributing industry. But when the workingman and his fellow workers start a store of their own to do their distributing to themselves, they get the experience. And when they carry on their own banking and insurance business, and organize their wholesale houses, and build their factories, and provide their own dwellings, theaters, and schools, telephones and transportation, they train themselves in their own affairs. They are then making themselves masters of industry. They are learning to carry on their own business in their own social interest. It is a constructive function.

Action-research characterizes the co-operative method. This means that the practices of co-operation are the product of direct contact with economic and social realities. Experience, trial, error, and tests result in the adoption of some methods and in the rejection of other methods. The co-operative way does not follow a predetermined philosophy; its philosophy is created out of the practices which it finds experimentally best to adopt. The co-operative way is a laboratory method, elastic, always growing and always changing, observing certain fundamentals which themselves are elastic.

THEORY AND METHOD

Co-operative democracy, since history began, has struggled for expression. In 1844 the Rochdale Pioneers, in England, formulated methods which were capable of being standardized and serving as the guide. It was not that they discovered anything new; co-operative societies, applying one or more of these methods which they adopted, had existed many years before the Rochdale period; but they combined the methods which time has proved essential to success.

The methods which they formulated and applied have come to be recognized as fundamental. The success of the movement has depended upon them. These Rochdale methods are:

1. Democracy of control.—Each member shall have one vote and no more.
2. Limited interest on capital.—Capital invested in the society, if it receive interest, shall receive not more than a fixed percentage which shall be not more than the prevalent rate.
3. Savings-returns.—If a surplus-saving ("profit") accrues from

the difference between the cost and the distribution price of commodities and services, after meeting expenses, paying interest (wages to capital), and setting aside reserve and other funds, the net surplus-saving shall be used according to the vote of the members either for the general good of the members, for beneficent social purposes, or returned to the patrons as savings-returns ("dividends") in proportion to their patronage.

The first of these methods helps to guarantee democracy. No individual or clique can easily get control. This differs from the practice of the profit corporations in which the individual has as many votes as he has shares of stock. Proxy voting is not permitted in the co-operative society. Where the membership is large and covers a wide area, the society is divided into districts, with district meetings and delegate representation at a central meeting. Democracy is the aim.

Democracy is more than a theory; it is a practical working method, necessary for the success of the co-operative way of business.

Modern capitalistic business has exalted property even above the interest of human beings. Before the courts in most countries, property rights are more jealously protected than human rights. Property can purchase either justice or injustice. Co-operation, on the other hand, stands for the recognition of human values. The two principles which co-operation has established—production and distribution for use and one vote for each member—are based on the placing of human interest above that of property. Production and distribution for use instead of for profit is a principle that now struggles for acceptance in the economic world.

The principle of one vote and no more for every member or shareholder of an economic enterprise is essential for the subordination of property to humanity. It is an ancient and natural practice.

The second method provides that the co-operative society cannot be used for purposes of capitalistic investment. No speculative profits are bestowed upon capital.

Co-operation does not provide a field for speculation. Money is put in the co-operative society by the member for a necessary purpose. It is not a means for getting return on capital in the capitalistic sense. There is no prospect of speculative dividends upon the investment, so dear to the investor in the stock of the profit-making corporation. Nor is there prospect of increase in the value of the shares, because in a co-operative society the number of shares is unlimited. They are bought and sold at par. In the co-operative society, it is not as an investor but as a consumer that one enjoys advantages. The value of organization is shifted from investor to consumer. The status of the investor becomes that of a mere lender. His loan is paid back to him as the reserve fund or surplus is developed, or when he leaves the society. Getting out of debt is always the aim.

As to the rate of interest paid on capital, the tendency is to hold it fixed and at a minimum, so that the speculative incentive to investment shall not prevail. Co-operation treats capital the same as capital treats labor; it hires it at the cheapest price. The capitalist system makes labor the servant of capital; the co-operative system makes capital the servant of labor. The interest rate paid shareholders is from 5 per cent down to 2½ per cent in Europe. In America, it is from 4 per cent down to 2 per cent. It is conceivable, and would be in the nature of co-operation, that interest be altogether eliminated. Interest is now paid because capitalistic business pays interest. In many co-operative societies no interest is paid. Money as a static thing, in such a case, no longer attracts money. The activities of the individual as a user and consumer, or as an employee, are the only means of obtaining the economic advantages of co-operative organization.

The third method abolishes the thing commonly called profits, by giving it back to the consumers who create it. Thus the business is carried on for service. Returning to the patrons who create it the difference between the cost and distributing price means production and distribution for use. The returning of this saving on the basis of patronage takes the profit motive out of industry.

The following methods are also commonly observed:

4. There shall be unlimited membership. No reason shall exclude a person from membership except that his membership would injure the society.
5. A co-operative society shall be composed of individuals who voluntarily join.
6. Business shall be done for cash.
7. A certain percentage of the funds shall be used for educational purposes in the field of co-operation.
8. There shall be political and religious neutrality.
9. Beginning with distribution or the rendering of service to the members, the society shall aim to expand its business into other fields of service, to produce the things the members need, and finally to secure access to raw materials.
10. Co-operative societies shall unite with neighboring co-operative societies to form a co-operative federation. Federations shall unite in districts, in states, nationally, and finally internationally.

Federation of societies prevents economic competition and hostility, avoids overlapping of jurisdiction, and makes possible mutual assistance among societies; for nonfederated societies, while they may be co-operative, are not co-operating, and are not a part of the co-operative movement, national or international.

The aim shall be to supply such needs of the members as a social organization can supply, to attain especially to the control of production, to encourage membership, to promote other societies, to create national organizations in every country, and to effect a union of the societies of the world into an international organization having the same common purpose as the primary societies.

In addition to the above methods, there are certain practices which are associated with them in co-operative administration. These are:

a. Each member patronizes the society in any commercial enterprise in which it engages.
b. Each member binds himself to the society by the investment of some of his capital or substance, if capital is needed.
c. Persons who have not capital to pay for initial stock may

allow the savings returns accruing from their patronage to
be applied to the payment for their share capital.

d. At each inventory, depreciation is charged off against the
property of the society.

e. Commodities usually are supplied to members at about the
prices prevailing in competing profit businesses.

There are many reasons for supplying commodities and service
at the prevalent market price and not at cost. One is the impossi-
bility of calculating cost at the time. The most important is that
such a policy supplies surplus capital for the business. It makes
expansion possible, permits assistance to other co-operatives, and
prevents a cause of competitive business hostility.[2]

Where the society needs capital, it is customary in the United
States to pay members their savings-returns in the form of stock
certificates instead of cash. This is an equitable method, for it
returns to the members an increase in their ownership of the
business and is a more direct way of getting money than by borrowing it from the members. They patronize themselves into the
ownership of property. They gain by spending. At this point it
becomes obvious that co-operation represents private ownership.
Co-operation is private business as contrasted with state or public
business. It is an outstanding example of free enterprise.

Co-operative societies do not *sell* to their members; they *produce, buy,* and *distribute* for their members. The members put in
the necessary initial capital with which to buy goods for themselves. The goods are bought. When each member goes to the
shop to get some of the goods, which are his and for which he
has already paid, he again leaves with the manager an amount of
money sufficient to replace what he takes away. To this he adds
the difference between the cost price and the current selling price,
and apparently pays the current retail price. This difference is
essentially a loan to the society. It constitutes his saving. It is
given back to him as a surplus-saving at the end of a period.

The same principle that applies to commodities applies to serv-

[2] See the Author's pamphlet, *Who Owns the Cooperative Surplus Savings,*
1945.

ices—produced, bought, and supplied. It applies to banking, insurance, health protection, recreations, and everything else.

Sometimes people co-operate to make only one purchase such as a shipload of coal or a house. After the first payment, the transaction is closed. But they have not sold themselves anything.

Co-operative societies do not aim to make profits. Their primary purpose is not increase of income but decrease of outgo. They make savings. The profit merchant buys from a second party and sells to a third party from whom he makes profit. The co-operative society is its own third party. People who unite their capital to buy more cheaply do not make profit from one another.

Co-operators have made the mistake of using the language of profit business. The old nomenclature is not applicable to co-operation. "Sales," "profits," "rebates," and "dividends" are no part of co-operative business. The co-operative society makes surplus-savings and gives back savings-returns to its members. Dealings with nonmembers introduce another element; here the transactions are profit-making and the nomenclature of profit business may be employed. But this is not the purpose of a co-operative society.

Additional capital is developed by distributing at a price which gives a surplus-saving. This accumulates in the treasury, and every three, six, or twelve months it is reported upon to the members and disposed of. After setting aside funds for interest, expansion, reserve, education, and other purposes, the balance is applied to the general social benefit of the members, or it is returned to the members in proportion to their patronage. The profit-making stock corporation returns this surplus to the stockholders in proportion to their ownership of stock; the co-operative corporation returns it in proportion to patronage. The question had always been, "Should the profit, the unearned increment, the surplus value, go to the stockholders or to the workers in the industry?" The co-operative method says, "To neither; but to the consumers who create it by paying too much."

Thus we see the members of the co-operative society receiving back a part of the money accumulated from their patronage. The British call it "dividend"; the Germans, "return benefit"; the French, "returned overcharge"; the Americans, "savings-return."

Its size depends upon patronage. The large family that has spent most with the society receives back most. In Great Britain many families find that the dividend suffices to pay their house rent. Some families use the dividends to purchase a home or to educate the children. In Great Britain, the dividend paid on purchases averages about 10 per cent. The family that makes all its purchases from a successful society often saves 20 per cent as a result of the existence of the society. This does not mean that a dividend of that amount is paid. It means total savings in fair prices, weights and measures, and other benefits accruing from a society connected with its own manufacturing wholesale. The saving calculated on investment is still greater.

Also there are the additional advantages of insurance, recreations, and education which the use of collective capital makes possible. Many co-operative consumers save not only the retailer's profit but the profits that would have gone to wholesalers, jobbers, commission houses, and manufacturers. Some make an additional saving in transportation costs by virtue of their societies' ownership of shipping facilities.

Many societies encourage their members not to draw out their savings-returns but to leave them with the society as loan capital to receive interest. The banking departments of many societies are built up by these funds. Millions of working people are accumulating snug savings in this way. Co-operation may be described as a means of shunting off the golden stream of profits from the hands of traders into the pockets of the consumers. The saving of co-operation is not the saving of privation so strongly recommended to the poor; it is saving by spending. The more the co-operator spends, the more he saves. Many co-operators in the United States have been able to immigrate to the new country with the "dividends" from the European "store." These people are convinced co-operators; they have found from experience what it does for them. They know that had they made their same purchases at the profit store, there would have been no dividends for them. The lesson is simple and easily grasped. The profit of other business has become transformed into their savings.

To what does all this come? What is the end toward which co-operation is moving? As it expands, it would seem that the result might be a state of society in which the ownership of property by an individual cannot be employed as the prevalent method of escaping the performance of service. The result, it would seem, is to set everybody to work, to glorify service instead of property, to eliminate the parasitic profiteer and the exploited proletariat, and by so doing to establish not the dictatorship of the proletariat but the dictatorship of humanity.

Briefly, this is what the consumers organized in co-operation tend to do in the economic world:

1. Substitute the service motive for the profit motive.
2. Make impossible the large privileged incomes from rent, interest, high salaries, speculation, and dividends.
3. Make more people workers.
4. Make more people owners.
5. Encourage thriftiness and the sense of responsibility that go with ownership.
6. Set the people as neighbors working together for their common good.
7. Train the people to administer their own industries in their own interest.
8. Substitute mutual aid for rivalry and antagonism.
9. Win back for the people the long-lost control of their food supply and of their other natural needs.
10. Decentralize the control over the lives of the people and place that control with the individual, the family, and the local community.
11. Lessen the need of governmental functions and thereby promote the decline of the dominance of the political state.

THE POSITION OF THE ORGANIZED CONSUMERS

Theoretically, consumer co-operation is based on the interests of all the people. For this reason, it should not recognize classes or create class antagonisms. It does not condemn profit business. It recognizes the value of the methods of business administration which have been worked out, and then it proceeds to make use of them in the interest of all.

There is a social morality in the organization of consumers which is, perhaps, more important than can easily be conceived. Although the consumers organize for their mutual interest, their interests are wide and permanent rather than circumscribed and temporary. The consuming masses are interested in the total good of society, for they are society. It will be found that they are willing to defer immediate advantages for future good. Experience has shown that the organized consumers concede to others when such concessions make for harmony and the public welfare. This attitude is different from that of other economic movements which are mainly concerned for their own circumscribed class and which are often at the expense of the public. This is not because consumers are unlike other mortals, but perhaps because their outlook is broader, since they embrace all humanity and all human interests and classes.

Profit business can influence the demands of the consumers to a certain degree, but the public is not wholly plastic. Should the people decide that an exclusive vegetable diet should be used, the beef trust and the organized workers in the meat industry would be organized in vain. The consumer's word is the last word. When the people preferred oil lamps, the candle industry faded out; when they preferred to buy gas and electricity, the lamp business went down. When the people find a way to get their power and heat out of the sun, the atom, the wind, the tides, or the streams, coal with its dirt and smoke will cease to be an economic factor and the unions of coal miners will have no further reason for existence. But the organization of consumers is fundamental and permanent.

There are no vicissitudes and fluctuations in store for the organized consumer, caused by improvements and advancements. Every useful invention, every laborsaving device, is in the interest of the consumers. Nothing good need be suppressed. The consumers' interests move always forward. They ultimately will decide what uses shall be made of the earth. The decision rests with them. They are the natural authority.

Whatever evil befalls a people, the consumers bear the brunt. Many of the disorders that are disturbing the world today spring largely from the measures which are taken by profit-making interests and the governments which are their agents to defeat this natural tendency of the consumers to control their own affairs. Tariffs, passports, visas, armies, and navies are artificial barriers erected by governments and often prevent people from co-operating in their own behalf.

There are many tests which may be applied to the co-operative principle. The first and most natural test is that which contrasts the co-operative method with the profit method of carrying on business.

In the co-operative society, the owners are the consumers, and the industry is carried on wholly for them. It was their money that started it, and any advantages accruing from the industry are theirs. Customers who own the business are jealous of its success. Pride in the enterprise is for its patrons; and the patrons maintain the business. All business is addressed to them.

Where proprietor and customers are one and the same, a simplification of business is attained. Business then changes its nature; it becomes distribution, production, or other activity for the purpose of service. It possesses the simple and primitive character of doing things to supply a need. It enlarges into a greater social organism the family, home, and garden, in which were once produced the family food and clothing. When the co-operative store is not succeeding or is threatened with disaster, there is an organized mass anxious to protect and save it. Owner and patron are willing to make sacrifices in its behalf. When the interest in front of the counter is the same as that behind the counter, an effective moral principle is introduced into business.

The co-operative store is a social unit made up of many individuals with one main interest; the profit store is a dual enterprise divided between two interests which are fundamentally antagonistic. People have no motive to cheat themselves; it is the other who cheats them. People have every motive to help themselves; the best help the other gets must come likewise from himself. In the co-operative store the masters serve the masters.

Everybody is a consumer and a consumer all the time. He is wholly a consumer in infancy, old age, when sick, and during the nonworking hours. Nearly everything produced is made to be consumed. Food, clothes, and houses, if not used, are futile. In the

fields of art and science, which have their value in the exercise
and in the opportunity for expression which they give the individual, production is largely for the producer, who becomes a
consumer in their joys and satisfactions. This is true of the recreations and leisure-time activities. Action here is for the enjoyment
of the body and the mind.

Production is work; consumption is pleasure. People produce
because they have to; they consume because they want to. Science
and invention are rapidly changing this relationship. Production
is becoming easier. Less and less labor is required. In time an
hour or so a day of labor from each worker will suffice to produce all that is needed. Science and the machine will do the work.
As civilization advances, labor will grow less and the joys and
satisfactions of consumption will increase. The important things
will be products of leisure. They will have a consumative as well
as a productive value to the producer. Leisure, not work, is the
aim of civilization.

In the field of labor and services for others, justice is most possible in that society which approaches nearest to that condition in
which each individual is a producer as well as a consumer. He
who produces more than he consumes is exploited to the degree
of the difference; and he who consumes what others produce, to
a degree more than he produces, is a parasite to just the extent of
the difference. It is to the abolition of this exploitation and this
parasitism that the co-operative method addresses itself.

The performance of service may be harmonized and equalized
with the consumption of things. This harmonizing of labor and
consumption is an aim of the co-operative method. An ideal of
the co-operative democracy is that the craftsman be employed by
the society to perform the best work he can, to make the best
things he can. His living is guaranteed by a salary. The things he
makes are not sold in the market for profit. They belong to the
society for which he works and of which he is an equal member.
The members who use the products of the society pay the price
they cost. Work under these circumstances is true service. The
worker gets all the value of the wealth he creates, minus what is
reserved for the social and the common purposes in which he

shares. The service which the individual performs gives him his standing in the co-operative democracy.

Co-operative business is nonprofit business because the "profits" are given back to the members who create them. They are abolished. This is true in retailing, in federated co-operative business, called "wholesaling," in manufacturing, and in the services. But profit is made by the co-operative employee. Here is the same profit motive as prevails throughout profit business. The worker produces his labor at the lowest possible cost by supplying his needs co-operatively so far as possible. His body is a profit-making industry. He buys food, housing, and clothing at the lowest price to produce labor power which he sells at the highest price he can get. In making the difference between the two prices he is animated by the same motives as the capitalistic manufacturer. He is called the "ultimate consumer," but the ultimate consumer who works for wages is engaged in profit business.

The profit motive will be eliminated when the co-operative employee receives no stipulated wage but takes what he needs from the co-operative society whenever he needs it, and desists from work when he will. This is the condition that existed in the primitive agricultural family back in the days when the farm was run to produce things for the consumption of the family—when nothing was bought or sold. It is a condition prevailing in many families today and in certain religious and economic orders. The co-operative way is moving in this direction—toward a civilization without price or profit.

The word "profit" is often used to denote "advantage" or "enjoyment." With that meaning every worth-while aim is to get "profit." In this discussion "profit" is used in the economic sense of the difference between two prices. In this sense co-operatives are not run for profit but for the service of the members. But the co-operative employee is in business for profit. In the chapters on co-operation and labor we shall see how his relationship to the co-operative that employs him differs from the relationships in profit industry.

Co-operation is radical. Those who desire that the prevalent economic and social conditions continue to be dominant should not enter the co-operative movement.

As any movement grows older and becomes established, it tends to become conservative. But neither age nor success seems to deprive co-operation of its fundamentally radical character. The conduct of directors and managers in large wholesales and other commercial departments of co-operation seems conservative. This conservative tincture is natural. A movement which must carry on intimate relations with capitalistic commerce cannot proclaim its radicalism. The directors of the great national wholesale societies are prone to talk like conventional businessmen. Their duties are peculiar and difficult. But whatever may be the outward signs displayed by representatives of the movement who come in contact with the capitalistic world, the fact is not altered that these societies are carrying out the dream of the Rochdale Pioneers—they are radically changing the methods of business.

The co-operative movement takes a positive stand. It frankly asserts that it means a change in the motive and method of industry. That it does not compromise is to be seen in every country. This position is well illustrated in the inaugural address by M. Llewelyn Davies before the Fifty-fourth Congress of the British Cooperative Union, of which she was president. She said:

"These two ideas, democratic control of industry and the abolition of profit-making, mark out co-operation as nothing less than a revolution, so fundamental, vital, and transforming is the change it is effecting in the economic structure of society. It is obvious that co-operation is far more than a reformist movement. We are working for no patchwork modifications, for no 'reconciliation of capital and labor,' for no 'infusion of a better spirit' into old industrial forms. We are laying the foundations of a new industrial civilization. . . . Co-operation is surely subversive enough for the violent revolutionary, orderly enough for the pacifist reformer. It holds the glamour of future possibilities for the idealist, while at the same time the most practical materialist could not reasonably be dissatisfied when he notes what has already been accomplished."

An eminent economist recently has written: "The growth of the consumers' co-operative movement has been one of the relatively unnoticed marvels of the past generation."

The radical tendency of this movement is not wholly in the supplanting of the profit method in business; its influence, in the

direction of the elimination of political functions, is no less fundamental. As co-operation grows, the functions of the state decline.
This movement is the one force that is meeting and opposing the
expanding of governments into the economic field. Thus the co-
operative movement fulfills the radical demand of changing the
motive of industry from profits to service, and does what libertarianism theoretically dreams in moving toward the fading of
the state.

The idea prevails that advocating the destruction of the capitalist system is radical. This is not the co-operative idea. Co-operation is not set up to destroy anything. It starts where things are not
done well, where needs are not supplied, or where profit business
is failing. It becomes established only where it is needed, where
it is adapted to the situation, and where it functions efficiently.
There it takes hold, penetrates into the economic consciousness,
and makes a fundamental change. Co-operation is constructive
radicalism—like the oaks which send their roots into the empty
soil of the barren plain and build an oaken grove where none had
been before.

The prevalent notion that radicalism means violence, cataclysm,
and a general upset of existing conditions is refuted by the co-
operative method. The movements which are accompanied by these
phenomena are not essentially radical. Communism, fascism, and
anarchism are not making radical and enduring changes in society.
The cataclysms, the expansions of the state, and the chaos which
they engender are ephemeral and insecure. Most of what the
world acclaims as radical, in the light of events, is highly reactionary. It moves in a circle back to the conditions it aimed to
supplant.

In co-operation, the root of things is changed by processes
which are evolutionary and, hence, slow. The change brought
about by the co-operative movement is peaceful and, in general,
permanent. Co-operation is never found taking destructive steps
to attain a good end. It makes use of constructive measures. The
test of radicalism is not in the amount of noise and chaos, but
rather in the fundamental quality of the changes it accomplishes.

Chapter II

THE BEGINNINGS OF MUTUAL SELF-HELP

THE ROCHDALE PIONEERS

CO-OPERATION and experiments in co-operative organization are old. The pages of history are rich with the records of man's search for practical means of working together for service and in the spirit of mutual aid.

The Rochdale Society of Equitable Pioneers in England was the beginning of the standardized co-operative movement. No long and expanding series of successes had ever followed any efforts at co-operation before them. They did not originate each of the Rochdale methods. They looked about and saw many plans in operation. They took several of these and combined them. This combination is their great contribution. The methods they made use of have proved, when combined, to constitute the essentials of co-operation. The Pioneers formulated the technic for applying these methods together. After painstaking development of their ideas they put them into operation. They opened their store. They carried out their plans. They succeeded. And from that day on there has been no recession in the progress of the methods they inaugurated.

Before they organized their society, the state of the weavers in the mills at Rochdale was pathetic, but typical of working conditions in capitalistic industry. After a life of toil, the poorhouse was the destiny to which they looked.

They decided upon a new plan. All their lives they had been exploited by traders. They would become themselves traders and, indeed, capitalists. They would add to their already burdensome work the duties of merchant, banker, and millowner. They would take over the functions of the captains of industry. These poor weavers! How they would have been laughed at by the owners of the mills had their ambitious talk been heard beyond the walls of their little meeting room!

When the twenty-eight of them, after more than a year of saving, had accumulated the sum of £28, they began their experiment. The ground floor of an old warehouse was rented on Toad Lane. They had about £14 to invest in a small stock of flour, oatmeal, butter, and sugar. They opened their doors for business on a cold night—the longest in the year, the 21st of December, 1844.

They felt like a band of conspirators—which they were. They were conspiring against poverty and the forces which created and subsisted upon poverty; and those forces were the mightiest powers in the British Empire.

These weavers not only acted together from the beginning, but they held together even when adversity came upon them. They received no aid outside their own efforts; and here was one of the reasons for their success. To accept financial aid has often been a cause of failure in co-operative undertakings; to sacrifice, endure, and develop self-reliance have ever been potent factors in building success.

The men were stanch. The allurements of the private tradesmen failed to divert the women from their shop or to dissuade them from their ideals. They realized that loyalty was the keystone. They walked long distances to carry home their purchases from their store. By the end of the year 1845, the Rochdale Society of Equitable Pioneers had 74 members and a paid-up capital of £180. Their first year's business totaled £710. Rochdale then had a population of 25,000.

Each applicant for membership, on his admission night, was required to appear in the meeting room and declare his willingness to take four shares at £1 each and pay a deposit of not less than threepence per share, to pay not less than threepence per week thereafter, and to allow all interest and surplus-savings that might be due him to remain in the funds of the society until an amount had accumulated to his credit equal to the four shares of the capital stock. Thus with the payment of a shilling, a member entered upon a simple agreement to make himself worth £4 by making his purchases at the society's store.

They planned a reorganization of the state and society. They declared that, "as soon as practicable, this Society shall proceed to arrange the powers of production, distribution, education, and government; or, in other words, to establish a self-supporting home-colony of united interests, or assist other societies in establishing such colonies."

Progress was slow. In 1847, when times became hard and prices went higher, there was great distress in England. The membership in the society increased rapidly. More distress next year resulted in greater increase of membership and capital. During the "hungry forties" it was demonstrated that "co-operation is the enemy of poverty." The "respectable and influential" threw obstacles in the way; but the society went on. The poorhouse ceased to be the destiny of Rochdale weavers. They wore better clothes. They looked better. They began to have the little luxuries which had ever before been denied them.

They became the educational center from which co-operation radiated throughout the world. In the early days of co-operation in Great Britain the newly organized societies had no better light than that shed from Rochdale.

The Pioneers aimed to do, and they did, the following unusual things: "Supplying the purest provisions they could get; giving full weight and measure." They asked for no credit nor gave any, and thus discouraged debt among working people. They applied the plan of giving the surplus-savings to the people who had made the purchases.

They announced: "The intention of extending co-operative commerce and manufacture by the establishment of an Industrial City, in which crime and competition should cease."

All members of this society had the democratic privilege of one vote for each person, three-quarters of a century before the state accepted this principle. Women had the right to receive their savings-returns as their own and to own shares long before the state permitted married women to have property. From the beginning women enjoyed their right of voting with men. The society devoted 2½ per cent of its savings to education. It added commodity after commodity to things it distributed. A reading room and then a library soon developed. The old basement was outgrown. Recreation, banking, and insurance were undertaken. Workingmen from far away were sent to study these methods. Similar societies sprang up with equal success. And the Rochdale

Pioneers expanded into the movement which has extended over the world.

Fifty years later, in 1894, at the jubilee celebration of this single society, the membership was 12,000, the funds £400,000, the amount of yearly business was more than £300,000, and the yearly "profits" £60,000. In 1934, the Pioneers' Society had 44,-000 members, £569,000 capital, and did a business of £657,000—this in a town of 96,000 population. From 1844 to 1934 the business turnover had amounted to a total of £30,000,000, and the surplus-savings distributed totaled £4,000,000. The society continues to prosper and expand.

Such has been the course of this single society. The Rochdale Pioneers might have acknowledged defeat, as the poor have usually done. They might have yielded to fate and resigned themselves to the hardness of life. They might have looked to the government to care for them. But, instead, they did the great thing—they grappled with life, and they won. At Rochdale began a new economic era. A different method of industry was devised. A way was found to guarantee that measures should be fair and the scales should balance true.

The records of the Pioneers reveal that this result came about quite by chance. Their plan was the building of a workers' commonwealth. They aimed to attain an association of producers. There is no evidence that they had a consumers' philosophy. The purpose of their retail shop was to make their wages go farther and to get capital for their producers' enterprises. The plans for a producers' economy failed because of one expedient—selling at the current market price, accumulating a surplus saving, and returning it to the consumers in proportion to patronage. This turned the co-operative movement into an association of consumers. But much confusion still prevails as to consumers and producers. The Pioneers built better than they knew. Out of their efforts grew a movement addressed to no special class, industry, or occupation, but to the interests of all people.

Chapter III

CO-OPERATION THROUGHOUT THE WORLD

CO-OPERATION IN MANY LANDS

IN those countries which came under the control of Fascist, National Socialist, and other totalitarian regimes during World War II, the consumer co-operatives were either destroyed or deprived of democratic independence. Only a skeleton movement survived. The physical properties were taken over by the various governments or were permitted to maintain a pseudo-co-operative existence. After the war, in those countries not remaining in the control of totalitarian governments, an extraordinary rehabilitation of the co-operatives is taking place. This growth of co-operation is greater than at any other period in its history. The common people seem to have realized the dangers of the totalitarian state, and are turning in the opposite direction. They prize their co-operatives as never before. Rather than asking governments to do things for them, they are using the co-operative method. In this they see free enterprise, their own private ownership, and a way that obviates the expansion of political government into the field of business. These changes are taking place so rapidly that the facts and figures in this chapter must be looked upon as only temporary. They pertain to 1947.

Argentina (Pop. 12,000,000). This country has about 120 distributive societies, with a membership of 200,000; about 85 societies for the production of electricity for their 215,000 members; also there are banking and insurance societies. The largest consumer society is the Workers' Household Society of Buenos Aires, which has a membership of over 10,000. Agricultural credit societies are multiplying. The educational union publishes an official organ and other literature. The National Union of Distributive, Building, and Credit Societies is steadily expanding. A national wholesale is developing. The country has about 800 co-operative societies of all kinds, with 500,000 members. There is a good co-operative literature.

33

Australia (Pop., 6,403,000). This country has well-developed and extensive agricultural marketing organizations out of which the consumer co-operative movement is growing. In New South Wales are many societies with distributive stores. The New South Wales wholesale has an expanding membership and business. Prosperous societies are at Kurri Kurri, Newcastle, West Wallsend, Wollongong, Woonoona, Sydney, Lithgow, Cessnock, Millicent, and many other places. The Maitland West Cooperative Bakery has over 1,500 members. In Victoria are many consumer societies. In South Australia is the Adelaide Cooperative Society, established in 1870, and several other store societies. A substantial co-operative bank, organized in 1905, is in operation in Melbourne. Co-operative insurance is expanding. Thus scattered over Australia is a growing movement which is now united in the Australian Cooperative Union.

Austria (Pop., 6,500,000). The Union of Austrian Consumer Societies was the largest co-operative union in Austria, before World War I. Before 1933 over one-third the population of the country were served by the co-operative societies. The Co-operative Society of Vienna had a membership of over 170,000. It had 144 distributive stores. The number of employees was 1,700. The society had 172 dwellings which it rented to members. Among its various departments were carpenter shops, locksmith shop, blacksmithy, saddlery, laundry, bakery, dairy, coffee roastery, and wine cellar. The Vienna society had joined with the municipal government to distribute fuel, and together they formed the largest distributor of coal in Austria. It had also united with the city government to distribute meat. The Vienna society provided for more than half the population of the city.

The co-operative movement in Austria was not politically neutral. The German-Austrian Union was distinctly a Socialist organization. As a result of this political aspect, Austria had also a neutral or antisocialistic union with bakeries, mills, housing, and credit banks.

In the field of housing, the Socialist government of Vienna showed preference to municipal housing as against co-operative housing. The co-operative houses were neutral while the municipal houses were occupied by government officials and Socialist party leaders who naturally enjoyed preferment.

The Fascist regime which was imposed upon the co-operatives in 1934 was largely instigated by the profit traders. The co-operatives were compelled to join the Shopkeepers' Trade Associations and submit to their control. Co-operative managers had to be appointed from the stores of private traders. All surplus savings had to pay the full profit tax. Co-operative societies were forbidden to supply goods to any department of the government. Restrictions were placed upon co-operative education, propaganda, the admission of new members, and the formation of new societies. The protests against this policy became so strong that in December, 1935, the government restored to the co-operatives their autonomy. The movement at present is in a condition similar to that in Germany—hope and reconstruction within a broken shell.

While the co-operative societies were denied democratic control and their co-operative quality was destroyed by the German National Socialist regime in 1938, as soon as Austria was liberated from the Germans the co-operators again took possession of their societies. They held their first post-bellum co-operative congress in 1946. The principle of political neutrality appears in the following resolution of the congress: "It is self-evident that religious, cultural, and political aims should be confined to those institutions designed for them. Co-operative societies are not the proper ground for the pursuit of such aims." The People's party, in 1947 the strongest in Austria, is promoting parliamentary legislation, providing for the co-operative ownership of industries, and opposing state industry. Austria's Socialist president, Dr. Karl Renner, said: "In an economy controlled by the state, there is not only the danger of bureaucracy but also the greater menace of the creation of new class differences and a new type of exploitation. Such stateism can even be transformed into state slavery."

Belgium (Pop., 8,130,000).   For forty years the workers of Belgium spent much time experimenting with productive workshops. Then about 1880 they became inspired with the idea of consumer co-operation, and the co-operative movement began. The leaders of Belgian co-operation are interested not only in establishing co-operative societies but in using co-operation as a means to unite the workers' political and trade-union movements.

The movement began with consumers' bread bakeries instead of stores, and it has given especial attention to social development and to political propaganda rather than to the paying of savings-returns. The surplus-savings are used largely for doing for the members of the co-operative societies what the socialized state would do. Old-age pensions, life insurance, insurance against sickness and unemployment, maternity benefits, and medical and nursing care are provided. Those beautiful buildings in Belgium, called "the houses of the people," are owned by the co-operative societies. These community centers are used for meetings, dramatic presentations, schools, and recreation. The Belgian societies are schools where the members are taught politics, art, history, economics, and temperance. The Maison du Peuple in each district is the symbol of the triple alliance of co-operation, politics, and labor.

The co-operative movement in Belgium continued to progress during World War I. The total membership of societies at the end of the war was greater than in 1913. The 1939 statistics show 82 consumer societies with 300,000 members in the Belgian Co-operative Union (Office Coopératif Belge). At the end of World War II, the statistics were not materially changed. The sales of co-operative societies affiliated with the wholesale society were 684,000,000 francs for the first six months of 1946, an increase of 90 per cent over the same period of 1945.

The Vooruit, the pioneer Belgian society in Ghent, has a large membership. Its Festival Palace was opened in 1915. The Belgian Wholesale has a variety of manufacturing enterprises. The society of Liége has some 70,000 members, with 250 branch stores and 80 recreational and educational centers. It owns a hat factory, a confectionery factory, a chocolate factory, and twenty bakeries. The Belgian Insurance Society (La Prévoyance Sociale) has insurance policies in the hands of 1,200,000 members.

The close affiliation of one group of Belgian co-operatives with the Socialist party and the labor movement results in a parallel development of nonsocialistic and neutral societies. The nonobservance of neutrality by much of the movement is responsible for this division.

Brazil (Pop., 40,300,000).   There are 870 co-operative agricultural associations in Brazil. A co-operative credit fund is maintained by the government to help finance co-operatives. This is advanced by the Ministry of Agriculture. In 1946, Brazil had 600 consumer societies, with 250,000 members, and 300 credit societies.

Bulgaria (Pop., 5,500,000).   Co-operation in Bulgaria had made constant progress since 1907, when state control was relinquished. In 1939, the National Cooperative Union (Napred) consisted of 58 societies, with 70,000 members and 9,000 employees. The total yearly turnover of the retail societies affiliated with it amounted to over $400,000,000; and the wholesale department of Napred did a business of $425,000,000. The wholesale had extensive productive works, chiefly for flour milling, canning, oil refining, cheese making, sugar refining, and the production of cereals, wine, cotton goods, tobacco, eggs, milk, lumber, wool, silk, and synthetic rubber. It handled 72 per cent of the cotton. Health societies with clinics and hospitals and 277 co-operative drugstores were prospering. It had rice plantations and electric power plants. It produced electricity which lighted a town, its flour mill, and the railway station. It imported lamps of the Northern International Wholesale, which were becoming the most widely used lamps in Bulgaria. The Central Co-operative Bank had affiliated with it 900 credit societies, 74 distributive societies, and 35 others. Credit societies rendered much service to the agricultural population. The Co-operative Insurance Society had 180,-000 members and $500,000,000 outstanding insurance. All the co-operatives were united in a National Committee of Bulgarian co-operation.

While the Bulgarian movement was originally connected with the Socialist party, it had gradually become independent, and was strictly neutral and nonpolitical. It gave much attention to education. Its leaders aimed to expand co-operation sufficiently to prevent either communism or fascism from becoming dominant in Bulgaria. As a result of World War II, the country has fallen under Russian Communist domination, and its co-operatives subjected to the uncertain eventualities of that regime. In 1946 there were in existence over 3,000 co-operative agricultural societies, with 300,000 members. People's co-operative banks had 312,000 members. Consumer societies in Napred had 275,000 members. If the people of Bulgaria could gain self-determination, the co-operative way of business would soon become the dominant economy of the country.

Canada (Pop., 10,000,000).   The Canadian movement began with the establishment of the Cooperative Union of Canada in 1909. This organization has driven home to a pioneer people the meaning of co-operation. It has zealously promoted education, standardization, and protection of the co-operative societies. The province of Saskatchewan has the first minister of co-operation to be appointed by any government. In an agricultural country such as Canada the farmers' marketing organizations naturally predominate. The three western provinces of Canada have developed a keen co-operative spirit following their successful experience with farm marketing associations. They are now building up consumer store societies. They have a co-operative consumer-owned gasoline refinery and are developing other productive enterprises. Each province has a co-operative wholesale. Scattered across the country are growing societies. Nova Scotia has a vigorous movement. It is promoted by the University of St. Francis Xavier, the Extension Department and the Department of Economics of which go out among the people to show them how to organize co-operative societies, and stand by until they succeed. This is a rare example of the economics faculty of an educational institution, materially affecting, for their good, the lives of the people and the economics of the community before the very eyes of the students and the public.

One of the most substantial societies in the Western Hemisphere is the British Canadian Cooperative Society, at Sydney Mines. It has over 3,500 members, and a business in its five branches above $1,000,000 a year. During the forty years of its existence, this society has given back to its members—the workers of Cape Breton—over $1,000,000 in cash savings-returns besides paying interest on capital.

Ceylon (Pop., 5,313,000).   The co-operative movement

started in 1912 but grew slowly until 1942. In 1942 there were 2,036 societies of all kinds, with 91,988 members. In 1945 there were 6,383 societies, with 1,033,228 members. The 1,811 credit societies lend money to consumer and to marketing co-operatives. There are 161 agricultural marketing societies, with 15,400 members. The growth of consumer co-operatives has been extraordinary. In 1942 there were 38 consumer societies, with 17,000 members. In 1945 there were 4,032 such societies, with over 1,000,000 members and a wholesale society. This rapid growth resulted from the collapse of profit business merchandising during that period. The consumer co-operatives now furnish foodstuffs and clothing to two-thirds the population. Women play an important part in this movement.

The government maintains a Department of Co-operative Development. This department conducts schools for the education and training of co-operative executives. In 1943, the emergency food distribution of the Municipal Council in Colombo was given up and the city divided into 105 districts, in each of which the public was invited to form a consumer co-operative. Since then, the entire population of 350,000 people get their rations from the 105 co-operative stores. The co-operative method is now the predominant method of food distribution.

China (Pop., 475,000,000). The Chinese are naturally a co-operative people. The modern co-operative movement, however, has only recently penetrated their country. The seed of the movement was sown at the close of World War I by Prof. S. Y. Hsueh. It is based on Dr. Sun Yat-sen's idea of a planned co-operative economy. Since 1927, when the Nationalists came to power, the movement has had the support of the government. In 1931 there were 2,796 societies of all types, with 56,000 members. In 1946 there were 165,331 societies, with 18,928,548 members and $1,500,000,000 capital stock. About 13 per cent of these are consumer supply societies and 80 per cent credit societies. The Co-operative League of China was started in 1940. It promotes education, and held its first national congress in 1942. Its president is Prof. M. S. Shaw. A national co-operative wholesale was started in 1940 by government loans. The offices of the league are at a suburb of Chungking in the mountains, one of the famous scenic spots of China. This salubrious location has now become the center of co-operative education. The Industrial Co-operatives make machinery, chemicals, paper, textiles, and cotton thread; produce woolen and silk goods; and tan leather.

Consumer co-operative stores are often in the farmhouses of the members, where no costs are incurred. Members take turns in the service. Sales are from one to four dollars a day. These stores are important as meeting places of neighbors. The war developed many productive societies. A national co-operative bank was started in 1945 by the Co-operative League.

Some educational institutions give courses in co-operation. There are several co-operative weekly and monthly periodicals, and a co-operative union which issues effective literature. In 1922 the Ping Ming Co-operative Society was formed at the Fuh-Tan University in Shanghai, where students, professors, and townspeople united. The society published a weekly paper, *The People,* and conducted a co-operative bank and stores.

Colombia (Pop., 7,850,000). This country is making extraordinary co-operative progress. It has passed a law giving special consideration to co-operative societies—preferential shipping conditions, retail co-operatives to fix retail prices, credit societies to fix interest rates, and co-operatives in general to exercise control over the regulation of industry.

Czechoslovakia (Pop., 14,720,000). Modern co-operation began in 1850 among the textile workers, who took this means to lift themselves out of their terrible poverty. The political chaos due to the splitting up of Austria-Hungary in 1919 into national states affected the movement acutely. The united work of seventeen years was terminated by the dismemberment of Austria by the Allies after World War I. The political, racial, and economic cleavage gave rise to four distinct movements: (1) Central Union of Czech Co-operative Societies; (2) Union of German Economic Societies; (3) Socialist stores movement, and (4) Catholic stores movement. The first two were members of the International Alliance. The Czech Union had 250 consumer societies, with 400,-000 members. It had a bank, over 400 housing societies, a number of credit societies, and the Co-operative Insurance Society. The wholesale of the union had two flour mills, two bakeries, a clothing factory, a brick and tile works, a food factory, and several others. The German Union had 150 societies, with 270,000 members. The wholesale of the German Union had five warehouses in Bohemia. It had factories for the preservation of fruit, a laundry, a ribbon factory, a malt-coffee factory, a small-wares factory, an underwear factory, a flour mill, chemical laboratories, and a dozen other industries. The differences of races and creeds were ignored by the co-operatives and from 1918 to 1940 they moved onward together and enjoyed great expansion.

The largest single consumer society in Czechoslovakia was the Consumers' and Savings Society Budoncnost (The Future) situated in Moravian Ostrau. Although private merchants had resorted to every conceivable measure to destroy this society, it continued to grow. In many districts no profit stores were to be found, but only the stores of the Budoncnost. It had over 200 stores and its own bakery and flour mill. It employed 800 people, paid no dividends, and was neutral in politics.

Before the Nazi conquest there were more than 17,000 co-operative societies in Czechoslovakia, with 4,000,000 members. About 8,000 were credit societies. Many were housing and agricultural societies. There were 1,700 co-operatives for supplying electricity. There were 1,800 consumer distributive organizations, of which 800 were agricultural supply societies. The membership of the consumer societies was about one million. The movement was politically neutral, but gave its support to candidates who were most favorable to co-operation. The government was, on the whole, not hostile. A state flour monopoly existed, in which the government supplied 51 per cent of the capital. The remaining 49 per cent came from the co-operatives, farmers' marketing societies, millers, and flour dealers. Prices were thus controlled. The Nazi developments in Germany had the effect of drawing the German-Czech and Czech movements closer together to work in harmony and collaboration. The whole national movement continued to expand until 1939.

After the collapse of the German control, an immediate recovery of the co-operatives took place. The first notable change was a unification of all the societies. The old lines that had separated them had broken down. Societies which had previously been separated by religious, political, and racial differences joined in a common national union. The only force preventing the unlimited expansion of the co-operatives is that of foreign government interference. At the beginning of 1947 there were over 4,000 consumer societies, with 1,000,000 member families. They are not divided as before but united in the Central Co-operative Council. The Ministries of Education and Agriculture are establishing courses on co-operation to teach young people co-operative methods. If the people of this country can rid themselves of foreign government interference, they can convert Czechoslovakia into a co-operative democracy.

Denmark (Pop., 3,600,000).   Denmark has led in co-operative agriculture. The agricultural purchasing and sales societies, dairies, bacon factories, butcheries, etc., exceed the distributive societies whose development has been of later date. Most needs of the people are met through some form of co-operation. From the country, the movement entered into the towns. Some 90 per cent of the farmers and the majority of the members of Parliament are members of co-operative societies.

In the National Union (Kooperative Faellesforbund) are 1,800 retail consumer societies, with 400,000 members and 5,500 employees. The total membership of all types of co-operative societies is 2,000,000, and employees 2,400. More than half the total commerce of the country is carried on by marketing and consumer co-operative societies. Co-operative dairies handle more than 90 per cent of the milk. Co-operatives handle most of the pork and butter exported.

The Danish Cooperative Wholesale Society (Faellesforeningen for Danmarks Brugsforeninger) had productive enterprises for hosiery, chemicals, leather, shoes, clothing, underwear, bicycles, rope, tobacco, soap, foods, and candy. It is a large dealer and tester of seeds.

The Danish Cooperative Bank (Dansk Andelsbanken) is the central credit institution of the consumer co-operatives. There are 1,800 co-operative consumer stores in Denmark, which distribute 15 per cent of the goods consumed. The Danish people turn to the co-operative method to solve their problems. They tend more and more to do this instead of turning to the state.

The largest single society in Denmark is the Copenhagen Consumers Society (Hovedstandens Brugsforening), with a membership around 50,000, about 400 employees, 95 stores, and several important productive enterprises. The co-operative housing associations are noteworthy. Co-operative health and insurance societies and sanatoriums for protecting the health of the members also lend strength to the movement.

Egypt (Pop., 14,218,000). The co-operative movement began in 1923. In 1946 there were 2,000 societies, with over 1,-000,000 members—1,636 agricultural societies and 361 consumer societies. During the past twenty years, the membership, capital, and turnover of the co-operatives have increased more than twenty times.

Estonia (Pop., 1,100,000). Before World War II the Republic of Estonia had a steadily growing co-operative movement of 300 societies, with 150,000 members. They did 25 per cent of the retail business and supplied 90 per cent of the agricultural requirements of the country. A wholesale was composed of 180 societies. Its factories produced lumber, wines and alcohol, packed fish, etc. It had the largest paper factory in the country. Insurance was well developed. The Co-operative National Bank was a central bank for all co-operative bodies. The government was sympathetic. Then came the German invasion followed by the Russian invasion, both of which confiscated the property and "liquidated" the co-operative leaders who were in favor of democracy. The co-operatives now are under Russian control.

Finland (Pop., 3,630,000). Finland has two unions of co-operative societies. The older, the General Co-operative Union (Y.O.L.), operates mainly in the rural areas. It has a wholesale called S.O.K. It carries on many manufacturing enterprises. Among these are clothing, preserves, coffee, chemicals, brushes and brooms, paper, lumber, flour, macaroni, etc. Its match factory successfully competes with the international match trust. The Central Union of Distributive Societies (K.K.) operates mainly in the towns and cities. Its societies own many farms. It also has a wholesale (O.T.K.). The two unions have 500 societies, with a total membership of 800,000 individuals. They have 3,000 stores and supply one-half the goods distributed in Finland. One of the most successful societies in Northern Europe is the Elanto Society of Helsingfors. The co-operative bank is owned by the 800 credit societies. The growth of co-operation has been rapid in Finland. This is one of the most highly co-operatively organized countries. Its co-operators have not only done much for Finland, but those who have migrated to the United States have become leaders in the American movement and have built some of its most substantial co-operative institutions.

France (Pop., 41,830,000). During most of the eighteenth century the French working class sought for a solution of their economic problem at the point of production. Then they hoped for the political socialization of the means of production or for its control by the organized workers. The progressive sentiment that swept through Europe, in 1848, expressed itself in the formation of productive societies in France, but did little for co-operation. Co-operation may be said to have begun at Nîmes, in 1885, when a small group started the consumer movement. Professor Charles Gide joined this "school of Nîmes," and in the course of time clarified and described the principles of co-operation. Indeed, Professor Gide did more than any other man to impress upon French thought the true meaning of this subject. It was he who prevented the movement from allying itself with the Socialist party. In 1947, Premier Paul Ramadier said: "The co-operative movement must take its stand to prevent government control of national economy. State interference threatens the liberty of the individual."

There are 4,000 distributive societies in France, with a membership of 2,500,000. Of these societies, 1,120, with 1,000,000 membership, belong to the Fédération Nationale des Coopératives de Consommation. The societies in the federation have about 25,000 employees.

The co-operative wholesale, Magasin de Gros, is composed of most of the societies of the federation. Among its activities are 13 grocery warehouses, 5 wine warehouses, 4 shoe factories, 3 canning factories, a soap factory, a chocolate factory, a clothing factory, a coffee roastery, and a sawmill.

The co-operative society of Paris maintains 300 establishments, comprising grocery stores, butcher shops, restaurants, cafés, pharmacies, etc., with a membership of over 75,000.

An important part of the French co-operative movement are the recreational centers for children and the restaurants and hotels. The French co-operatives deal principally in foods. They distribute 6 per cent of the perishable food (milk, meat, bread) and do 12 per cent of the national retail trade in groceries.

Germany (Pop., 62,500,000). An early co-operative venture in Germany was a store at Eilenburg, started in 1849, after correspondence with the co-operative association in the United States which had opened its store in Boston in 1845. Assistance to this German movement can be traced directly to America. But the store movement grew slowly. It was the co-operative banking movement that initiated the wave of inspiration that spread over the country. The Germany of 1850 was essentially a land of production on a small scale, of peasant farmers, craftsmen, and independent tradesmen. The co-operative bank first stirred these people. The consumer movement was retarded by the Socialist teaching that "any reduction in the cost of living brings with it an equal reduction in the rate of wages." This doctrine had a profound influence on German thought for fifty years, and directed the working people into politics and profit-sharing enterprises. Only after the last decade of the nineteenth century did the consumer movement make progress.

After the Revolution, in 1918, working-class co-operative stores steadily increased in number. The reputation which the co-operative movement won as the protector of the economically weak proved of the greatest value to the masses of the German people. Before World War I, restrictive laws, regulations, taxation, and commercial discrimination in favor of profit business were all directed by the state against the consumer distributive societies. This was in sharp contrast with the policy of favoritism and state aid shown by the government toward agricultural marketing organizations.

Consumer societies had become sufficiently numerous, in 1903, to unite to form the Zentralverband Deutscher Konsumvereine (the Central Union). The Grosseinkaufsgesellschaft Deutscher Konsumvereine (Co-operative Wholesale) was founded in 1894. Banking, distribution, and housing steadily developed during the first third of this century.

The difficulties of the German co-operative movement after the Armistice, in 1918, seemed almost insuperable. Still the membership and trade of societies more than doubled between 1914 and 1933. At that time a fourth of the population were included in the societies. The central union, the wholesale, and their affiliated consumer store societies had over 50,000 employees. There were 900 consumer store societies.

In addition to these consumer societies, there were 21,602 co-operative banking societies, 6,842 societies for purchase of raw materials, 4,171 home-building societies, and various other co-operatives, which made a total of over 50,000 such organizations.

The Central Agricultural Loan Bank of Germany had 68 branches and 750 employees. The shareholders included 5,757 Raiffeisen banks.

Co-operation in Saxony, as though to retaliate for governmental abuse in the early days, in 1933 had 150 societies, with 700 stores, 160 of which were in Dresden. The German Wholesale was organized in Saxony, in 1901, and in Saxony established its first industries. In 1933 more than one-half the population of Saxony were supplied by the co-operatives.

The Consumers' Building and Savings Society, Produktion (the consumer society in Hamburg), was an example of one of the best German societies. It started with 700 members in 1899. At the beginning of World War I it had 80,000; in 1933 it had over 130,000 members. Nearly one-half the people of Hamburg were supplied by it.[1] It carried on a large banking and insurance business for its members. The motto of this society was: "All by the people and for the people."

The Berlin society, with 150,000 members, was similar to that in Hamburg. It was destroyed by the Nazis.

The Grosseinkaufsgesellschaft (G.E.G.), up until 1933, was steadily increasing in membership and business. In 1933 it had

---

[1] With production as its ultimate purpose, it already had the following productive enterprises: the largest bakery in northwest Germany, a big slaughtering and meat-packing plant, preserve and canning works, coffee roastery, mineral water bottling establishment, foodstuff factory, furniture factory, woodwork and frame factory, tinware factory, and a brick factory. It owned a 1,600-acre farm with a creamery. It had 275 stores, 40 automobiles, 100 wagons, 30 barges, and 2 tugboats. It had 150 blocks of buildings containing over 1,500 dwellings.

over 1,000 member societies and employed 5,000 persons. The motto of the German Wholesale was "Production for the organized consumers." Some of its factories were the best and most beautiful in the co-operative world.[2]

The wholesale carried on a large banking and insurance business. It was the banking department for the movement, and put aside capital for reserve, benevolent, pension, and insurance funds. It had ten warehouses. Offices and warehouses were maintained at Hamburg for foreign and domestic purchases, from which port distribution was made to the thousands of stores through their headquarters in various cities.

The central office of the union in Hamburg had a printing establishment which employed over 600 people, and was one of the largest and most perfectly equipped printing plants in Germany.

The progress of the German movement during World War I and the five years of blockade proved its strength. The German Union at its Nuremberg Congress, in 1917, went on record as follows: "This wholesale murder and this continued destruction of the work of civilization must cease. Larger and larger grows the number of those who in their hearts have realized the truth of the old German co-operative motto: 'Co-operation is Peace.'"

The scientific efficiency which was characteristic of the German people was applied to the co-operatives. German co-operation made use of every sort of technical expert. The talent for organ-

[2] These included soap factories at Gröba and Düsseldorf; weaving and clothing factories at Oppach, Dresden, Seifhennersdorf, and Leopoldsgrun; macaroni factory, wooden box factory, and chemical factory at Gröba; match factories at Gröba and Lauenburg; brush and broom factory at Stutzengrun; mustard and malt-coffee factory at Chemnitz; cigar factories at Hamburg, Frankenberg, and Hoehenheim; cigarette factory at Stuttgart; tobacco factories at Hamburg, Burgsteinfurt, and Nordhausen; textile factory at Oppach (Saxony); meat-and-fish packing, candy, and chocolate works at Altona; woodenware factory at Dortmund; food factory at Madgeburg; fodder mill at Minden; and a sausage factory at Elmshorn. At Hamburg also were a coffee-roasting department, a spice mill, wine cellar, coffee, cocoa, and spice packing industries. At Gröba were also a coffee-roasting industry, and coffee and cocoa packing. At Mannheim were coffee roasting, and tea and coffee packing. In 1925 it acquired a large and modern fruit-preserving factory at Stendal. It also had a timber industry, a factory for shop-fitting and furniture, machine shops and other industries. Its fish-packing industry at Altona employed over 100 persons.

ization and the genius for administration in Germany were found more and more in the co-operative movement.

While in many other countries the co-operative societies were taking an increasing interest in politics, in Germany the opposite was coming to pass. The co-operative congresses passed resolutions favoring political neutrality, which meant nonparticipation in politics. The German Wholesale report (*International Cooperative Bulletin,* June, 1922) contains these significant words: "The year 1920 witnessed the beginning and 1921 the completion of the liberation of Germany's economic life from the shackles of state control. We have always held that co-operation cannot develop under bureaucratic oppression, but must have complete freedom."

German co-operation by 1933 had more than recovered from the war. The conditions which the Allies had inflicted upon the German people and the provisions imposed by the Treaty of Versailles made life in Germany difficult. But when thus afflicted the suffering people seemed to learn to act more in the spirit of mutual aid. They helped one another to lift themselves out of the distress into which governments had plunged them. To this end they were making effective use of co-operation.

In the meantime, oppressive conditions of the Versailles Treaty were making economic recovery impossible. The people resented the conditions under which they suffered. They could not go on forever at the mercy of external and hostile forces. A change inevitably had to grow out of the conflicting circumstances. It obviously had to move in the direction of communism or fascism. The Germans had their choice, and cast their lot with fascism. This is what politics did to Germany. The Nazi government, which was the result, in 1933, then proceeded to take over the co-operatives. They were put under the control of a government appointee, restricted, and harassed. Much of this was at the behest of the Nazi merchant class. But the members of the co-operatives were not as well served as when they controlled their own business. Dissatisfaction continued. With one-third the population accustomed to conduct its own distribution of supplies, there remained in the minds of these people a desire to have back their societies free from government dominance.

Before the rise of national socialism the co-operatives distributed 12 per cent of the goods consumed in Germany. There were 12,000 retail stores. After World War II, the co-operatives in the zones controlled by the French, English, and Americans were permitted to re-establish themselves. Little information of the Russian zone is allowed. It would seem that the members are not permitted freedom of election, but leaders and managers are appointed by the Russians. The Berlin society has been split up into small societies. The great preserve factory of the German Wholesale has been dismantled and moved to Russia. It had employed 700 people and produced 30,000,000 pounds of preserves yearly. The 1,700 acres of farm lands owned by the wholesale, employing 150 people, where fruits were grown for the factory, have been broken up in the process of "land reform." The co-operatives are close to the hearts of the people. No government has yet succeeded in doing away with the co-operative idea. As in Russia and Italy, the co-operators of Germany look toward their emergence from government domination. The reconstruction is now in process.

A conference of co-operative societies, held in Hesse, in July, 1946, passed the following resolution: "In the terrible situation in which the German people find themselves today, the consumer societies, children of misery and suffering themselves, apply their tested principles in an attempt to help the masses out of their economic distress and to restore to them their faith and the consciousness of their own strength." These societies now represent the hopeful feature of economic recovery.

Great Britain (Pop., 44,700,000). Many factors have contributed to the success of British co-operation. The Rochdale Pioneers made by no means a lone and isolated experiment. First, there were the many societies that preceded them and whose mistakes and successes taught them much. Dr. William King, a physician of Brighton, from 1828 to 1830 published a little magazine, *The Cooperator*, in which he set forth a philosophy of co-operation and the methods necessary for success. He is often designated as "the father of British co-operation." He said: "Co-operation is a voluntary act, and all the power in the world cannot make it compulsory; nor is it desirable that it should depend upon any power but its own." Robert Owen and a small group of religious men, the Christian Socialists, contributed much to the idealism of the movement. Among them were men of wealth and influence who promoted education and favorable legislation. Charles Kingsley, a clergyman, and John Stuart Mill, an eminent economist, were among these. Later came E. Vansittart Neale, a lawyer, who rendered great practical service. Most of the influential men who were active in discussion and organization affecting co-operation in the nineteenth century thought in terms of labor rather than of consumption. Dr. King was the outstanding exception. He was apparently the first to comprehend consumer co-operation. Later, J. T. W. Mitchell amplified this conception of the consumer and gave it its larger and practical application.

Just outside the co-operative field were men whose labors contributed notably to the understanding of the economics and sociology of this subject. Adam Smith and Richard Cobden clarified much that had to do with co-operation before it developed a philosophy of consumer economy.

As the movement expanded, the need of federation of societies was soon felt. A congress of co-operative societies was held in London, in 1869, which grew into the Cooperative Union. The union was created as a federation of societies for education, propaganda, and protection. Practically all the societies in Great Britain are now members. It may be regarded as the soul of the British movement. Today the co-operative societies in Great Britain have a membership of 9,500,000. In terms of families, this means more than one-half the total population. There are 1,065 retail societies.

The 1,150 retail distributive societies which were members of the Cooperative Union of Great Britain in 1924 distributed £177,000,000 worth of commodities to their members; in 1946, over £365,000,000. The "profits," or more properly, the surplus-savings, in 1924, amounted to £15,500,000; in 1946, £25,-000,000. In addition to this, members have free or low-cost life insurance and many other benefits. At the beginning of 1925 the retail co-operative societies had £94,000,000 capital, and 134,419 employees. At the beginning of 1946, they had £175,000,000 share capital, and 330,000 employees. The London Cooperative Societies have 900,000 members.

The consumer societies own 68,000 acres of farm land in Great Britain and rent 9,000 additional acres. They are the largest dealers in butter, sugar, bacon, and dried fruits, as well as of tea, in the empire.

Most of the industrial life and accident insurance in Great Britain is written by their co-operative insurance society. Its annual premium income is over £14,000,000, its assets exceed £70,000,-000 and are steadily increasing.

The English Cooperative Wholesale Society was formed in 1863, and now consists of over 1,000 societies. It represents the economic center of the movement and is the largest single distributive business in Great Britain.[3]

Scotland has 1,000,000 families in membership in its co-operative societies. This is more than half the population. The Scottish Wholesale performs services similar to those of the English C.W.S. It is the greatest distributive business in Scotland. Its factories at Shieldhall, Glasgow, are models of efficiency. It carries on fifty-eight different industries. Its annual business amounts to over £40,000,000.

These two wholesales jointly own 35,000 acres of tea plantations in Ceylon and India and plantations in other countries. In 1940 their tea business was more than 80,000,000 pounds. This is the largest tea business in the world. These two societies are also the largest importers of grain, butter, sugar, and dried fruits in Great Britain.

Co-operation in Ireland and Wales continues to expand as in England and Scotland. The number of employees of the British consumer societies has steadily increased for one hundred years. This labor is better paid and works under better conditions than

[3] In 1913, the C.W.S. had £2,000,000 paid-up share-capital; its sales amounted to £31,371,976. In 1934 it had £12,000,000 share-capital; and its sales were £90,000,000. In 1946, its sales were over £200,000,000. It produced £54,000,000 worth of goods. The deposits and withdrawals in its Banking Department in 1945 amounted to £1,300,000,000. The bank's assets in 1934 were £81,000,000. In 1946 they were £236,400,000.

The C.W.S. has palm olive estates in West Africa. It owns its own steamships. It has purchasing offices in the large commercial centers in every part of the world and depots in various European countries, North America, Africa, and Asia. It is the largest single purchaser of Canadian wheat in the world. Its flour mills are the largest in Great Britain.

the labor in competing industries. Much consideration is given to education, British societies annually appropriating £250,000 for this purpose.

Greece (Pop., 6,200,000).   Before World War II, the approaches to co-operation in Greece had been through the workers' guilds, copartnership productive societies, and agricultural associations. A law gave special consideration to co-operative societies, exemption from state and local taxes (such as income tax, tax on real estate, etc.). The government gave rewards to persons who organized co-operative societies which were successful and enduring. Rewards were granted to individuals who devoted themselves to work in the co-operative movement. Courses on co-operation were given in public schools. Most of this work was in the interest of producer copartnership enterprises. The consumer movement was slowly taking form. There were 3,450 consumer societies. Of these, 2,500 were credit societies, 400 distributive, and 300 housing societies. Their membership more than doubled in the ten years before the Italian invasion. The restoration of co-operatives and the building of new co-operative societies have been the outstanding constructive processes going on in Greece coincidental with the civil warfare following the restoration of the monarchy in 1946.

Guatemala (Pop., 2,480,000).   The government maintains a Department for Co-operative Development and carries on education and propaganda in the interest of co-operation. The number and effectiveness of co-operative societies are steadily increasing.

Holland (Pop., 8,000,000).   Holland has 4,000 co-operative societies of all kinds. The Holland Cooperative Union has 200 affiliated societies, with a membership of over 300,000. There are 500 consumer societies, with 1,400 retail stores. The Holland Wholesale in Rotterdam embraces 350 societies, with 360,000 members. It has a soap factory, a flour mill, a sweet-cake factory, and factories producing oleomargarine, chocolate, clothing, cigars and tobacco.

The movement was badly split by political factionalism. Since the union was subject to much Socialist influence, there was also a neutral movement started by the Catholics. Each had its own national union. The societies of both unions were members of the wholesale. The trend toward neutrality aims ultimately to unite the two unions. The total membership of all societies is tending toward a single organization. The Hague and Rotterdam have strong local societies.

Hungary (Pop., 8,680,000). The co-operative movement in Hungary developed along with that of Austria. Agricultural and credit societies were organized first. Then the industrial workers organized.

Hangya (The Co-operative Wholesale Society of the Federation of Hungarian Farmers) thrived before and after World War I. The total membership of its societies was over 1,000,000. It had 2,000 affiliated societies. With the exception of a few workingmen's societies, nearly all the members of Hangya were farmer consumer societies. The wholesale of Hangya had two flour mills, a soap factory, a candy factory, a chemical factory, a brush factory, a rope factory, a match factory, a cutlery factory, and a distillery. The Civil Service Co-operative Society in Budapest, which had 80 retail stores, supplied 20 per cent of the inhabitants. It had 40,000 members. It had a slaughter house, a large shoe repairing business, and a beehive factory. It distributed milk, owned vegetable and fruit gardens, and a factory for preserving fruit.

Industrial workers constituted the Union of Hungarian Workers Co-operative Societies and its wholesale. Its largest society was the General Distributive Society of Budapest, the largest retail society in Hungary. Its two largest warehouses served the members in grocery stores, butcher shops, dry goods stores, and a restaurant.

The co-operative bank, Diligentia, was formed in 1921; each of the stores of the society acted as a branch to receive deposits. The bank had over 30,000 depositors and a growing capital. The Hungarian movement was neutral, and had no relation to the political parties. It was largely agricultural in membership.

The Nazis did to Hungary what they did to other countries. Since World War II, there has been a movement to rehabilitate the co-operatives, impaired by the antidemocratic efforts of the Communists.

Iceland (Pop., 100,000). Iceland has over 40 societies with a membership in some cases of two and three thousand each. It has a union (Samband Islenskra Samvinnufjelaga) with a wholesale. More than half its population are supplied by the co-operative societies, and three-fourths of its business is done by the co-operatives. Most essentials, such a groceries, coal, oil, building materials, and agricultural supplies, are distributed by the co-operatives. The consumer societies have productive enterprises for the weaving of cloth and the manufacturing of shoes, clothing, and other necessities. They operate slaughter houses, refrigerating plants, dairies, fishing stations, hot houses, a cod liver oil factory, and other enterprises. The first co-operative society was established in 1882. Iceland is one of the most highly co-operatized countries in the world—and, perhaps, the most civilized.

India (Pop., 339,000,000). The first co-operative society in India was a credit society organized by a British government official in the eighties of the past century. Since then the movement has developed slowly, but has continued mainly in the field of credit. Able Indian leaders of the movement are trying to create initiative and self-reliance among the people. In the province of Madras are 15,724 co-operative societies of all types with 1,743,000 members, 10,000 rural credit societies with 637,000 members, and 2,284 consumer co-operative stores.

There are more than 175,000 co-operative associations of all kinds in India, with 5,000,000 members, and £75,000,000 working capital, statistically known. The total number of societies is, perhaps, much larger. The majority are agricultural credit societies. Agricultural marketing societies are increasing. Societies for combating malaria are very successful. Consumer distributive societies have been developed especially during the past fifteen years. "This represents a public feeling against the injustices suffered at the hands of profit business." There are also many societies for social services such as arbitration, health protection, and "better living."

Italy (Pop., 44,000,000). Italy had many and various co-operative organizations. The Cooperative League of Italy before the fascist regime of 1923 had over 4,000 consumer societies, with a collective membership of over 500,000 families. The Fascists,

upon coming into power, attempted the destruction of these societies. Those which were under Socialist influence were destroyed
and their leaders killed or imprisoned. The Fascists burned, plun-
dered, and wrecked the property of co-operative societies connected with the league. Many co-operators were killed and hundreds assaulted. Appeals to the government for protection and
redress were unavailing. It was the societies of a distinct political
character that were damaged. Participation in politics had much
to do with their destruction.

After the first wave of ruthlessness, the value of the co-operatives was realized and the membership insisted upon the continuation of their business. Fascist leadership was then demanded by
the government, which proceeded to appoint a majority of Fascists
to each board of directors. Under Fascist control the societies then
proceeded to function. The membership and the business expanded. By 1939 there were fully as many societies as before
1923. The membership of the consumer societies had increased to
750,000, and was growing. This was particularly true of central
and northern Italy; although the societies were expanding also in
the southern provinces and Sardinia. In some rural districts the
only business was co-operative. The former Cooperative League
had been succeeded by the Fascist Union of Cooperative Federations. The Cooperative Wholesale had expanded and had begun
manufacturing. Fascism cannot be said to have destroyed Italian
co-operation; it only succeeded in making it wholly Fascist—or
nationalistically Italian. In 1947 there were 17,000 co-operative
societies of all kinds, with 2,500,000 members. Among these
were 7,500 consumer societies, with 1,000,000 members. The
new constitution of Italy, adopted in 1947, provides: "The Republic recognizes the value of the co-operative movement, favors
its development by the most appropriate means, and watches over
the maintenance of its character and proper objectives."

Jamaica (Pop., 1,051,000). The study circle method has
done much to advance co-operation in this country. These groups
in time form credit unions and then buying clubs as beginnings
in co-operative practice. Farmers' marketing and credit co-operatives predominate.

Japan (Pop., 65,000,000). The co-operative movement in

Japan originated among the farmers and small producers as credit societies in the middle of the last century. Most societies still are credit co-operatives, of which there are 15,000. The first consumer society was in Tokyo in 1878. Consumer commodity societies consist chiefly of agricultural purchasing organizations; they purchase materials for the farmers' needs and for their personal and domestic consumption. Fairly satisfactory state laws regulate these societies. Consumer societies, with stores, are developing in the towns among salaried workers and wage earners. In 1937 there were 210 such societies, with 150,000 members. Eighty per cent of the farmers are members of co-operative societies. The consumer societies have over 5,000,000 members. Health societies numbering 120 are highly successful. They employ 1,000 of the 50,000 doctors of Japan. In 1940 there were 14,000 co-operative societies of all kinds, with 7,000,000 members. In 1945 the total membership had declined about 5 per cent. Co-operatives produce 20 per cent of the silk of Japan.

There are a national union and a wholesale. The wholesale is a federation of over 1,000 societies. The Agricultural Central Co-operative Bank is one of the largest banks of Japan.

Latvia (Pop., 1,900,000). Latvia had 500 consumer societies, with 150,000 members. Half of these belonged to the central union, Konsums. This union had a wholesale with several productive plants, including a tar factory, a fertilizer factory, several tanneries, a sawmill, a flour mill, and a machine shop. The national co-operative bank, established in 1920, had 400 organizations, with 100,000 members. Besides the above, there were societies for housing, education, fire insurance, cattle inspecting, bee cultivation, etc. Between 5 and 25 per cent of the net surplus-savings was used for educational and social purposes. This country, which between the two great wars had been making extraordinary progress in culture, education, and economy, has been deprived of democratic freedom and made a Russian vassal state as a result of World War II.

Lithuania (Pop., 2,390,000). The Lithuanian Co-operative Union had 400 retail affiliated societies, with 100,000 members. The wholesale had several warehouses, a slaughterhouse, and meat-packing plant. Lithuania had about 200 co-operative credit societies and banks. There were also a central co-operative bank and the Jewish Central People's Bank. The co-operatives handled 84 per cent of the salt, 76 per cent of the sugar, 60 per cent of the cement, all the fertilizer, and all the agricultural machinery.

For twenty years, as independent republics, the three Baltic States made great cultural and co-operative progress. The re-entrance of Russian control has robbed them of self-determination and the rights of democracy.

Mexico (Pop., 16,400,000). The co-operative movement in Mexico has experienced many adversities, but it goes on. It has suffered especially from being complicated with the politics of the government. In Yucatan, the government has undertaken the promotion of co-operation without a realization of the difficulties in attempting to mix incompatible elements.

New Zealand (Pop., 1,500,000). The New Zealand movement is similar to that in Australia. The Cooperative Union and Wholesale Society is an efficient federation. It publishes *The New Zealand Cooperator.*

Norway (Pop., 2,814,000). In 1947 the Norway Co-operative Union (Norges Kooperative Landesforening) had 850 societies, with 250,000 members, over 1,000 distributive stores, and 5,000 employees. There were 104 bakeries, 67 butcheries, many boot-repairing shops, a flour mill, and several other factories. One of the largest distributive societies is that of Oslo. It has a model bakery and an up-to-date sausage factory. The society at Bergen is sixty years old.

The wholesale society of Norwegian Distributive Societies is steadily growing. Politically the movement is neutral. The Insurance Society (Samvirke) has a membership of over 100 societies and an increasing business. The wholesale has an electric lamp factory, a chocolate factory, a margarine factory, a coffee roastery, and a tobacco factory. The circulation of the journal *Kooperatören* is around 100,000. Co-operative reconstruction is progressing rapidly. A national co-operative school is in operation.

Palestine (Pop., 1,000,000 Arab; 600,000 Jewish). Co-operation was introduced in Palestine by the Jews. The Hamaschbir Society at Tel Aviv, formed in 1916, has many distributive stores. Hevrath Ovdim is a federation of 200 societies, most of which are retail distributive. There are co-operative insurance societies, transport societies, restaurants, schools, credit societies, and housing societies. Credit societies have 50,000 members. Agricultural, productive, and marketing companies also are prevalent. Co-operative factories, either consumer or producer owned, manufacture agricultural machinery, tools, boots and shoes, rubber goods, woolen yarns, flour and other foods. The co-operatives exported 300,000 cases of citrus fruits in 1946. Co-operative land settlement societies are of unique social importance. The movement is growing steadily and is making a profound impression on the people. Conscious of the advantages which the Jews are obtaining from their co-operative associations, the government for the past fifteen years has encouraged the Arabs to organize co-operatives.

Panama (Pop., 467,000). The new constitution of the republic of Panama in 1946 provided that the state shall "encourage and supervise producer and consumer cooperatives, and for this purpose shall set up the necessary institutions."

Peru (Pop., 6,147,000). According to the last report of the Department of Cooperation of the Ministry of Agriculture, Peru has 47 consumer societies, with 15,000 members. The consumer movement is larger than the farm marketing movement. Both are growing.

Philippines (Pop., 12,604,000). The National Co-operative League of the Philippines has over 600 co-operative consumer societies in its membership, with over 225,000 families as members. The paid-up capital of these societies amounts to $2,000,000.

Poland (Pop., 32,000,000). The total number of Polish consumer societies, before the German-Russian invasion (1938), was over 6,600, including 5,000 credit societies. The Union of Polish Consumer Societies had 846 organizations, with 275,000 members. When to these are added the agricultural and marketing associations, the total number of co-operative organizations in Poland amounted to 10,000, with more than 3,000,000 members.

The wholesale department of the national union had a number of productive plants and a 500-acre farm for producing poultry and eggs. The publishing department put out a large amount of periodical and other effective literature. The sales of the retail societies in the union amounted to $30,000,000 in 1938. The wholesale's sales were $18,000,000. It produced flour, soap, and other things. The business of the co-operatives was steadily increasing. The co-operatives distributed more than 12 per cent of the food sold in Poland before World War II.

As in many countries in which the political government is unsettled, people of Poland were turning to co-operation as the means of expressing the united social will. Peasants were joining in "economic unions" for the purchase of the things they needed and for the sale of products. Some of the best brains of the country had been turned away from the political movement and drawn into the "economic movement" which had lifted up the peasantry and given them education in self-government.

The trend was indicated by the election in 1922 to the presidency of the Polish Republic of Stanislaw Wojoischowski, who was one of the founders and for many years a director of the Union of Polish Consumer Societies, chairman of the Guild of Cooperation, author of books on co-operation which have had a profound influence on the development of the movement in Poland, and, at the time of his election, was professor of co-operation in the Commercial High School in Warsaw. The government encouraged the co-operatives. All the societies were confiscated by the Russians and Germans except in an area of about half the country where the dairy and other agricultural societies were permitted to function during the war. There the co-operative spirit kept alive. Notwithstanding the subjugation of the co-operatives, the Polish Cooperative Union (Spolem) actually increased its membership during the war. From 1939 to 1945 the number of its societies and their membership more than quadrupled. The reconstruction of the Polish co-operatives is one of the wonders of after-war history. Eighty per cent of the distribution of consumer goods is now in co-operative hands. Spolem handled such relief supplies as came to Poland after the war. The people as never before insist upon being permitted by the governments that are attempting jurisdiction over Poland to develop their co-operatives to supply their needs.

Portugal (Pop., 6,650,000). There was little of a co-operative movement in Portugal before 1920. In that year, a National

Union of Cooperative Societies was organized at Lisbon. The wholesale purchase of goods was entered into by the union. The federation now comprises over 200 societies. The movement expands slowly.

Puerto Rico (Pop., 1,544,000). The co-operative method is advancing in this country. There are 20 co-operative societies, with 30,000 members mostly for farm marketing and credit. There is one farmers' co-operative purchasing association, with 2,500 members and $3,000,000 yearly business. A new law in 1946 created the Department of Cooperation in the university and a co-operative office in the Department of Agriculture and Commerce.

Rumania (Pop., 18,053,000). Rumania had 5,000 credit banks, with a membership of over 1,000,000 before World War II. The banks had district federations with a Cooperative Credit Banking Central at Bucharest. The 2,000 consumer societies, with 300,000 members, organized into the National Union and Wholesale were steadily growing. Co-operative insurance was also expanding. After the war a surge of co-operative interest came from the people. By 1946 there were 1,035 new societies of all kinds, including 774 new farm supply societies and 144 consumer societies. Immediately after the war the government asked the co-operatives to do the major part of the distribution of relief. The present Russian influence leaves the situation uncertain.

Russia (Pop., 182,000,000). Russia before World War I was not only weak in consumer co-operative societies, but those which did exist were discriminated against by the government. With the weakening of the government during the war, the societies increased until the Russian co-operative movement became the largest in the world. By 1918 the number had increased until there were 26,000 consumer societies. Up to 1918 the Moscow Narodny, or People's, Bank was the financial center of the movement. It constituted a joint federation of local credit unions and consumer and peasant agricultural societies. In 1918, the bank had a capital of one hundred million rubles, and deposits amounting to six hundred million rubles. During the last year of the war, this great institution, set aside, all told, four hundred thousand rubles for cultural and educational activities. The Russian agricultural societies conducted distributive stores for their members. There was a large and rapid growth of consumer societies among the peasantry during the war.

In September, 1918, a co-operative university was opened at Moscow. Over a million and a half rubles were required to cover its first year's budget; this was contributed by the co-operative societies on a basis of a percentage of their turnover. The aim of this unique educational institution was to train co-operative workers. In 1918, 65 per cent of the food of Central Russia was distributed through the co-operative movement.

When the Bolsheviki came into power, in 1918, the co-operatives were the chief instruments of distribution. The new government itself at once undertook the task of controlling the production and distribution of food and other essentials. This followed from the Marxian philosophy. Accordingly, the government, by various decrees, began to exercise control over the co-operatives. By the Bolshevist decree of April, 1918, every consumer was compelled to become a patron of his local consumer co-operative. On March 20, 1919, another decree effected the consolidation of all the consumer societies and stores, as well as the co-operative productive agencies, into one nation-wide Consumer Commune.

In 1920, all distributive agencies, co-operative or nonco-operative, were confiscated by the state. The property of the societies became the property of the government. The Moscow Narodny Bank was closed. In short, the vast network of the co-operatives in Russia—consumer, banking, and agricultural—the greatest voluntary co-operative movement in the world, was completely absorbed by the political state. As a voluntary movement, it disappeared. It was confiscated without compensation.

Then came the demonstration that socialization of industry by a political government was difficult. The political appointees proved inefficient. Bureaucracy and politics contrasted poorly with the former economic independence. The membership resented the change. As a result of the failure of state-controlled "co-operation" to function effectively, the Soviet government nominally re-established the autonomy of the co-operative societies by the decree of April 7, 1921. The Centrosoyus again became nominally independent of the government. But actual freedom from the political state was never restored. The Soviet government proceeded to keep control of the co-operatives by the use of the multitude of expedients available in an autocratic government.

The co-operatives continued to expand. Most retail distribution in Russia was through their agency. Their factories and schools increased. But they were all subject to Communist control, and so far as possible were used by the government to promote its policies and programs. What was called co-operative education was dominated by political propaganda.

In 1935 a government decree was issued abolishing the co-operative stores in the towns. Their assets were confiscated by the government without compensation to the 9,881,000 members. They are now state stores. The rural societies, with 41,000,000 members, still survive. It remains to be seen whether the government will become strong enough to take over these.

Two conflicting forces are to be seen operating in Russia. There is the dogmatic insistence upon the virtue of the all-dominating state, which is a natural product of Marxism. This would have crushed the co-operatives, had it been able, and left nothing but state business. There is also the undestroyed desire for voluntary action. There is still the hunger for freedom which keeps alive the spirit of co-operation. This ultimately may prevail.

Communism is an utopian ideal. Its aim is a society with communal ownership and administration by the working class. Communism in Russia under autocratic dictatorship has acquired a new meaning. It is state socialism plus a purpose to use force to establish and maintain a political dictatorship of a minority of the proletariat, if a majority is not available, and to employ force to maintain the economic system which it would administer. The Russian experiment shows that, while the abolition of the state is a theory of communism, it is a remote possibility in the communist program. This form of state socialism, when discovered in action, is found attempting to strengthen the autocratic and coercive state on every hand. The state takes the place of the capitalists and itself becomes the one big capitalist corporation. This spells corporate monopoly. The ownership of property vested in the state places the officeholders in the personal position of the capitalists. The political officials are the privileged class. Democracy is made impossible and the working class is destined to eternal conflict with the autocratic political government.

Co-operation cannot exist together with communism. The fact that communism has not been attained makes possible the modified co-operation which prevails in countries whose politics are dominated by Communists. Here the consumers maintain in their own interests co-operative associations which the state, as a matter of political expediency, finds it best to countenance. Communist government regulates and controls the co-operatives as far as possible, or as seems wise; and takes to itself the credit arising from institutions which it would destroy, were it stronger or they less popular.

Most industrial production in Russia is carried on by the government in state-owned factories. The consumer co-operatives are permitted production in small factories. There are 11,000 small industries making clothing, shoes, harness, barrels, soap, etc.

After the confiscation by the government of the urban societies in 1935, the country and village societies continued to expand. By 1947 there were said to be 30,000 societies of all kinds—19,000 consumer societies and 11,000 industrial producer co-operatives. These latter consist of workshops and small factories. The consumer co-operatives have over 200,000 stores. The total membership of all societies is said to be 75,000,000. By the decree of November 9, 1946, the consumer and the producer co-operatives were all brought more closely under state control and even administration, and compelled to give more attention to supplying city consumer needs. This apparently was in response to the failure of the state-owned stores adequately to serve the consumers.

Spain (Pop., 23,650,000). At the First National Congress of Cooperatives in Spain, in 1921, a National Federation was created. Its Fourth Congress was held in 1935, and reported progress from 482 affiliated societies with 157,000 members. This was a mixed federation, 131 societies being other than consumer distributive organizations. The total business in 1935 was $17,000,000, on a paid-up capital of $2,500,000. The consumer co-operatives worked in relation with the producers. The strongest movement was in Catalonia, a district of textile workers, where a regional wholesale was in operation. A national wholesale was in process of development at the beginning of 1936.

An example of what consumer co-operation can accomplish was in the Catalonian fishing town of Puerto de la Selva. This was a co-operative community, and differed from neighboring towns in its absence of poverty and in its general appearance of well-being. The store, the café, the hotel, the theater, the insurance, the credit, the school, and health protection were administered by the co-operative—even the issuing of its own money. Spain had a steadily increasing number of co-operative medical clinics, bakeries, and restaurants. Its insurance and banking societies were expanding.

Upon the establishment of the republic in 1931, co-operation grew steadily and enjoyed protection at the hands of the government. After the civil war in 1934, the reactionary government discriminated against co-operatives; since 1945, co-operation has made but difficult progress under the Fascist regime.

Sweden (Pop., 6,162,000). Sweden has a co-operative union (Kooperativa Förbundet, formed in 1899) with a general wholesale. From 1926 to 1942, the membership of its societies doubled. In 1947 K.F. had over 700 affiliated societies, with 6,500 stores and a total membership of 900,000. The total business of its retail societies amounted to 1,000,000,000 kroner. Banking and insurance are carried on by these societies, as is distribution. There are more than 30,000 co-operative employees. The co-operatives do more than 40 per cent of the consumer goods business of the country. The total membership of all co-operative societies is 2,500,000.

The fire insurance society, Samarbete, the accident insurance society, Valfard, and the life insurance society, Folket, are growing and successful co-operative enterprises. *Konsumenbladet,* the official weekly organ of the union, has the largest circulation of any paper or periodical in the country. K.F. is the largest publishing business in Sweden. Educational courses are given by mail and in the people's high schools. K.F. conducts a college for co-operative education near Stockholm. Much attention is given also to employee education. The societies do not participate in politics.

The wholesale has a coffee-roasting plant, bakeries, fish canneries, factories for margarine, cash registers, galoshes, automobile tires, chemicals, fertilizer, shoes, foods, viscose, textiles, earthenware, porcelain, etc.; and two flour mills, the largest in Sweden. Its defeats of the Swedish margarine, flour, rubber, and electric lamp trusts are national economic events. It produced for the consumers 350,000,000 kroner worth of goods in 1946. It is the chief manufacturer of rayon yarn. Its bathtub factory has a capacity of one tub every two minutes. Its cash register production lowered the costs 50 per cent and saves the people of Sweden 100,000 kroner a year in the cost of paper rolls alone. The Stockholm society is characterized by its beautiful stores. It is the largest retail society. It has 85,000 members with 400 stores, including a department store in the central business section.

The government has appointed the Swedish co-operatives as distributors and price regulators of all imports into Sweden. Most electric current of Sweden is distributed by consumer electric supply associations. There are 1,500 such organizations. Housing is also highly developed. Fifteen per cent of the people of Stockholm live in co-operative houses.

Switzerland (Pop., 4,066,000). The pioneer Rochdale consumer society was opened in 1851. The Zurich society, established in 1851, was the first to employ the word "Konsumverein." Swiss statistics show 669 distributive, 404 water supply, 400 electric and gas supply, 775 credit societies, and 7,180 farmer co-operatives.

The Union of Swiss Consumer Societies is composed of 534 societies, with 500,000 member families and 2,000 stores. The Swiss Union (Verband Schweizerischer Konsumvereine) was established in 1890 and conducts a number of factories. Its printing plant and shoe factory at Basel, flour mills at Zurich and Vevey, and meat-packing plant at Prätteln are models of equipment. Other successful enterprises are furniture making and banking. The Central Co-operative Bank of Switzerland, with 200,000,000 francs capital, is the depository of the consumer co-operatives and the trade-unions. It promotes co-operative housing. Much attention is given to co-operative education. More than 9,000,000 copies of daily, weekly, and monthly co-operative papers are issued yearly. The nine publications of the union are of high literary excellence. In German Switzerland, half the population are connected with the co-operatives. The Swiss Wholesale is the commercial side of the union. Co-operative insurance is conducted by the Swiss Union, with the active support of the trade-unions. Housing societies are well advanced in Switzerland.

Switzerland has many towns that are almost wholly co-operative. For example, the city of Basel comes near to being a co-operative community. Most of its population are embraced by the co-operative society, which has the largest and best stores in the city. Here is to be seen an example to which civilization might aspire.

The Swiss government has not shown hostility toward the co-operative movement, but has on the whole been friendly. Swiss societies are neutral in politics and accordingly have no split in their movement.

Turkey (Pop., 13,650,000). In 1946 there were about 1,000 co-operative societies of all kinds. They included 560 rural credit societies, 80 agricultural marketing co-operatives, 144 handicraftsmen's societies, 154 consumer co-operatives, and 49 housing associations. The credit societies have 170,000 members. The marketing co-operatives perform certain purchasing functions. Housing co-operatives are performing excellent service, many school co-operatives supply student needs. Co-operative education is well advanced in the schools and colleges.

The United States of America (Pop., 141,000,000). The American Indians carried on much of their economic affairs on a co-operative basis. They pooled their properties and administered them in common. This practice created communal strength. The United States government compelled them to discontinue it and required each Indian to hold his property separately. A more enlightened Indian Administration in the 1930's tried to restore to the Indians their ancient co-operative rights.

Co-operative colonies settled on the land in the eighteenth century. They were occupied in farming and other productive work, and buying in common. The Mormons long practiced co-operation in Utah.

William Bryan, founder in 1828 of the Brighton, England, Cooperative Society, came to America in 1829 and founded a co-operative society with a store in 1830 at or near Hudson and Leroy Streets, New York City.

Another beginning of co-operative organization in the United States was in 1845 when the Workingmen's Protective Union opened its first store in Boston. Since that time the working people have made continuous attempts to establish co-operative societies. These old societies lacked the fundamental qualities of co-operation. Those which could be regarded as co-operative were wanting in co-operative education. Their members rarely understood the nature of their enterprises. Most of them failed.

The building and loan associations represent another form of early co-operation which extends over a long period. The first organization of this sort was the Oxford Provident Building Association founded near Philadelphia in 1831. The first struggling societies were practically all destroyed by the public demoralization incidental to the Civil War. Co-operative banking and credit associations date back to the early part of the nineteenth century.

While co-operation was making its remarkable progress in Europe during the past century, it advanced slowly in this country. The chief reason for this slow progress is that until 1916 there was no national central source of information such as existed in each European country. The people started societies that were not really co-operative in method; and they attempted to run them without guidance. Besides this, there are economic reasons. A new country with limitless opportunities breeds the spirit of individualism. Profit-making business and the quest for the dollar dominate the public mind. Each individual hopes to get more than his neighbor in the competitive struggle. In no country has the urge of individual profit-making become so strong and the opportunities so great.

In the United States an unsocial individualism has prevailed. Each one hopes for something to which his fellows are not to attain. Each is exhorted to "make his way"; that means to get ahead of others. He does not want the others to "get ahead" with him, or his purpose would be defeated. The result is a psychology opposed to working together for the good of all.

Co-operation in the United States has to do with a mixed population. People of alien races with different customs and languages do not always mix well.

Fluctuations of population are caused by the newness of the country. The people are restless. They do not remain to live in the neighborhood where they were born. They do not grip fast to a locality. The presence of frontiers to the westward, toward which a fluid population could move, was an obstacle to the stability necessary for co-operative organization. People who are not long in contact with one another, but are always having strange neighbors, develop an individualistic and suspicious nature.

The slowness of co-operation in the United States is due also to the fact that poverty is so overshadowed by wealth that the escape from poverty always seems possible because of the abundance of money. The idea that any man can grow rich by his own individual actions has deterred people from uniting in a project which is based upon an acknowledgment of the need of mutual aid, and in which the early rewards are so meager while the efforts are so great. These American conditions are incidental to a new and wealthy country.

The strenuous competition among private tradesmen and the allurements of advertising have won the people to a habit of shopping and bargain hunting until these have become prevalent forms of American recreation. While competition has kept prices down and has made it possible to find reasonable prices, it has prompted the tradesmen to offer every inducement and enticement for the sake of trade. The people are satisfied with the service which profit business gives them. Also, they want bigger and quicker returns from their investments than co-operation offers.

The United States is the land of the great god "Business." The laws, as well as the public psychology, are adjusted to the profit-making system. The influential elements in each community are the boards of trade, merchants' associations, and chambers of commerce. These organizations are composed of the prominent citizens. They dominate the schools, the press, and the public thought, as well as the industries. And these bodies, found in every community, are generally opposed to the co-operative movement. Often the methods that can be used by a powerful organization to destroy a weaker one are resorted to by these elements to suppress co-operative associations.

Another serious hindrance to co-operative progress has been the multitude of spurious "co-operative" societies. They have varied from the fanciful schemes of well-meaning dreamers to the most unscrupulous frauds. These enterprises have taken millions of dollars from working people, who are left hostile to true co-operation.

There is another side. For over fifty years there poured into the United States a stream of immigrants from countries having well-established co-operative movements. These people brought with them not only the knowledge of what their native societies were doing but they brought a co-operative spirit. There have survived from that early period many societies scattered over the country. A few of these date back forty and fifty years. The immigrant people united with the native stock and promoted co-operaion.

The farmers have done the most of any one class for co-operation in the United States. This is partly due to the fact that until 1921 the farmers were the largest class. Unlike Great Britain and the other industrial countries with a wide co-operative development, it has not been the industrial workers but the farmers who have taken the lead. Much help has come from the agricultural population who emigrated from Denmark, Germany, Norway, Sweden, and Finland. But old American stock has also done much for this development. The strength of the co-operative movement is now in the rural districts. The native-born are taking an important part.

In the New England States there is an increasing number of consumer distributive societies. Most were established in the present century. They have stores, restaurants, bakeries, consumer creameries, and other enterprises. In the Middle Eastern States, New York and Pennsylvania lead. The Central States have many societies. Ohio, Illinois, and Indiana are in advance. In Michigan, Wisconsin, Minnesota, and the Dakotas there are still more societies. Here are many Finns and Scandinavians.

Among the Western States there is a growing movement.

Nebraska, Kansas, Missouri, Colorado, California, and Iowa are outstanding. Some of these in the past five years have become great centers of co-operation. Oklahoma, Texas, Maryland, Virginia, and North Carolina have large and successful consumer societies. Every state has a growing co-operative movement. This growth is mostly among the farmers who are turning to consumers' co-operation. The consumer agrarian movement in this country begins with the joint purchasing of farm supplies, and then moves on to the supply of domestic and personal needs.

Two national federations of societies constitute the consumer co-operative movement of the United States. The Cooperative League for thirty years has represented the educational and promotional interest of co-operatives, and National Cooperatives, organized in 1932, has represented the business and commercial interest. They are composed of wholesales and national or regional federations. The League is the U.S. member of the International Cooperative Alliance. National Cooperatives represents the U.S. in the International Cooperative Wholesale Society. The consumer societies which possess the best understanding of consumer economics and are most concerned for national and international co-operation of co-operatives are in membership in these organizations. The majority of societies in the U.S. do not yet qualify for this membership. They cannot be regarded as of the consumer co-operative movement, for isolated unfederated societies are not constituents of a movement. But co-operative education and understanding are slowly modifying these disqualifications.

Among the members of these two organizations are the following consumer-controlled co-operatives with the location of their central offices:

American Farmers Mutual Auto Insurance Co., St. Paul, Minnesota.

Associated Cooperatives, Oakland, California.

Central Cooperative Wholesale, Superior, Wisconsin.

Central States Cooperatives, Chicago, Illinois.

Consumers Cooperative Association, Kansas City, Missouri.

Consumers Cooperatives Associated, Amarillo, Texas.

CUNA Supply Cooperative, Madison, Wisconsin.

Eastern Cooperatives, New York, New York.
Farm Bureau Cooperative Association, Columbus, Ohio.
Farm Bureau Mutual Auto Insurance Co., Columbus, Ohio.
Farm Bureau Services, Lansing, Michigan.
Farmers Cooperative Exchange, Raleigh, North Carolina.
Farmers Union Central Exchange, St. Paul, Minnesota.
Farmers Union State Exchange, Omaha, Nebraska.
Indiana Farm Bureau Cooperative Association, Indianapolis, Indiana.
Industrial Arts Cooperative Service, New York, New York.
Midland Cooperative Wholesale, Minneapolis, Minnesota.
Pacific Coast Student Cooperative League, Berkeley, California.
Pennsylvania Farm Bureau Cooperative Association, Harrisburg, Pennsylvania.
Utah Cooperative Association, Salt Lake City, Utah.

Most of these are district federations with wholesales. They are controlled by the retail societies which own and run them for their own service. The retail societies constitute their membership and control them by the same Rochdale methods as the retail societies are controlled by their individual members.

The above societies own 179 mills and factories including 10 up-to-date gasoline refineries, in seven states, with a capacity of 70,000 barrels a day. They own 1,664 miles of oil pipe lines, 489 oil wells, and maintain 1,425 oil service stations. They have 100,000 acres of oil lands under lease. These figures are constantly increasing. The co-operatives are now the largest independent oil refiners in the country. Their retail distribution of oil in 1946 amounted to $365,000,000.

One of these federations, composed of 1,028 retail societies in eight states, with its headquarters in Kansas City, has shipped, at cost, petroleum products of its own manufacture to the co-operative wholesales of Estonia, Bulgaria, Scotland, France, Belgium, Norway, Holland, Sweden, South Africa, Egypt, Australia, Canada, China, Czechoslovakia, Italy, Siam, Switzerland, and Tunisia.

Societies carrying on petroleum business tend to expand into other fields. In 1945, for example, a North Dakota petroleum association bought a garage with an apartment and a hotel. A Minnesota petroleum association bought a general merchandising store. An association in Minneapolis, operating six gasoline stations, acquired an automobile repair garage, and a coal, feed, and lumber business, and four food stores.

Besides petroleum, they conduct many other industries. Their fertilizer factories have broken the trust prices in Ohio and Indiana. Their feed mills and flour mills have made it possible for farmers to get these commodities at cost. They have factories for producing tractors and farm implements, milking machines, chemicals, paint, milk products, cereals, and the canning of vegetables. They own coal mines and have recently acquired 6,000 acres of coal fields in Kentucky containing an estimated 12,000,-000 tons of coal. They have bakeries, printing and publishing plants, coffee roasteries, and plants for producing reliable seeds. The astonishing discovery is made that many of these factories pay for themselves in savings in from one to three years.

The 20 regional federations in this membership did a total wholesale commodity business in 1946 of over $200,000,000. This business has been increasing at the rate of 25 per cent a year. The 20 regional federations have 4,522 retail societies operating 5,500 retail stores, doing a total business of $700,000,000 in 1946. Their total membership exceeds 2,000,000. In 1945, the net surplus-savings amounted to 5.8 per cent of business done in retail stores, and 8.9 per cent in petroleum retail business. The increase of membership was 25.6 per cent.

Consumer co-operatives in the United States in 1947 totaled over 27,000 associations, with more than 6,000,000 members. They include 44 wholesale federations of farmer consumer commodity associations. They did $1,850,000,000 business in 1946. The 2,800 farm supply co-operatives have 1,700,000 members and do over a billion-dollar business.

A federation in the Northwest increased its business and its membership 75 per cent in the past year and leads in co-operative health organization. An Eastern States wholesale is one of the ten largest food wholesales in the U.S. It has 171 member societies. It has in its membership a society in New York City with 8,000 members, conducting seven restaurants, four food markets, an apartment house, bakery, and other enterprises. Another in Ohio, with $35,000,000 business in 1946, conducts over 500 educational study groups. The oldest of these regional federations, located in the Northern States, has a book publishing business and has in its membership a number of retail societies which are the largest business in their respective towns. It did $8,000,000 business in 1946. Its 225 societies have 300 stores and 32 oil service stations. A federation which covers the state of Pennsylvania is regarded as so sound a business that investors seek its shares in preference to capitalistic securities. A regional league in Texas, with a major oil business, takes leadership in the promotion of co-operative health associations. Its gasoline refinery has a capacity of 8,000 barrels a day. The federation in Indiana, with a business of $26,000,000 in 1946, owns the largest fertilizer plants and was the first to buy a capitalistic bank and convert it to its own co-operative service. Several of these federations have bought banks, insurance companies, and public utility corporations. A wholesale in the Northern States which began as an oil co-operative now has one of the largest grocery businesses in its district, with 460 retail societies doing $51,000,000 business a year. Their surplus-savings in 1946 amounted to over $3,000,000. The association with headquarters in Kansas City has the largest co-operative gasoline refinery, located at McPherson, Kansas, with a capacity of 17,500 barrels a day. Among its many other enterprises it has a lumber mill which produces twenty-two carloads of lumber a week. This association saved its members $1,665,000 on its $26,000,000 business in 1946; $15,000,000 worth of the materials it supplied came from its own factories. Its member societies did a business of $126,000,000 in 1946.

Outside the Cooperative League and National Cooperatives are many consumer organizations with other affiliations. Among these is the Grange League Federation, of New York, which manufactures and purchases for the use of its members more than $100,000,000 worth of materials a year. The National Council of Farmer Cooperatives is a federation of 107 such associations, with a total membership of 2,000,000 individuals. United Cooperatives is a large and successful wholesale.

The 825 rural electric co-operatives have electrified 1,500,000 farms, despite the opposition of the profit public utility companies. They are now buying old and established public utility company plants. This has recently been done in Ohio. In the Northwest, thirteen co-operative electric supply societies united in 1946 to purchase an extensive electric power system for $34,400,000.

The 10,000 credit unions, or co-operative banks, have over 3,000,000 members and $350,000,000 capital. Five thousand telephone co-operatives supply 350,000 families with service. Some 2,000 co-operative or mutual fire insurance societies have 10,000,-000 members and $170,000,000 yearly premium income, with outstanding insurance amounting to more than $6,000,000,000.

Co-operative health protection is represented in a steadily increasing number of health societies and co-operative hospitals, owned and controlled by the patients and prospective patients. Housing societies are multiplying. Co-operative lumber mills are supplying farmers with lumber at cost.

A feature of co-operation in the U.S. is what are called Campus Cooperatives. They are organizations of college and university students to supply themselves with housing, food, clothing, books, athletic goods, and other needs. Some rent houses for dormitory purposes.

Others own their own buildings. They conduct restaurants and have dining rooms in their houses. Most campuses have co-operative stores. These are all owned and run by students. Many have grown into big businesses.[4] Some of them make student living very cheap. A student co-operative in the University of Texas reduced the cost of living to $3.50 a week; and claimed they had made possible that "it is cheaper to go to college than to stay home." The University of Washington has so many of these that they have federated to form their own wholesale. There are regional federations of campus co-operatives. In 1945, five of these federations, representing 4,000 students, united to form the North American Student Cooperative League.

The total of producing plants owned and operated by consumer co-operative societies in the United States is as follows: 10 gasoline refineries, 489 oil wells, 1,664 miles of oil pipe lines, 11 oil compounding plants, 6 printing plants, 8 sawmills, 2 paint factories, 7 seed mills, 42 chicken hatcheries, 13 fertilizer factories,

[4] See *Harvard Cooperative Society—1882-1942*, by N. S. B. Gras.

2 flour mills, 5 coal mines, 2 coffee roasteries, 2 canneries, 7 bakeries, 8 soybean processing plants, 4 farm machinery factories, 4 food processing plants, 1 slaughterhouse and meat-packing plant, 7 insecticide and fungicide factories, 2 chemical factories, and 12 other productive enterprises.

Besides these organizations are other associations for retail store distribution, restaurants, housing, telephone, medical service, burial, recreations, etc. (See Forms and Expressions of Co-operation, page 82.)

Rochdale Institute, the national school for the training of co-operative educators and executives, and the training schools of the district federations carry on co-operative education. The district federations employ educational secretaries, conduct schools, publish their local papers, and promote much co-operative education. The larger retail societies do the same.

Outside the field of consumer co-operatives are 10,000 farm marketing co-operatives, with 3,000,000 members, doing a yearly business of $4,500,000,000. They supplied one-third the foodstuffs shipped abroad during World War II. The membership of these marketing associations learn to co-operate in marketing. Then they begin to realize that they are consumers also and proceed to use their marketing associations to make purchases for them, or they set up a separate purchasing association and thus get a larger understanding of the fundamentals of economics. The total business of all co-operatives in the U.S. was $13,100,000,000 in 1945.

In many European countries the Catholics have their own co-operative societies apart from those of the Socialists and Protestants; but in the United States there is no division; the Catholics are in the societies with the other classes. The aim of this national movement is to unite all elements, and to eliminate creedal and political antagonisms by maintaining strict neutrality. Racial groups in the United States have their own co-operatives, but in the course of time they take in members of other nationalities and lose their racial quality. The Finns, Germans, Italians, Poles, Czechs, Bohemians, Spaniards, Negroes, and Indians have their own co-operative enterprises. In Chicago is a large co-operative store connected with a Negro housing enterprise. Many successful stores and other co-operatives are conducted by Negroes in the South.

The lack of a national co-operative organization had been the early deficiency in this country. To meet this need, the Cooperative League of the United States was organized and started work in 1916, with headquarters in New York City, to federate into its body all genuine consumer societies. It collected information concerning co-operation in the United States; made surveys of failures and successes; published information; gave advice; standardized methods; created definite policies of action; prepared by-laws for societies; conducted a bureau of auditing and accounting; maintained an office in Washington for legislative information and advice; prepared study courses; published books, pamphlets, and periodicals; promoted district federations; and in every way possible advanced co-operation. The League is a federation of co-operative societies, governed by its constituent members. The best and strongest of the societies are its members. Through the League, the United States movement is connected with the International Cooperative Alliance. National co-operative congresses have been held under the auspices of the Cooperative League in 1918 and every second year since. The Cooperative League sent 22 delegates to the 1946 Congress of the International Cooperative Alliance in Zurich, Switzerland.

As a result of the work of the League, the knowledge of co-operation has penetrated to every state. The mistakes which characterized the pre-League period are becoming rare, and failures fewer. Co-operation is being discussed in colleges and universities, articles are constantly appearing in current periodicals, and the churches are advocating co-operative economics.

Venezuela (Pop., 3,027,000). This country has a growing co-operative movement. The agricultural and credit societies predominate. Much attention is given to co-operative education. There are many co-operatives in the schools among the pupils. In 1944 the republic of Venezuela issued Rochdale Memorial postage stamps to commemorate the one hundredth anniversary of the founding of the Rochdale co-operative store in England.

Yugoslavia (Pop., 13,930,000). Before World War II, this country had a General Cooperative Federation constituted of

16 co-operative unions composed of a total of 4,579 co-operative societies, with a collective membership of nearly 1,000,000 individuals. There were in all 11,000 societies of every kind. There were 65 co-operative members to every 100 farm families.

There was a variety of societies based on nationalities. The Union of State Employees' Societies of Belgrade comprised 88 consumer societies, with 22,000 members. The Union of Serbian Agricultural Societies of Belgrade comprised 705 consumer societies. Former Carniola had three unions. Former Croatia had a federation of 324 consumer societies. Slavonia had a union of 177 societies. There were many consumer health societies. The largest society was the Workingmen's Society of Laibach, established in 1895. It had 12,000 members. Much educational work was being done. The present Russian domination favors state ownership and control. The immediate status of the co-operatives is doubtful.

Other Countries. Co-operative societies, as above, are developing in other countries. There is apparently no corner of the world where co-operation is not found. Often, exploration brings to light surprising examples of societies in unexpected places. The natives of East Africa conduct highly successful co-operative societies. South Africa has a progressive movement with successful societies in many towns. A union and a wholesale have been established. Armenia has a growing co-operative movement.

Since 1918, the French Cooperative Federation has carried its educational work into North Africa with the result that a steadily growing movement exists in Algeria, Tunisia, and Morocco. The largest retail grocery in Algeria is co-operative. Tunisia has many co-operative handicraft societies.

The Malay States present all types of societies, including a Society for Better Living. Burma has over 3,000 credit societies. Siam has over 5,000 co-operatives, mostly credit societies. The Straits Settlements are multiplying their co-operative banks. The West Indies are developing producer organizations, out of which consumer societies are growing. In Haiti, the government is teaching the people how to set up co-operatives. Newfoundland is expanding its co-operatives, especially among the fisherfolk. It has 180 societies, of which 30 are consumer co-operatives doing a business of $1,000,000 in 1946. More than half the population of the island of Cyprus are served by co-operatives.

Ecuador has been developing co-operatives since 1923. In Uruguay, the National Cooperative Institute includes most of the co-operative societies. British Guiana, Chile, and other less conspicuous countries are developing co-operatives of promise. They seem destined to go through their periods of experiment, mistakes, and successes. The sooner societies join their national federation and the sooner it affiliates with the International Alliance the shorter seems to be the period of misadventure.

At the beginning of 1946, according to the International Labour Office, there were 143,000,000 persons in membership in co-operative societies of all kinds in 43 countries. Most of these memberships mean a family. This indicates that more than one-fourth the population of the world are embraced in these societies. Some 78,000,000 of this membership are in cities and towns. In the cities, 59,000,000 persons are members of consumer co-operatives supplying food, clothing, and fuel. Co-operative housing associations have 8,000,000 members. There are more than 6,000,000 members of co-operative credit unions.

The International Cooperative Alliance. The Alliance was founded in 1895. Representing the application of the co-operative principle in international relations, it aims to be a union of the federated co-operative societies of all countries. The executive offices are in London. Its objects are: (1) to collect information concerning co-operative principles and methods in all countries and to promote education and propaganda; (2) to maintain friendly relations between the members of the Alliance; (3) to collect co-operative statistics; (4) to provide information and to encourage the study of co-operation; and (5) to promote service relations between the co-operative organizations of all countries. Before World War II, the co-operative societies in forty countries were federated into national organizations, and these national organizations were federated in the International Alliance. It was composed of 193,000 co-operative societies, with a total of over 100,000,000 shareholding members. The total business of these societies in 1938 amounted to more than $20,000,000,000.

The Alliance holds an International Cooperative Congress at suitable intervals. Such congresses have been held at London (1895), Paris (1896), Delft (1897), Paris (1900), Manchester (1902), Budapest (1904), Cremona (1907), Hamburg (1910), Glasgow (1913), Basel (1921), Ghent (1924), Stockholm (1927), Vienna (1930), London (1934), Paris (1937), and Zurich (1946). This Zurich Congress was the first after World War II. It was composed of delegates from the co-operatives of twenty-four countries.

The Alliance is a nonpolitical league of nations without diplomats, secret sessions, protectorates, mandates, imperialism, or other political mechanisms. Its congresses represent a true league of peoples. Its Central Committee is elected from its national constituent members and meets at regular intervals. Its Executive Committee holds more frequent meetings. The Alliance continued to function through World War II, and added to its membership the national co-operative leagues of China, Australia, and New Zealand.

The *Review of International Cooperation,* the official organ of the Alliance, published monthly in three languages, has been issued regularly since 1908. The work of the Alliance is a factor in the promotion of international union, sympathy, and peace. The Alliance has also an International Cooperative Wholesale Society. An International Cooperative Banking Committee and an Insurance Committee are organizing international co-operative institutions in these fields.

International co-operative wholesaling is already far advanced. For example, the English and Scottish wholesales are the largest producers and importers of tea in the world. The Scandinavian wholesales jointly conduct the most successful electric lamp factory in their respective countries; they have coffee plantations in Java and other enterprises. Most of the international wholesaling consists in exchange of commodities among the constituent wholesales. This has become large international commerce and represents a form of international relations which, perhaps, portends more for world peace than the many peace gestures of the warmaking nations. At least, here is a steadily growing international commerce from which are absent the causes of war which characterize profit-business's international traffic in goods, credit, and natural resources.

The International Cooperative Wholesale Society and the International Cooperative Trading Agency are the organizations which are gathering within their scope these international commercial activities. They embrace the national wholesales of twenty-one countries, and are steadily expanding. They will naturally have as members all the national wholesales of all countries which have such institutions. One of the leading functions is the exchange of commodities among the various national wholesales and between agricultural productive societies and consumer organizations. The function of international co-operative wholesaling might well be to perform on a world-wide scale services which the member societies perform nationally. Buying and selling at wholesale for profit is not co-operation.

A modern 13,500-ton oil tanker is owned by the co-operatives and carries oil from the co-operatives of the United States to the national cooperative league of Sweden, which owns a gasoline refinery. This vessel is now in commission and is carrying on international co-operative petroleum commerce. At the last Congress of the International Cooperative Alliance, the International Petroleum Association was formed. The co-operative wholesales of twenty-two countries at once subscribed to its $15,000,000 capital. This highly significant international commerce owes the preliminary pioneering that was carried on for several years to the Consumers Cooperative Association of Kansas City.

The business of international wholesaling should be precisely the same as that of national wholesaling—serving constituent national wholesales without profit. The I.C.W.S. should move toward the production, manufacture, and distribution of commodities which can best be handled on so large a scale. Its province will include commodities which can best be produced and handled by an organization having in its international scope access to materials which are not naturally produced in many countries. Tea, rice, coffee, tropical fruits, raisins, currants, olives, oils, salt, fertilizer, lumber, coal, fish, hides, furs, flax, silk, cotton, petroleum products, and other such commodities, which are not produced in all countries where the constituent societies are located, would naturally best be supplied by the international so-society. The ownership of steamship lines, international transportation of freight and mails, transcontinental railroads, and other international utilities may in time come within is province—as co-operative and not as profit enterprises.

Besides international co-operation in commodities, the members of the International Cooperative Alliance have under consideration the development of international co-operative banking and finance, insurance, travel for recreational and educational purposes, and international co-operative education.

The United Nations Political and Security Committee, meeting in London, February 12, 1946, against the opposition of Russia, voted to admit the International Cooperative Alliance to consultative affiliation with the United Nations Economic and Social Council.

Chapter IV

FORMS AND EXPRESSIONS OF CO-OPERATION

Distributive Stores. The distributive retail store is the nat-ural and prevalent expression of the co-operative consumer so-ciety. In order to begin distribution to themselves, people have often organized upon a meager basis. They have put together a small amount of capital and purchased in quantity some one or more articles, which have been stored in an individual's house or other building, to be divided among the co-operating participants. There are many societies, composed of a few people, who have their little store in the house of a member. A member gives his services free. The home is the place of business and of meetings. This is the primitive method. There are many of these "buying clubs" in the United States. The store often follows as a result of a certain amount of education and experience. A definite organ-ization is then created, capital raised, and the larger enterprise launched.

In the United States, co-operative mail-order businesses are serving their members from illustrated catalogues. The colleges have store co-operatives run by teachers and students for provid-ing commodities, pressing clothes, lending credit, supplying hous-ing and board, and other services.

Most countries now have a national union, as we have seen, which provides all the necessary information and guidance. In countries which have a wholesale society, new organizations at once have a co-operative source of supplies where the members are guaranteed fair dealing. With educational guidance and a source of commercial supplies, success in such countries is assured.

In Europe, the co-operative stores are apt to be the most reliable stores in the town. Their goods are of a quality better than the average. Their buildings as a class are better than profit stores. Societies with as many as fifty or a hundred or more branches often have a building department, and carry out the details of construction of their own buildings.

There is in general a friendliness between societies which prevents overlapping. This means that each neighboring society recognizes the jurisdiction of the other, and does not attempt to establish stores in a territory occupied by another society. Of course, there are exceptions; rivalry sometimes exists between neighboring societies. Such business rivalry is distinctly opposed by all co-operators and everything is done to discourage it; it is regarded as contrary to co-operative principles. The national co-operative federations have rules to prevent it. The union of adjacent societies is constantly taking place. In some countries, while statistics show a decrease in the number of societies, they show also an increase in the number of stores and members.

Wholesales, which are federations of co-operative retail societies, in Scotland and some other countries establish some retail stores of their own where needed. Then gradually a society is built up around the store, and in time acquires its local autonomy. Where the wholesale treats the retail as a branch and continues to control it, without allowing the consumer patrons to acquire the ownership and control, business efficiency may be temporarily promoted, but democracy is defeated; and without democracy co-operation is defeated in the end.

It is customary for the stores of co-operative societies to handle everything the people want. Usually they begin with the things most urgently needed—food and clothing. From these, they expand toward the less commonly used articles. Large societies have department stores. In many European cities, the biggest department store will be found to belong to the co-operative society. Countries which are co-operatively weak often exhibit stores which are neither attractive nor efficient.

As one walks through the streets of a town, the co-operative store may not impress the stranger as peculiar. But it is different from the profit-making store. It is a social institution which is affecting the lives of the people—often more profoundly than they realize. It is the ever-present and living demonstration that business can be carried on for service by those who are served. It is the quiet and unsuspected school in which the people are training themselves for a different economic system.

Co-operative Wholesaling, Importing, and Manufacturing. Wholesaling is carried on by organizations which are formed by the federation of distributive societies or unions of distributive societies. In some countries producer organizations are permitted to be stockholders. But naturally wholesaling is distributive business in the interest of the consumers. A wholesale society is formed by the consumer societies taking shares and paying in share-capital. The members of the wholesale are the retail distributive societies. Each member society has votes in the administration in proportion to the size of its membership or in proportion to the amount of patronage it gives the wholesale. The wholesale is governed by a delegated body elected by the member societies. The administration of the wholesale is by a board of directors and commonly also an executive committee. These bodies are often full-time salaried officials. They appoint managers and other employees.

In some countries the wholesale is a department of the national union or league which also promotes education and protection. In other countries it is separate and independent. In others there is a close union between the two—as where the directors are the same in each.

One fundamental principle applies in all cases: a wholesale must be a federation of societies. Attempts of individuals to establish a wholesale, and then expect societies to patronize it, have not succeeded. Such experiments naturally are doomed to failure for the reason that a co-operative wholesale must be a community of interests the same as a consumer society; and the control must rest out among the consumers. The ownership and control cannot be centralized as in profit business.

Forty countries before World War II had co-operative wholesales. Many of these conducted banking and insurance service for their members. Wholesaling, like retailing, begins with distribution of the wanted necessities. In time, when large-scale distribution has been mastered, and often the wholesale finds itself buying the total output of factories, the next step is taken and the wholesale goes into production. Sooner or later, co-operative consumer wholesales reach this point. Then manufactories are added to the business. It would be difficult to find a necessary commodity not produced by these wholesales. The largest shoe production in Great Britain, the largest meat production in Switzerland, and the largest flour mills in Sweden are those of the co-operative whole-sales. Foods, clothing, hardware, furniture, chemicals, jewelry, watches, radios, and vehicles are co-operative products of many lands. The important fact is not that many of these industries are the largest in their respective countries, but that they represent production of commodities for the use of the people who own the plants, and not for sale by the owners to others. Better products are one of the results. The electric lamp bulbs made by the Scandinav:an co-operative wholesale are purposely made to last 25 per cent longer than the bulbs of the lamp trust, which are purposely made to last 25 per cent shorter time.

The next step in the progress toward the elimination of the profit motive is the acquisition of raw materials or the control of natural resources. The most important fact about the coal mines owned by co-operative societies is not that they are well administered, but that the coal is mined for and used by the owners of the mines. Forests for wood for matches, boxes, and lumber pur-poses are owned by several wholesales. Many thousands of acres of farm lands owned by wholesales produce vegetables and fruit for their canning factories. Some societies own herds of cattle for milk and meat production. Many own other livestock. The natural resources of the sea are in this category through the fish-ing boats of several European societies.

Many large retail distributive societies also conduct flour mills, shoe factories, shoe repairing, canning works, creameries, farms, and other plants. A growing tendency among co-operatives is the movement toward self-sufficiency; and wherever societies can sat-isfy their needs locally by their own efforts they tend to do so, leaving to centralized wholesales the services beyond the local capacity.

In the United States, an unusual condition prevailed during World War II, and still continues. Federations of consumer so-cieties purchase manufacturing plants in such a way that they cost nothing. The owners of a plant, or a bank, approach the co-opera-tive with an offer to sell. Since the government takes as much as 85 per cent of the profit, the business prefers to sell out to the co-operative which can make a go of it because it does not make any profit. A bank or the government lends the co-operative the money for the purchase. Then the co-operative makes an extraordinary discovery. After running the business, it finds that in the course of from one to three years the surplus-saving amounts to the capital cost of the purchase. The plant has paid for itself in that time. The capital investment and the interest are paid off and the co-operators find themselves the owners of many millions of dollars worth of manufacturing plants, free and clear, without themselves having taken a cent out of their own pockets. This has given rise to the co-operative slogan: "Own your own factory; factories are free!" Many of the gasoline refineries, oil blending plants, pipe lines, and factories for fertilizer, feed, flour, and farm machinery; coal mines; vegetable canneries; and a multitude of the other 179 manufacturing plants owned by co-operative consumers in the United States have been acquired in this way. Only by this experience have the co-operators been able to learn of the enormous profits made in the manufacturing business. They simply patronize themselves into ownership without paying any more than before for what they consume. This means reduction of the cost of commodities to the consumers.

Another peculiarity of co-operative consumer-owned manufacturing plants is that they do not fail. Factories owned by producers and by capitalist profit business fail. But factories owned and run by the people, who themselves use the product, are in a strategic position to the importance of which neither economists nor reformers have yet awakened.

Housing.   The form of housing which is most eminently co-operative is that in which the co-operative housing society owns the land and houses, and the members occupy the land and houses of their society. Each member puts in a certain amount of money or share-capital which, with loans secured from their own or other lending institution, provides the funds used to purchase land and erect houses. A single home is taken by a member, which is his in perpetuity or so long as he occupies it as a member of the society. For convenience and economy, instead of each owner having a sole ownership of one home, the responsibility is thus shared. This applies to raising funds, construction, upkeep, mortgage, and amortization. Gardening, central heating, central laundering, and other services are often performed co-operatively.

The co-operative housing society is a consumer society. After the dwellings are constructed, the board of directors and the executive committee supervise the administration. The members pay what is called "rent" at the current price or less. The word "rent" is used for convenience; but it is quite as incorrect as is the word "sell" when applied to the co-operative store. One does not rent from himself his own property. The member tenants make a monthly payment to the society. This fund is used to pay common expenses of upkeep, interest, etc. A part is set aside in an amortization fund and another part in a reserve fund for expansion. The balance is returned to the members in proportion to their payments; or the surplus-savings are used for social purposes, maintaining playgrounds for the children, beautifying the gardens, providing a central social building, etc.

Some societies, or federations of societies, having many members and, having developed a large surplus, maintain their own architectural bureaus, artisans, door and frame factories, brick kilns, cement works, tile and pipe factories, and painting establishments. All this is possible while the members are paying no higher costs for their housing than they would be paying to a private landlord. Houses are created thus out of funds which otherwise would be profits for somebody else.

Another form of co-operative housing enterprise is that promoted by the consumer distributive society. Many of these are societies with stores, etc., that use some of their surplus to build dwellings which are rented to their members. Co-operative societies in many countries have built blocks of apartment houses for their members.

Many European cities have housing societies. The Cooperative Garden City of Nuremberg is unusual in its charm. One of the best of these demonstrations in Switzerland is Freidorf, near Basel, a society which owns not only the one hundred and fifty houses and gardens, but the streets, the park, the school, the restaurant, and the recreation hall. In Switzerland, since World War II, three-fourths of the houses built are of co-operative construction and owned by consumer societies.

Some building societies, especially in England, sell the houses outright to the members. This at once introduces the possibility of the member becoming a real estate speculator and selling the house for more than it cost him or renting it to others at a profit. As soon as this happens, the co-operative feature disappears. It is on account of this that one sometimes hears of a co-operative housing society putting up attractive dwellings; but when one goes there a few years later, the co-operative society has disappeared. The London Cooperative Society, with nearly 1,000,000 members, in 1945 began the construction of 500,000 new houses, to be rented to members.

Permitting the ownership of a specific house and land to be absolutely in the hands of one individual invites speculative use of the property. And this is precisely what true co-operation aims to avoid. The attempts to prevent the sale or rental for profit of homes, co-operatively built but privately owned, have not been successful. The only housing whose co-operative character can be guaranteed is that form in which the private ownership is vested is an association of members, and each one has the private use of a specific part of the collectively owned property. He may be permitted to sell at par his share in the collective property; but in a real co-operative housing society, neither the buildings, the land, nor the lease may be sold by any individual. The mutuality of the undertaking is thus preserved.

The member has a lease instead of a deed. But the co-operative lease proves a better guarantee of permanent domicile than a deed. The dangers of foreclosure of mortgage and the sale of the house are better prevented by a nonprofit organization of houseowners, mutually banded together to perpetuate and protect their homes, than by a lone individual.

In the best societies, when a member must move away or sell out, the society buys back from him his shares and investment at cost. This also is done temporarily, if he wishes, with the lease. In the United States, societies have been destroyed by the increasing value of property; the members have actually voted to discontinue the co-operative principle, profiteer in their investment, and sell or rent as landlords, when they found that the value of their property had greatly increased.

It is for such reasons that a member of a consumer society is not permitted to own a shelf in the store, another a drawer, another the counter, another the scales, etc. Such specific ownership is fatal to co-operation.

In Italy and some other countries, housing has been promoted by the state, and there is comparatively little true co-operative housing. Municipal or city-owned housing exists in many places. Often, as in Vienna, the municipal houses are occupied by leaders and henchmen of the political party which happens to be in power. This is wholly different from co-operative housing.

It is an interesting fact that the co-operative houses often are better, cleaner, more homey, and less expensive than similar houses owned by municipal governments. In many cities, the rents of municipal houses are higher than those of co-operative houses. The reason is that the bureaucratic political method is more expensive than the simple and direct co-operative method of construction and administration. As a member said: "We are the owners of our buildings. We take an interest in them. We are here to stay. The renters of the city's houses are a different class of tenants. They have not invested any money, and they have less interest in beautifying their premises with flower boxes, gardens, or personal touches. The municipal dwellings look like tenement houses. They cost more to rent because of all the salaried officials which it takes to run them. We run our own." That describes the difference between co-operatively owned and politically owned enterprises.

In Copenhagen, for example, each housing group is a department of the main housing society. The rent is collected, the repairs and upkeep are made by a local committee from each group of homes. Each independent group elects its local officers and also two members to the central board. The central board decides on problems of larger finance, such as the purchasing of new property, the erection of new buildings, and the administration of its works and factories. The central board has an elected executive committee, with a full-time chairman and seven officers, who are paid for their services. Twice a year there is a general members' meeting of all the householders, to whom the central board makes its reports.

This Copenhagen society has 34 apartment houses containing 6,000 dwellings. It also has a charming suburban colony of stucco and brick cottages, each one surrounded by a garden. The members consider the homes as their own, for their society gives them a perpetual lease. In addition to their homes a series of co-operative shops for groceries, meats, hardware, and house furnishings is conducted.

Stockholm has over ninety co-operative apartment houses occupied by more than 90,000 people. Gothenburg has nearly half its population in co-operative homes. In these more co-operative countries, the member of a society, when he wishes to move, is transferred from one society to another and thus the change of residence is facilitated.

Leases are usually for ninety-nine years or more, with the privilege of transmitting the lease to one's heirs or family. Thus the sense of proprietorship and pride in one's home is preserved, while the possibilities of real estate speculation are removed. Co-operative housing is housing for home purposes only. Most people in American cities, nurtured in the theory of home ownership, in fact live in somebody else's house. The landlord about every ten years takes the total value in rentals. The tenants literally buy the house every ten years, give it back to the landlord, and let him then proceed to sell it to them again. The co-operative method applies the monthly payments to tenant ownership.

Among the best expressions of housing in America are the Amalgamated co-operative houses in New York, housing over 5,000 people. Co-operative housing leads to other co-operative ventures. This association maintains a food store, a generating plant for its electricity, laundry, milk distribution, credit union, and a wide social, educational, and recreational program. Its surplus saving in 1946 returned to each member the equivalent of a month's rent. A $10,000,000 co-operative housing project, Circle Pines, is in process near Minneapolis. A $5,000,000 project, East River Co-operative Houses, in New York was developed in 1945. Co-operative homes' are being built in Washington, D.C.; Racine, Wisconsin; and other cities.

At no other time in the history of the United States has there been available such a wealth of material and technical ability for the creation of homes; and at no other time has so large a proportion of the population been without homes. One-third the housed population live in rural hovels and city slums. The dominance of the price and profit system, as expressed through the builders and real estate dealers, obstructs co-operative housing.

The problem of adequately housing the people, it would seem, can be solved when the people themselves unite their resources in their own co-operative building societies; and then proceed to supply their own needs. Co-operative methods applicable to housing have been worked out and standardized by practical experience. When the standardized methods are used, success may be expected to follow.

Banking. By 1939, world affairs had come to a pass at which the commercial and the economic life was largely controlled by credit. This means that the banking business dominated the situation. The banker, like the potentate of old, sat in the high place, and withheld or gave life and privilege. He decided whether industries operate or be idle, whether men be paid or go hungry, whether war be prosecuted or peace declared. The bank had become the throne.

Money was the medium that connected labor and consumption in all fields except that in which the consumer actually produced for himself. Indeed, it had become more; it had become also the barrier which often separated labor and consumption. Money had come to represent the most potent form of property, and credit had come to be represented in terms of money. Credit was traded as a commodity. It was bought and sold. In this buying and selling of credit the people are at the mercy of the traders precisely as is the case with other commodities.

The working people, who are without credit, pass daily through their hands a golden money medium in a constant stream. Commonly as much goes out of one hand as comes into the other. That is the difficulty. How can these people cause just a little of it each day to stick to their hands, and thus begin the storing of reserves? That is what the banker does. Can the people do the same? We have seen that they have succeeded in doing this with their exchange of other commodities. Can they do it with money?

With the development of the co-operative movement has come this question. And it has been answered by applying to credit and money the same co-operative principles as have been applied to commodities for consumption. The co-operative store is an agency whereby 1,000 poor men make their dollar equal in purchasing power to that of the rich man's $1,000; and a co-operative bank puts the dollar of 1,000 poor men into a joint fund that gives them collectively the credit standing of the rich man's $1,000.

In the evolution of co-operative banking, there was also a pre-Rochdale stage. The same experimental period was passed through. Ineffectiveness and defeat were the rewards of the first attempts. Then came the Pioneers, who hit upon a plan that succeeded. And from that day to this, there has been a history of constant achievement.

The distress that swept across Europe after the Napoleonic Wars, and ended in the revolutions of 1848, called for the solution of pressing economic problems. Many people gave their minds to these subjects. Victor Aimé Huber (1800–1869) was the pioneer who explained the co-operative movement and showed its possibilities and ethical necessity to the people of Central Europe. He furnished the inspiration that gave rise to co-operative banking. A judge, Herman Schulze-Delitzsch, in Prussian Saxony, and Frederick William Henry Raiffeisen, a Prussian burgomaster, formulated and standardized the methods by which co-operative banking has attained success. These men saw the German people suffering for want of credit. The farmer and the small artisan were victims of the moneylenders. The people were not able to save and develop credit against a time of need. Schulze organized recreational, social, and welfare work among the people of his town. He helped establish a provident fund for the needy. And then, with the carpenters and shoemakers, he created an association for buying raw materials. It was a natural step from the supply of raw materials to the supply of money. In 1850, he established the first credit association. Gradually this grew into a co-operative bank. The Schulze system aims to stimulate thrift among its members. His idea was to help producers, such as artisans and farmers, with credit.

Raiffeisen formed a consumer distributive society in 1846, and in 1849 a moneylending society composed of prosperous citizens; but the element of charity in these societies, he found, weakened them. He then promoted credit societies on the basis of self-help similar to those of Schulze-Delitzsch. In 1869, he reorganized a society to provide rural credit which was based on mutual aid among neighbors.

The Raiffeisen banks have tended to develop more especially in the country. A characteristic of the Raiffeisen society is that it welcomes anyone as a member whose character is vouched for by his neighbor members even though he has not a cent. The borrower must be a member of the society, and the use to which he is going to put the money must be known and approved by the loan committee. Money is loaned on character. The borrower pays interest. The interest received from the borrowers is used to make good any losses or impairments that the paid-up capital may have suffered. Interest is paid on deposits but at a lower rate than is charged for loans.

The propaganda promoted by Raiffeisen was idealistic as well as practical. He had a vision of a growing movement that would play a large part in bringing about a better state of social justice and would make the working people independent of the state and of philanthropy.

The Raiffeisen bank in Europe is usually found located in a dwelling house, a workman's shop, a room in a barn, a small office, or wherever the treasurer happens to be. Small depositors—children, women, old men, artisans—come with their little amounts and their bankbooks and make their deposits. The borrower applies to the lending committee when he wants a loan. Sometimes the executive clerk who keeps the books receives a small salary. The Schulze-Delitzsch banks, on the other hand, are often seen in their own banking premises, with barred windows, clerks, and all the paraphernalia of a banking house. Some of them have large and extensive business connections. However, some of the Raiffeisen banks in the United States now occupy their own bank buildings.

From these beginnings and out of these practices has grown the co-operative banking movement that is to be found in every country. In many lands it has raised the poor peasant farmer from a state of poverty to independence and self-reliance. Districts in which the credit banks have been established have undergone a marvelous change. It is no wonder that a bronze statue of Raiffeisen was erected in front of his house at Heddesdorf, that thousands of farmers attended its unveiling in 1902, and that he is proclaimed in Germany the patron saint of agriculture.

The co-operative bank, credit bank, people's bank, popular bank, or credit union is today to be found in every part of the world. These banks carry on both small and large banking business. They differ somewhat in each country.

The surplus-savings ("profits") in these banks go to the stockholder members in proportion to their investments or deposits. Some believe that the most equitable distribution of surplus-savings is to divide them in proportion to patronage—to member depositors in proportion to deposits and to member borrowers in proportion to the amount borrowed. This is practiced by some banks in Belgium; it is a custom in France; and it is popular in Italy. The savings-return to be paid is best calculated on the basis of the amount of interest paid to depositors and received from borrowers. Although this latter method theoretically may seem most just, it has never come into general use. The usual method is to give the borrower his benefits in the form of a reduced rate of interest. Being also a member, he receives interest on his stock.

The most common practice is to pay a fixed rate of interest on stock, to give the net surplus-savings to depositors, to reduce the rate of interest to borrowers as the surplus-savings increase, and to require depositors and borrowers to be members.

The control of co-operative banks is democratic and in the hands of the members. Business is done largely with the members. The Raiffeisen type of bank has become the more popular. The credit unions of Denmark have been of especial service in lending money to the small farmers. These organizations are independent of the government, and represent a splendid type of self-help. In Norway and Sweden the co-operative banks have been of much service. In many countries, federations of co-operative banks have created a national central bank.

In Poland and some of the adjacent countries, the co-operative banks became the centers around which the economic life revolved. In some provinces of Poland these banks had gradually absorbed almost every form of financial activity.

Co-operative banking was introduced in America by Alphonse

Desjardins, at Quebec, in 1900. He brought his experience to the United States in 1905, and the first credit union law was enacted in Massachusetts in 1909. Credit unions have been promoted in this country especially by Edward A. Filene and Roy F. Bergengren. Most states now have a credit union law. A federal law was enacted in 1933. A national federation of credit unions in the United States is now in operation.[1] The following are the characteristics of these credit unions: (1) membership is open to persons having a community of interest with the group; (2) low membership fees, low-priced shares, and installment payments for same; (3) democracy of control; (4) loans only to members; (5) loans to officers only under exceptional circumstances; (6) loans only for productive purposes and urgent needs; (7) interest charge of not more than 1 per cent per month; (8) loans made on character as well as on collateral; (9) interest paid to fully paid shares of stock.

The low overhead costs make it possible for the member depositors to get back most all that as member borrowers they pay in interest. The weakness of the credit unions is that they encourage borrowing. That is debt. If when a member borrows he were required to pay back in installments twice the amount borrowed, borrowers would then be compelled to become savers, to increase their credit with each need, and thus capital would be expanded.

The total number of co-operative credit associations in the world in 1940 was around 120,000, the membership 50,000,000, and the annual business $15,000,000,000. All this has sprung largely from the work of Schulze and Raiffeisen. Outside this field is a large number of "co-operative banks," "savings and loan associations," and "building and loan associations," having enormous capital. With slight changes in method, these near-co-operatives could become real co-operative institutions.

A new field of co-operative banking which has experienced great growth in latter years is the banking department of the consumer co-operative association. Not only do members leave their savings-returns, but they bring their money and make banking deposits with their societies. The central wholesales in many countries carry on a central banking business, the local distributive

[1] Credit Union National Association, Madison, Wisconsin.

societies acting as branch banks. In 1946 the city of Salford, England, transferred its £5,000,000 yearly banking business to the Banking Department of the Cooperative Wholesale Society, withdrawing the city's funds from the local commercial banks. Already more than a hundred English municipalities had done the same.

The striking characteristic of all forms of co-operative banks is that they suffer no losses, or have losses which are so small a fraction of 1 per cent that they are taken care of by the reserves created for that purpose. In the United States, from 1929 to 1947, the losses among these banks, which made loans to working people on the security of character alone, have been inconsiderable when compared with the losses among capitalistic banks, in proportion to money invested. Banking business, which the average workingman thinks of as intricate and mysterious, becomes safe when carried on co-operatively for his service.

The banking departments of the British co-operative wholesales have loaned to municipalities as well as to their own co-operative associations. In public crises the co-operative banks have come to the rescue with their joint capital. The time has come for the co-operatives to carry on their own banking system, nationally and internationally, and not be dependent upon the commercial banks.

Co-operatives could issue their own money, based on a unit of labor and a unit of time, and backed by their ownership of vast properties. An international bank within the International Cooperative Alliance could solve many problems of exchange. Beginning with the co-operatives of forty countries now in the Alliance, the co-operative credit system could expand indefinitely. The future hopes of monetary practice depend upon the issuance of money not by political governments but by people in their economic organizations. A unit of money having a regular declining value would keep money in circulation, compel people to spend and use money to get things and services. The co-operative movement should be ready to lead in the reorganization of the prevalent vicious monetary system and move on toward the time when money shall serve only for accounting purposes and represent services performed or goods or property delivered.

Insurance.   Nearly every kind of insurance is provided by co-operative societies. The Joint Insurance Department of the English and Scottish Wholesale Societies carries on all sorts of insurance, including life, accident, fire, burglary, fidelity, employers' liability, livestock, plate glass, automobile, boiler, electric plant, etc. Its total assets amount to £38,000,000; its premium income in 1941 was £9,700,000; and its employees 8,266. Each year it shows an increase of reserves and of premium income.

The Health Insurance Section of the English Cooperative Wholesale Society has grown to a membership of 600,000. It provides free dental treatment, legal assistance for recovery of compensation, convalescent home benefits, and benevolent grants. It paid over £8,000,000 sickness compensation in 1941.

The co-operative societies of England are more and more employing the life insurance provided by the English wholesale. Every purchasing member of insured societies is thus insured without the payment of any premium by the individual. Retail societies insure their whole membership. The retail pays the wholesale one penny a year for every £1 of purchases made by its members. This simple system insures all. The amount paid to the widow, widower, or children is based on the average annual purchases for the past three years prior to the member's death. This insurance requires no medical examinations, no agents, no individual premiums, and no complex bookkeeping. It is simple and automatic. And its justice rests upon the fact that the needs of the family are judged by what it consumes. This insurance scheme promotes loyalty to the society.

Co-operative insurance in many countries offers special benefits. This is particularly important for the employees of co-operative societies. The amount of insurance guaranteed constitutes one of the advantages they enjoy over employees of profit business or of the government. The co-operatives make every effort to provide for their employees and members in times of calamity.

Practically all members of co-operative societies in Finland, Denmark, and Sweden have enjoyed the benefits of such insurance. This method of insurance has been steadily expanding in at least forty countries.

Co-operative insurance in the United States is largely agrarian. It is highly successful. The 2,000 co-operative fire insurance companies among the farmers in the United States carry insurance exceeding $6,000,000,000 on property valued at over $7,000,-000,000. This insurance is carried at about one-half the rate charged by profit-making companies. The credit unions are now adding life insurance to their functions.

Education. Education is a fundamental business of co-operation. The ideal of co-operation is that each country shall have a co-operative educational institution, and each district and local society some form of educational organization. There is a tendency for each co-operative society to have an educational committee. The function of this committee is to acquaint the members with the history, principles, and methods of co-operation. While the need is admitted, only a minority of retail societies have an effective functioning committee.

Large societies often maintain an educational secretary with assistants who are full-time paid executives. It is the general practice for co-operative societies to circulate a paper or magazine which reaches all the members; societies which do not themselves publish such a periodical are supplied with one by the national central union.

Co-operative schools and classes are growing in popularity. These are of two main types: (1) those which teach co-operation as a general cultural course for students of economic problems and (2) those which give courses for the training of co-operative executives and managers. The two naturally fuse into each other. Practically all national co-operative unions conduct such schools.

The British Cooperative Union organizes and conducts classes in all parts of Britain. It holds examinations, grants diplomas, gives prizes for excellence, provides scholarships, and conducts a co-operative college. It publishes a vast amount of literature. It conducts summer schools, weekend schools, and schools for children. It has lately been laying much stress upon children's education in "children's co-operative circles," "co-operative comrades' guilds," and "junior choirs." It organizes both junior and adult choirs, and has published two co-operative songbooks. It publishes a number of co-operative dramas. Lantern slides and lectures also are provided. It produces its own cinema films. Its courses of training for executives prepare people for important co-operative positions.

The Swedish union has similar schools and carries on similar work. Its co-operative college, near Stockholm, trains executives and administrators. Swedish co-operative education penetrates all parts of the country, and is constant and intensive. Switzerland also maintains an excellent co-operative college.

In the United States, the Cooperative League for thirty years has shown societies how to organize educational committees. Rochdale Institute, the national co-operative college, has its headquarters in Chicago. It conducts courses also in other cities. It gives general cultural courses and trains co-operative employees, educators, and executives. It prepares study courses on co-operation for schools and groups. District leagues conduct summer schools. Some train executives. Teachers from the Cooperative League have lectured in practically all the important colleges and universities in the country. The states of Wisconsin, Minnesota, and South Dakota have enacted laws making the teaching of consumer co-operation compulsory in high schools, vocational schools, state universities, teachers' colleges, and country normal schools; and all teachers of economics in such institutions are required to be informed on this subject. Teachers of economics in several American colleges give lectures on the subject to their classes. Many schools and universities in Europe have a chair of co-operation.

In South America are chairs for the teaching of co-operation in the Institute for Cooperative Studies of the University of Cauca, Colombia; in the Cooperative Institute of Bolivia; and of Panama. The University of Bogotá has a professorship of co-operation. Cuba has a National Institute of Cooperation. The same exists in Venezuela, Uruguay, Ecuador, Peru, and Argentina. A resolution establishing a chair of co-operation in the National University of Lima says: "This resolution was based on the necessity of transforming the Peruvian economy, of accomplishing this transformation on a cooperative basis, and of giving the orientation of the cooperative movement solid, economic and scientific foundations." The oldest chair of co-operation in South America was founded in 1925 in the Faculty of Economic Sciences of the University of Buenos Aires.

There is a chair of co-operation at the School of Economics at Ankara, and courses at the University of Istanbul. Centrosoyus, the Russian co-operative league, has three co-operative colleges with 950 students, 42 technical schools with 9,000 students, 47 co-operative schools with 5,000 students, and a school for the training of co-operative teachers with 125 students.

The pupils in many schools in France and other countries organize co-operative societies for the supply of school necessities, thus obtaining practical co-operative education. There is still another form of co-operative education: there are schools providing instruction outside the field of co-operation, but conducted as co-operative societies. The consumers—the students—organize the schools, finance them, and control and administer their affairs. This is the real expression of consumer co-operation in education. A number of such schools have existed in New York for preparing students to take civil service examinations.

In the United States the co-operatives have been instrumental in having courses and lectures on co-operation introduced in colleges and universities. In 1946, the Belfast Cooperative Society gave £2,000 to Queen's University in Belfast unconditionally.

Recreation. People are interested in recreation as the next most important matter after the vital hungers. The recreational committee is an important adjunct to every co-operative society. In the United States, the Cooperative Society for Recreational Education conducts a national convention each year and several regional schools during the year. The Cooperative League circulates a number of co-operative films which are both educational and recreational. The best education is rich with recreational possibilities. The choir and orchestra are found in many consumer co-operative societies. The United Cooperative Baking Society of Glasgow has bands and a children's chorus of several hundred voices. The society of Ghent has three bands. Several English societies own theaters or cinema buildings. The society of Helsingfors owns an island in the harbor for recreational purposes. Several American societies have recreational parks.

In many countries, farms with mansions and manor houses are acquired and used for recreation. The Swiss Union's Recreation Home in Weggis, the mansion and grounds at Shornells of the

Woolwich Society of England, the fine old mansion house at Whympstone, with its 2,500 acres of grounds, of the Plymouth society are all examples of the tendency to satisfy recreational needs.

Throughout the world the co-operative society is found aiming to have its own central building, and, as soon as it gets it, provisions are made for recreation and education. The motion-picture show is found in hundreds of co-operative buildings in Europe. Many co-operative films are produced. A number of co-operative dramas have been written. Walking clubs and every sort of recreational organization are found in co-operative circles. Some American co-operatives, like many European societies, employ a recreational director.

Most co-operative recreational work is carried on by consumer societies, but many special recreational societies exist. These have been organized to carry on some special form of recreation, such as motion-picture shows, alpine clubs, sailing, and athletic clubs.

A Co-operative Press. The press is rarely impartial; it is usually the instrument of the owners and advertisers. With few exceptions, the daily press is controlled by profit-business interests. The press reflects their opinions and serves them. So well is its propaganda value understood that certain forces often own the press for the specific purpose of creating public opinion. But to maintain the profit press as a financial success it must serve also the advertisers.

There is one form of periodical which is organized for its readers. A paper owned and controlled by the consumers—the readers—is in a position to serve their interests. Consumer-controlled printing and publishing is widespread, including the United States, where many societies and institutions publish books and periodicals for the use of their members.

Let us not make the mistake of thinking, however, that a press is co-operative when it is owned and run by a political government or by an organization of printers. The first will be found to be the organ of the dominant political party. The second form of publication will be found serving the interest of the restricted group who own and print it. Its policies are those of the few owners, and its profits are limited to the producers. The truly co-operative press is that which represents the consumer. It, too, will be found loaded with propaganda in the interest of co-operation, but it serves consumers and no class.

Co-operative publications may be issued by societies already organized and existing for general distributive purposes or by special societies organized for publication purposes. The latter are operated upon precisely the same basis and by the same methods as the former. Several countries have a co-operative publishing society, owned by the co-operative distributing societies. The United States has such an organization, the Cooperative Publishing Association; also a co-operative publishing business owned by authors, the Island Press.

In Europe the co-operative press has become a fact. In all countries with a well-developed co-operative movement, there are a good number of periodicals issued by the co-operative societies. There are some 78 national co-operative publications; in addition to these, there are several thousand papers and magazines published by local societies. Among the latter are a number of dailies. The *Cooperative News,* the largest co-operative paper, was started in England in 1871, and has appeared every week since that date.

Printing and Publishing. Because of their interest in education, co-operative societies have early occupied themselves with printing and publishing. Many local co-operative societies have their own printing plants. Many of the national co-operative unions have large printing establishments, with many employees, and print co-operative books, periodicals, papers, and stationery. The Swiss Union does printing of a highly artistic character. The Cooperative Press of Great Britain does much of the printing for the British co-operators. Its shares are mostly owned by consumer societies. This Press, founded in 1869, has printing and bookbinding establishments at Manchester, Newcastle, and London. Its annual business amounts to £300,000. It maintains a fund which pays to employees upon retirement an annual pension.

Bakeries. Baking is one of the fundamental needs which is promoted by the co-operative method. The Belgian movement began with bakeries, and these bakeries have been the veritable mother's breasts from which the growing movement has taken its sustenance. The bakery represents the simplest and most natural approach to production for use. In practically all countries the consumer bakery is an early expression of co-operation.

So successful has the bakery been in the hands of these associations of consumers that in hundreds of cities and towns in Europe the bakery of the co-operative society is the best bakery—the best equipped, the cleanest, and the largest. The societies of Stockholm, Helsingfors, Budapest, and Basel have model bakeries. One-fourth the bread supply of Great Britain comes from the co-operatives.

Most co-operative bakeries are conducted by distributive societies which have other enterprises—especially stores. The bread is sent to the stores for distribution. But some bakeries are organized exclusively as baking societies. Such a one is the United Co-operative Baking Society of Glasgow, Scotland. It was organized in 1869, and its first bakery was started with one oven in a little house on a back street. Now it is a federation of 212 co-operative societies.[1]

One striking effect of co-operative bakeries is that they keep down the price of bread made by private bakeries. Wherever they appear they become a challenge to the profit bakeries. Another effect is that they improve the quality of bakery products. At the present time the co-operatives of Great Britain are supplying bread, made of American wheat, at one-half the price of bread in the United States, and paying bakers a wage equal to the American bakers' living-wage scale.

It has often happened that these bakeries are boycotted by the flour mills or wholesale sources of flour. When private profit bakeries feel the pinch of the better quality and lower prices which the co-operative bakeries establish in a community, they

---

[1] It has £500,000 share-capital, distributes £1,600,000 worth of bread and cakes a year, and makes a yearly surplus-saving of £60,000. It devotes £1,400 a year to cooperative education, carries £50,000 worth of goods in stock, and has £300,000 reserves. It uses 30,000 tons of flour a year and puts out 800 tons of bread a week. It has 120 ovens with the most modern machinery. Besides its central bakeries in Glasgow, it has bakeries at Clydebank, and at Belfast, Ireland. Among its members is the Scottish Wholesale Society from which it gets flour; and since this latter society is a large producer of flour, the access to source material is close.

resort to this method of compelling millers and dealers to refuse to supply the co-operative bakery with flour. Such action as this has rarely succeeded in doing permanent injury to a co-operative bakery. It was an attempt of this sort in Switzerland that resulted in the Swiss Cooperative Union's securing possession of the large flour mill in Zurich, and producing its own flour. This experience has been repeated in several countries.

Restaurants. Restaurants are established by consumer distributive societies and also as separate and independent enterprises. Many large societies maintain restaurants for their employees. Among these is the British Wholesale with its restaurant in the Manchester headquarters, capable of feeding 1,000 people at a time, and its restaurant in its London headquarters. Many wholesale societies have restaurants in their factories.

A combination of restaurant and service kitchen exists in the Amsterdam Cooperative Kitchen. This was started in 1903. It has over 1,500 members and sends out nearly 1,500 dinners daily to families at their homes. The restaurant serves also about 400 people twice daily.

Some consumer societies in the United States have excellent restaurants. Consumers' Cooperative Services, in New York City, is an example of the independent co-operative restaurant for middle-class working people. It has seven restaurants and 8,000 members. It gives especial attention to the service of clean, pure, and wholesome foods. Profits made from nonmembers are used for education and expansion.

The most common restaurants are those which are conducted by consumer societies having stores and other distributive enterprises. They are multiplying steadily.

Laundries. The co-operative laundry has naturally developed to meet the consumers' need. As with bakeries and other businesses, they are found in two forms: the laundry run by the distributive society which has stores and other enterprises, and the laundry which is organized as an independent society. The British co-operative distributive societies are establishing more and more laundries. Some of these have become large institutions, equipped with the most modern machinery. Some societies federate to form a district laundry society. These are again united in the National

Federation of Cooperative Laundries. Denmark has a nation-wide network of co-operative laundries. The 400 co-operative laundries in Sweden reduce the costs of laundering to one-fourth the charges in the profit laundries and employ methods that result in an enormous saving of fabrics washed.

Transportation. The transportation of people and commodities was originally carried on for service. Later much of it was undertaken for profit, and railroads and express companies developed. In many countries, the disadvantages of the profit system in transportation became so patent that governments have taken over these enterprises. This is still in process, and the socialization of the lines of transportation steadily continues.

The co-operative societies have as yet little to offer in the way of examples which approach in magnitude the private or state-owned railroad lines. There are many motor omnibus and charabanc lines which are run by co-operative societies. Co-operative transportation societies run much of the transportation in Palestine. The French co-operative wholesale society owns a couple of hundred railroad cars which run on other people's rails to carry freight for the society. Many other European societies own freight cars. The British wholesale has oceangoing vessels. A single society, for example, in England (the Plymouth Society) owns for transportation purposes 215 motor vans, 45 motor trucks, 100 railroad cars, 17 sightseeing automobile omnibuses, 7 touring cars, 9 milk trucks, 113 milk wagons, a sailing vessel, motor barges, etc. One can travel pretty much over the whole of England in the motor buses of the co-operative consumer societies. Locomotives and steamboats are owned by many societies. American societies own tank trucks for milk and for pretroleum products. Swiss co-opertives conduct railroads. In the Gulf of St. Lawrence, a co-operative owns and operates the buses, ferries, and airplanes which provide transportation for the islands.

The ability of associations of consumers to conduct big affairs is patent. About the first successful steam railroad was from Middleton to Leeds in 1804, and was organized, owned, and run by fewer people all together than are present today at any poorly attended members' meeting of the Leeds Cooperative Society. If private stockholders can finance and promote a railroad for profit, co-operative stockholders might do the same for service. It is only natural that ultimately the international wholesale should use its own vessels for its growing international transportation. In countries such as Denmark, Sweden, and Finland the co-operative societies are fully competent to assume control of the railroads—certainly as competent as a railroad commission. In a country such as the United States, where running railroads for profit purposes approaches its end, the travelers and shippers of each state, organized into co-operatives and federated nationally, are the natural material out of which ownership and control may be built. They have already bought and virtually paid for the railroads many times. By co-operative methods, the ownership might be consummated and put in the hands of the real purchasers.

Transmission of Verbal Communications.—Although the post, telegraph, telephone, and wireless communications are destined shortly to come under the jurisdiction of the socialized state, the co-operative societies might administer these essential industries. This is a difficult field. What success the co-operative societies will have in developing it is a problem wrapped in the uncertainties of the future. This we know: the people as consumers, in their voluntary associations, have developed postal and telephone services. Many rural co-operative telephone companies in the United States, and in Russia both telephone and postal service, have testified to the fact. About the first telegraph line was put up, owned, and run by Gauss of Göttingen in 1833. It did not even have a company. What an individual can do it would seem possible for an association of consumers to do.

Wireless transmission is in the same category. A boy of fifteen can carry on wireless communications with his neighbors and with the outside world. Possibly it is not beyond co-operative societies to do the same. Need people be intimidated by the politically-minded who insist that this business is too intricate for the simple consumers in a co-operative democracy, but must be run by the superior intellects of a political government?

The Cooperative Radio Association of Catalonia, in Spain, dates back to 1924. It was conducted for the cultural advantage of its members and broadcasted good music, theatrical performances, lectures, and other educational and cultural programs. These included co-operative education. Members paid two pesatas (28 cents) a month. The power of its transmission permitted it to be heard all over Europe. Members received a daily bulletin since the daily press, influenced by the commercial broadcasting companies, refused to publish programs. This association was a member of the Spanish National Cooperative Federation, which was a member of the International Cooperative Alliance.

A federation of co-operative societies in Washington, D.C., U.S.A., the Potomac Broadcasting Corporation, representing 20,000 consumers, is developing a broadcasting station at the nation's capital, with programs featuring music, education, art, and good literature.

Electric Power and Light.—This public utility has reached its zenith as a profit business. In many countries it is becoming a state function. In others it is found that distribution of elecricity is best undertaken by the co-operaively organized consumers. This is the case in Denmark. Much of the distribution in Sweden is in the hands of consumer co-operatives. The United States is moving in this direction, with some 825 electric supply co-operatives. An increasing number of farmer co-operatives supply their members with electricity. These co-operatives put up their wires and install their equipment. Some buy electricity at wholesale from municipalities which manufacture more than they need, some purchase from the federal government's newly created plants, some buy from public utility companies, and some manufacture current for themselves in their own plants.

Petroleum Products.—Consumers have had to look to profit-business for the distribution of lubricants, fuel oils, and gasoline until the farmers in the United States organized co-operatives for this purpose. This began at the close of World War I. Minnesota led in the development, but now these societies are in almost every state. This is the first co-operative business in the United States that has grown so large as to give "big business" some concern, and caused it to resort to every expedient to stop the co-operatives. These oil-distributing societies are usually organized independently, but many farmers' organizations are adding this business to their other undertakings. In the United States the supply stations of over 4,000 oil-distributing co-operatives compete with the profit companies. Their 1,500 oil service stations are highly successful. They lay aside reserves, expand their plants, conduct education, and give to their members savings-returns of over 25 per cent on the investments.

The first co-operative oil and gasoline association was started at Cottonwood, Minnesota, in 1921. Five years later several such retails federated and formed the first co-operative oil wholesale. They put together their money and bought the first tank car of gasoline. The expansion of this oil business has been constant and was accomplished largely by pooling the savings from the business. Comparatively little original new capital has been put in. These people have saved by spending. They have spent their way into the ownership of big business. The millions of dollars of equity in co-operative gasoline refineries, blending plants, and oil wells in the United States has cost most of the owners nothing.

The official publication of the profit oil industry has made the statement that, "Unless we can learn to compete successfully with these co-operatives, they are destined to become the oil-distributing business of this country." It is precisely in the difference between their methods that the difficulty for profit business lies. The co-operatives have their laboratories and are having produced for themselves the commodities they want according to their own specifications. Tests prove that they are getting the best gasoline and oils used in the country.

Coal.—The outstanding example of coal mining under consumer control was the Shilbottle mine of the British C.W.S. This is the best-administered coal mine in Great Britain. The government took possession of it during World War II with the approval of the co-operatives. An increasing number of coal mines in the United States and other countries are owned by co-operative societies. Many thousands of co-operative societies distribute coal. Many own coal cars and barges and bring coal from the mines. In many towns the larger part of the coal distribution is in the hands of the co-operatives. In the United States the time has come when the national wholesale or district wholesales could purchase coal mines and develop the business on a large scale. Co-operative societies also make contracts with mines to take their total output.

Milk.—Co-operative societies in many countries distribute milk to their members. Milk of higher nutritive value, greater cleanliness, and lower price is commonly the result. Reports of Health Departments of many cities show improved quality, reduced sickness rate, and increased milk consumption, as a result of the control of milk by the co-operatives. In many European cities the co-operative is the major milk distributor. In Great Britain, U.S.A., and some other countries, consumer societies have their own pasteurizing and bottling plants. One-fourth the milk of Great Britain is distributed by the co-operative societies. Milk is added as a matter of course to the business of food stores. Distribution of milk by the municipality was once much advocated and practiced in some towns in England; at the beginning of World War II, there was no municipality in the milk business, but most of the large co-operative societies had their creameries, pasteurization, and distribution. The result is increased price to the farmer producer and lower cost to the consumer. The Milk Board of Massachusetts has criticized the Society of Maynard for selling milk with more butter fat than the law requires—for selling milk that is too good. A small percentage of consumer societies have cattle and lands and produce milk for their members.

Undertaking.—The exploitation of bereavement has long been, and continues to be, a fruitful source of business profit. Co-operative societies in many countries have established undertaking and funeral departments to protect their members from the wiles of that ancient cult—the morticians. British societies have carried this service far, with their own coffinmaking, funeral parlors, and vehicles. In the United States are over a hundred societies providing this service. The undertakers, with much legislative influence, continuously oppose them, even to securing from a State Department the refusal to grant a charter to such a co-operative on the ground that "a corpse is not a consumer." Still the number of these co-operatives increases. They make a great saving for their members. A burial society in Oklahoma provides undertaking and funeral service for $38, for which the professional morticians charge $240.

Other Expressions of Co-operation.—Many other activities are not here described. Health care, courts and the delinquent, science and art, and invention are discussed in Part V. Many societies own hotels for the accommodation of their traveling members and their friends, especially in Great Britain. The United Cooperative Baking Society of Scotland has recently bought the Grand Hotel in Glasgow. Campus housing co-operatives, organized by college and university students, are notable institutions in the United States. (See page 74.)

Near-co-operation.—In the borderland of near-co-operative societies are many which call themselves co-operative but which violate one or all of the Rochdale principles. Some pay dividends on stock; some permit stock to vote; in some the majority of stock is owned by one man who may be manager; some are organized under laws that place the control in a few hands, and some purposely provide for autocratic control. These societies are often started in good faith by individuals who believe that these methods are better than the Rochdale co-operative methods.

Then there are the "co-operative societies" started by companies and corporations for their employees. These take the place of the "company store," of which the workers are often suspicious. The employers organize the store for the workers, provide the building, and sometimes furnish much of the capital. Often the business is run by Rochdale rules. But usually the whole affair is so under the wing of the employers, either from the acceptance of a rent-free building, or capital, or managing personnel, that the co-operative idea is not carried out. These organizations have the merit that the workers save some money, and often the demerit that lower wages are accepted in consequence. They usually obligate the workers to the employers and thus prevent strikes and other expressions of unrest. On the other hand, they give the workers first lessons in co-operation. The workers may wonder if the store would not serve them better if they were wholly responsible for it and absolutely independent. This thought is likely to come sooner or later. It came in the case of the restaurants, started by factory owners in France, after World War I, and it came in the industries in Russia. In fact, the Russian co-operative movement, among the industrial workers before the Revolution, owed much of its motive power to the societies which were started by the factory owners and later were converted by the workers into true Rochdale societies.

Building and loan associations and many mutual insurance companies are on the borderline of co-operation. Institutions such as the nonecclesiastical churches, social clubs, athletic associations, and other nonprofit organizations belong in this category.

Part II
CO-OPERATION AND THE STATE

Chapter V

THE INDIVIDUAL AND THE CENTRALIZED STATE

LIBERTARIANISM

WHILE hunger for freedom is widely prevalent, the desire for security causes people to sacrifice their liberties; and the desire for power prompts people to deprive others of the very liberty they want for themselves. Approval of coercion is general. The people for so many generations have suffered restrictive law that it is accepted as inevitable. In the development of a society which prizes industrialism, the individual has lost control of the job at which he earns his livelihood. It has passed to other hands. So gradually and insidiously has this control been lost that its loss is scarcely noticed. But that loss means the difference between freedom and dependence. It begins with the body, but shortly it strikes into the soul. In modern society two important developments have come about in connection with the privileged control of industry and property: one is antagonism among individuals; the other is dominance of individuals by centralized authority. A competitive struggle in the presence of a waning democracy is the result.

The natural tendency among animals of the same species and among human beings is mutual aid. Co-operative democracy finds its fundamental principles in a book by the naturalist, Peter Kropotkin, entitled *Mutual Aid*. This scholarly work is the introduction to the co-operative principle in society. Self-reliance and federalism, the sovereignty of each group, and the construction of the larger composite social body from the small and simple group were the leading ideas as recently as the eleventh century. But since that time the conception has changed. The votaries of Roman law and centralized authority succeeded in paralyzing this ancient Greek idea which had given to families, clans, villages, and towns their local autonomy.

From that time it has been taught from university, pulpit, and court bench that the salvation of society must be sought in a strongly centralized state under semidivine authority. Centralized government has come more and more into power, and local autonomy has decayed. The absorption of social functions by the state favored the development of a narrow, irresponsible individualism. As the obligations to the state increased, the citizens were more and more relieved of their obligations to each other. The state taught the individual that his responsibility was to the state, and that the state would protect the individual. Neighborliness and brotherhood gave way to citizenship and patriotism.

The citizen now pays taxes, and that rite absolves him vicariously from his ancient responsibility to do things for himself. As a result, there arises the theory that man can and must seek his own happiness in a disregard of the needs of others. Justice and the consideration for others may be left to the state. The new law tends to leave the citizen free from the old and natural human obligations. They have become the business of the state.

It is against this centralization of authority that we need be warned. We need not oppose organization, but the organization we approve should be the natural and voluntary grouping of energies to secure results beneficial to the individual. Society might wisely seek for a nonauthoritarian organization of common interests which would abolish the existing antagonisms between individuals and classes. Release from the restraints of authority might thus be attained.

Do not minorities need protection from the oppression of majorities as well as majorities need protection from minorities? Is there not need to exalt the individual in contrast with the exaltation of the state? Is bondage to the state essentially different from bondage to an autocratic ruler?

Libertarianism maintains that, when centralized powers dominate the mind and the conduct of man, this means his enslavement; and that not society but the individual should be the main consideration.

The generally accepted theory is that the security of society depends upon "law and order." There is a prevalent idea that if the restraints of the law were removed—policeman's clubs, soldiers' bayonets, battleships, armored cars, poison gases, bombing airplanes, and the electric chair—people would fly at one another's throats and chaos would reign. It is possible that such forces have an effect which is the opposite of that which they are supposed to possess. Social conscience and harmony are possibly not promoted by these instruments. Despite them, the peace and security of society may depend upon the goodheartedness, the inherent sense of justice, the prudence and goodwill of human beings. Anthropologists have long since discovered this fact in studies of primitive peoples. Man is naturally not only kind but generous toward his fellows. When he is not deprived of the things he needs—food, love, clothing, housing—he finds in kindness to others a source of satisfaction for himself. Deprivation, exploitation, and coercive law create the antagonisms which make him hostile to his fellows.

The punishments and forcible restraints of governments are largely called for because of the existence of an inequitable distribution of the resources of nature. To maintain an established state of inequity the forces of government are invoked.

In the present society the removal of force is not to be advocated as a first step. Force is a symptom. First must come the institution of a social system that makes for equity. Then the use of coercive force in society will become unnecessary, for then there should be no class which is attempting to hold more than it needs and which requires protection against another class which is deprived of its needs.

The philosophy of libertarianism is based upon the theory that all forms of government rest upon violence and are therefore harmful as well as unnecessary. It demands the absence of government in the political and coercive sense. It is opposed to the authority based on force. Much of all this is a negative philosophy. It lacks a constructive plan for the organization of society. It needs alliance with some positive building method to make it complete.

Its opportunity is to connect with the co-operative way of social organization to get a positive impulse. Then men may forget their grudge against the state. When they have created something better than the state, the state will cease to be a source of concern to them. If they would reduce the power of the state, the best way is to do a constructive piece of work that will make the state less necessary.

The co-operative movement offers a philosophy based on liberty, unrestricted by man-made law. It is the philosophy of a society regulated by voluntary agreement instead of by political government. It is the one movement directing the world away from the expansion of the political state.

SOCIALIST AIM, METHOD, AND END

The socialist aim is a society in which democracy prevails; in which the worker is rewarded with the full value of the service he performs; in which production and distribution in the main are for service and not for profit; and in which the people are equal citizens in a democratic state in which private income from interest, rent, and dividends has been abolished. The chief methods offered by socialists for the attainment of these ends are the capturing of the political government by the ordinary political election, by the revolutionary overthrow or the disintegration of the capitalist system, and by the gradual socialization of industries.

Victory, by winning a majority at the polls, by revolutionary uprising of the proletariat, or by both, is the means by which many look for the attainment of the "co-operative commonwealth." Idealism and the desire for a better and more just organization of society have always characterized socialist propaganda.

Karl Marx and the leaders who worked out the socialist philosophy had so deep a concern for the hardships of the working classes that they were prompted to concentrate their attention upon labor as the all-important function to be protected and improved. As a result they failed to recognize the relation of industry to the society of consumers, and were chiefly concerned for the worker at the point of production.

The early socialists advocated producers' partnerships as a means of capturing the industries for the proletariat. They believed also in the idea of a superstate as a great centralized organism. They believed that such a state could be created out of the present political organization of society. This attitude has prompted the promotion of government ownership and directed the attention of the working people toward control of the political government.

By voting for these principles the citizen is voting for the expanded political state. This may not be what is wanted, but it is what this voting always brings when it wins. While Marx and the modern socialists have favored a free society and desire that the political state shall ultimately melt away, it is difficult to see how the creating of state socialism can bring about that result. In fact, there is danger that the socialized state may be further from a free society than is the present capitalistic state. It may be more difficult to create a free nongovernmental society in the presence of an established socialized state than in the presence of the unstable capitalistic states which now exist.

As a result of socialist propaganda, people have been more and more persuaded as to the deficiencies of capitalistic industry and have demanded government control and then government ownership. In response to this demand, and also as a result of inefficiencies of the capitalist system, governments have taken over more and more economic functions until there are few types of industry and few social functions which governments somewhere in the world have not undertaken. But the striking fact is that it has not usually been socialists or socialist governments that have taken over these things. The steady political socialization of industry is being put into operation by the existing capitalistic governments and government officials, both of which are theoretically opposed to socialism. Inasmuch as capitalistic political parties dominate most of the governments, they control the situation; and in the interest of keeping themselves in power they give the people as much socialism as the people demand, or as the deficiencies of the profit system make necessary. There is every indication that they will continue to do this; and, by so doing, they keep ahead of the socialist parties and effectively prevent them from coming into power. Capitalism leads to socialism and is actually installing socialism.

In the presence of the disabilities of capitalism, the capitalistic politicians are adjusting themselves to the inevitable changes. They are found beginning to approve of state socialism. The reasons are obvious. (1) The more functions the state has to perform, the more political jobs there must be. (2) The collection of commercial charges for public utility services can be transferred to taxes and all pass through the politicians' hands. (3) Unprofitable businesses can be turned over to the government. (4) The tendency is toward capitalistic consolidation and monopoly in one big corporation—the state.

When reformers have succeeded in convincing the public that the government should run the railroads or telephones, or when these businesses break down, it is the existing political government that takes over these industries, and often runs them in such a way that the details are worked out to the advantage of the former private owners of the industry. It has been the reformers' advocacy of government ownership that has played into the hands of their opponents, and left the reformers standing on the outside watching the enemies of reform putting socialistic plans into practice.

Voting at election does not bring about the change of an economic system. Economic systems are changed only by the natural course of evolution. Revolution may appear as an incident in the course of such a change, following the collapse of a prevalent system, but a permanent change is wrought by the edict of neither premiers nor voters. Nor does the earnest belief in a theory qualify or prepare workers to direct the industrial affairs of a nation. Something more than belief is necessary.

The socialism which Russia had imposed upon it by force consists essentially in the substitution of one big capitalist—the state— for a multitude of smaller capitalists, with an autocratic government prevailing.

Socialism exhorts the people to vote at the polls for candidates who, when they get a majority, it is hoped will make the "great change." "It is within their power to change the present hellish conditions between the rising and setting of the sun" is a current doctrine. But if in any industrial country these reformers should win a victory at the polls and should attempt to change the present conditions "between the rising and setting sun," by a socialization of industry, that country would be thrown into great disorder. If the government should proceed immediately to take over the industries, chaos would be the result. For that reason such victories in Denmark, Holland, and other countries have never been followed by socialism.

Sudden revolutions, both political and economic, fail because the present owners of the property control the surplus wealth, the surplus food, the guns, and the powers of coercion; and only those who are trained to run industries can run them. It is not a question of what is right or what is wrong; it is a question of the action of forces which cannot be controlled nor changed overnight. Apparently the way to change the economic system is to go to work day by day and change the economic system.

Experience shows that there is no easy way. By electing some other person—to go to a capital city—to instruct the thing called the government—to do it is a devious way. If the people want a change, they must train themselves to do things themselves in the way they would want them done in a changed society. As to voting, the most important voting is being done every day in the economic elections. Shall I buy this or that, patronize this shop or that, rent an apartment or build a house, walk or buy a ticket and ride? The political voting which comes once a year is wholly predicated upon the results of these economic elections daily taking place.

To begin at the bottom, to obtain experience, and to move on is to get the kind of training that fits men to administer industries for the people. The method is slow and arduous. It cannot be gotten out of books, nor lectures. It requires pains, work, and patience. There is no short cut. There is no easy way. And without this training, victory at the polls and revolution fail. Victory without the people behind it—people who can run industries—is doubtful victory. The captured industries cannot be held unless they can deliver the goods to the people. And if the people have been sufficiently trained by experience to run their industries to supply their needs, they will find that they have captured industries without a victory at the polls and without revolution.

Let us suppose that the people of some country voted by a majority for the socialization of the industries. Suppose that the majority elected to parliament were for it. Or suppose that the capitalist system went to smash. Would those who are now conducting the industries easily change their policy and serve the people as consumers? They would if their education or experience had given them understanding of the methods and meaning of consumer ownership and control of industries in the interest of these same consumers.

Many workers are now giving up the doctrine that their hope is to capture the political state and organize to control industries in the interest of the workers. They appreciate this program as an end, but not as a means. They have tried it. They have seen election victories and revolutions fail to bring the desired results. Experience has taught that a political revolution does not bring economic freedom. More and more the workers now are turning to the co-operative method as a means of building up a new society. At the same time they do not relinquish their interest in trade-union organization nor in political action. But they have learned no longer to look to them exclusively to bring the reorganization of industry for which they hope.

Some writers speak of a "socialism of producers" and a "socialism of consumers." In general it is the former that answers to the conventional socialism; the latter is co-operation. But factually, co-operation, while social, is surely not socialism. So far as its relation to government goes, it is diametrically the opposite of socialism.

As a theoretical program, the socialist movement harmonizes with co-operation, but methods and results are different. Socialist congresses pass resolutions "recognizing the high value and importance of the organization of consumers for the working classes, and urge the workers to become and remain active members of the cooperative distributive societies." In some countries the socialist movement is close to the consumer co-operative movement because of similarity of theoretical aims. The harmonizing of socialism and co-operation is seen in many European countries. Usually the socialists are promoters of co-operation. So, too, are the members of other political parties.

There is growing up among socialists, a moderate school of sentiment which demands that socialism shall unite with co-operation and strive for the co-operative administration of all personal, domestic, and local affairs, and leave to the state only the large and extensive public utilities. Most socialists are not yet ready to believe that co-operation can do everything. In all countries in which socialism is strong, the socialists are learning practical lessons from co-operation which are winning them away from the old doctrine of the glorification of labor and of the state. They are going to the school of co-operation and learning the "socialism of consumers."

A newer socialism is now offered, a democratic political state with only honest and socially minded officeholders, responsive to the public interest and promoting co-operation and other nonpolitical public services. This is impractical wishing. If it should come about, it would no longer be a political state but an industrial democracy, which is the antithesis of a political state.

There is a danger to co-operation in being made love to by socialists. A recent socialist book, published in England,[1] which enjoys popularity among socialists, makes clear the socialist attitude. It treats co-operation as a temporary development among consumers, to build up nonprofit business, ultimately to be taken over by the socialized state. The acknowledgment is made that the socialist state will be coercive as in Russia. Voluntarism is scorned. The author says: "Socialism cannot tolerate the existence of voluntary cooperation in the economic sphere" and "Under socialism cooperation would no longer remain voluntary." The socialist directors of the British and Scottish wholesales have passed resolutions advocating that the government take over the major functions of the co-operatives.[2] American socialists approve this fate for co-operation, that it is ultimately to be swallowed up by the state. To meet this socialist threat, to preserve voluntarism and the freedom of the individual, and to prevent the development of the all-powerful coercive state is the task of the co-operative way.

Socialism is a theory. In dominant operation it becomes communism. Communism is socialism in working clothes. Communism abolishes parliamentary and democratic methods and resorts to force, however ruthless, and intrigue, however unscrupulous, to put and keep itself in power. This is upon the assumption that the

[1] *A Century of Rochdale Cooperation*, by Joseph Reeves.
[2] See article by the Author, "Cooperatives to be Absorbed by the State," *Review of International Cooperation*, May, 1943.

end justifies the means. Socialism, despite dreamy theories to the contrary, moves toward the autocratic state in business. It produces things at one cost and sells at a higher price; the difference between the two being profit, which it enjoys in the place of collecting taxes. It thus makes for the restoration of the profit motive. It creates a privileged class in its officeholders. It establishes one big monopoly, the state in business. It reestablishes and fixes upon society the out-standing evils of capitalism. Cooperation is the one effectively functioning movement in the economic world that is radical. Social-ism when attained is highly reactionary.

Socialists are mild-mannered reformers in the presence of a capi-talist society. But let a socialist government prevail, and their atti-tude wholly changes. Then they become the master race. Socialist potency asserts itself, and becomes the major threat to the existence of co-operatives.

Chapter VI

THE NATURE AND DESTINY OF THE STATE

GOVERNMENT, NEITHER DEMOCRATIC NOR BENIGN

WHEN profit business, which performs useful service, fails adequately to supply public needs or becomes bankrupt, the government gives it assistance and ultimately takes it over. This is the way of the expanding state.

There is a prevalent opinion that if profit-making business is not the best agency to carry on industry, then the state should succeed to that function. The idea is widespread. Hence, we may well make some examination into the nature of the state and inquire whether its character is such as lends itself to the promotion of the people's business. In this discussion, I shall not attempt to separate the state, which is the institution, from the government, which is the agency through which the state functions.

The state is a compulsory organization of the people into a body politic, presumably to secure the prevalence of justice by self-imposed government. As a matter of fact, the state was created as an organization in which the dominant forces in society protected themselves against the suppressed forces. The state developed as an institution for the protection of privilege. Its perpetuation depends upon force. A state without repressive laws, police, soldiers, and jails is not conceivable. When we go back far enough we find that states and governments started not so much as movements of the people, but rather as the efforts of a privileged class—chiefs, kings, lords—to have their privileges, which were got by force of arms, legalized and made secure.

The state, from its beginning, has been a physically powerful social organization. It could do much for its citizens. It did more for those citizens in whose interest it existed. It protected their property and their privileges against the demands of the unpropertied and unprivileged. It made laws or interpreted laws in their behalf, and if it neither had laws nor interpreted laws in their behalf, its officials often acted in their behalf in defiance of the laws. The concern of the state has been for property rather than for people. The state has looked upon property as the most important basis of social organization; and it still does.

When we depart from the interest of the few, who own most of the property, and consider the many, we find that the state at times favors them also. But the things the state does for the masses, although apparently in the interest of the masses, are chiefly in the interest of the few. Discontent, strikes, unemployment, poverty, crime, disease, prostitution, and slums are all disagreeable. The world is small, the poor are near neighbors of the rich, disease is contagious, growling mobs are annoying; therefore, it is wiser to do some things for everybody. And so the state does good things—not because of natural virtue in the state, but because of expediency.

In some lands the state is responsive to the will of the people, to a large degree. Yet in all lands, the dominant voice in the control of the state is not the people but those few who control the credit, property, and industries; or, if they are not, they become the dominant voice in the course of time. Should the people in their co-operative societies become the chief owners of the property and industries in any country, it will be found that they become controllers of the state.

With the property-owning minority as the dominant influence in the banks, the press, the courts, the police power, and in the fields where the masses earn their living, the thinking and willing and even the voting of the majority are not free. Generation after generation of thought control and patriotism compels approval of things as they are. This is illustrated by the action of the masses as the propaganda and news agencies of the government make the people ready for war—on either side. The people are not free to act through the state because they are not capable of acting together, politically, in their own interest. They do not know how to move together to operate the intricate political machine and make it serve them. It is beyond their genius. That they can is a theory but scarcely a fact.

All this applies especially to national governments, to governments far removed from intimate contact with the people. In many countries the town and municipal governments are responsive to the will of the mass of the people. Especially in villages where there are no large industries to dominate the politics, the village government often is highly democratic and serves the interests of all the people. Privilege, corruption, and inefficiency creep in when the area governed becomes large, when the government is not close to the people, when government becomes centralized, or when a minority element owns dominant industries in the community upon which the majority depend for their livelihood. The closer the people keep to the principle of a society of neighbors who have common economic interests, the better is their community control, whether it be political or voluntary.

Surely it is good for the social morality that the people strive to have better laws and a better machinery of government. There is no objection to the people capturing the state and trying to bend it to their common good, if they can. But we may as well acknowledge the fact that they cannot succeed until they have got control of the economic machinery upon which the lives of the people depend. There is no such thing as political democracy without industrial democracy; and this industrial democracy seems to be developing, and capable of expanding into all society in the consumer co-operative movement. This would seem to offer the way to co-operative democracy.

Politics usually is remote from the lives of the people. The government is away off somewhere; the people think of it as foreign to them; it is surely remote from their daily problems of bread and butter and the crying baby. The politicians make the people think that political affairs are the vital matters. But the people are absorbed with the real problem of making the family wage pay the rent and buy shoes and potatoes. The economic life is closer.

I am not unmindful of the steady improvement in political conditions in many countries in the world; but I am also mindful of the fact that these improvements were preceded commonly by economic improvements. Measures for political democracy are seldom yielded until the people have already obtained economic power sufficient to compel the government to grant their demands. Who controls the man's means of livelihood controls the man.

If the people, as consumers, were organized democratically

they would not need to bother so much with legislative bodies. They could have what they want irrespective of legislation. A solid mass of people with economic power, if they wish, can make their own laws, and if they have sufficient solidarity, they can enforce them. This is seen in operation every day. Law is the indicator that records the location of the economic power.

For a citizen to prosecute a state for its crimes is a futile undertaking. The state may commit murder—either retail or wholesale. Were it possible to hold it to account, as the individual is held to account, the governments would become the archcriminals at the bar of justice the world over. The growing power of the state has been described by Herbert Spencer as "the coming slavery." This is based on the fact that the state has demonstrated itself to be the greatest of tyrants in the suppression of liberties and justice.

The conflict between the citizen and the state is an unequal one. It is also demoralizing. It furthermore creates an unctuous hypocrisy in the agents of the state. The free spirit of the individual is constantly subjected to insult by the arrogance of officeholders, who have behind them the authority and arms of government.

Political hypotheses are built upon the idea that the purpose of the state is to do good for its citizens. This is the protective coloring of the state. And it is true that it does and must do much that is apparently good for the citizens. Good must be the state's most conspicuous quality. Whenever things are going bad with the state, it proceeds at once to bestow some benefit upon the people. It has always been so. Gladiatorial entertainments, bullfights, monuments in the public places, parks and playgrounds, free education, drinking fountains, free lunches, old-age pensions, the franchise, free hospitals, the dole, and social legislation are the prices the state pays to the people. The more of these things the state does, the better does it protect itself. The reason the state is not more prodigal with its benefactions is because they apparently come out of the pockets of those who control the government; and those interests are often so unwise as to oppose the benefactions that would save them from the collapse of their economic system and their state.

"Fidelity to the Republic is the first duty of the citizen" is a typical constitutional requirement. This political demand takes precedence over fidelity to justice or to ideals. It assumes that the state is superior to the fundamental virtues.

Government has its place. Respect for government cannot be denied. But it might be confined to those who need it. If the state should suddenly cease its existence, I am sure society would find itself in a bad predicament. The lame man cannot suddenly be deprived of his crutches, nor the slave of his master. The lives of the people have been adjusted to the state.

For want of other organization, the state provides many necessary things. The people turn to their government to build bridges, to provide electricity, to maintain lighthouses, to issue weather reports, to prevent animal diseases, to regulate traffic, to control quarantine, and to do a thousand other good things. The people need the state and its government because they have not organized themselves to do things. But they could do all these things independently of the state, if they only knew it.

The people maintain the state as it is; it exists with their approval, and serves them in such manner as they desire—or, at least, deserve. It has defects, due more to the apathy and indifference of the majority than to the wickedness of the minority. Its deficiency is that it is capable of being controlled by a minority and used in the interest of the minority. But this can be said of any institution in which the majority is indifferent.

There are three attitudes toward the state with which this discussion is concerned: capitalism and the static state; socialism and the expanding state; co-operation and the fading state.

The important matter is that if we would have a fading state there must be efficient organization of the people to take its place. As co-operative business expands the state has less to do. Should co-operative society bring about more just conditions, better living, and a higher culture, the functions of the state would then grow less, and the vanishing point of the state would be the peaceful end toward which society might tend.

When the Swiss Consumer Cooperative Union got control of the meat trust of Switzerland, the laws against bad meat, the courts and penalties for selling diseased meat, and the inspectors to prevent fraud became unnecessary. Consumers find no advantage in supplying themselves with bad food. It is always somebody else who finds that advantage. With every additional function performed by the co-operative consumers the government loses a multitude of functions.

The state now exists, and clings to the body of society as a parasite. It takes its sustenance from the weakness of society, from the inability of the masses to do things for themselves. But as society makes itself more healthy, as the people become more efficient in their own affairs, the grip of the parasitic state is seen to relax.

Chapter VII

CO-OPERATION AND GOVERNMENT OWNERSHIP

FOR PRIVATE PROPERTY

A TENDENCY is abroad which is making for state ownership of property. So-called radical literature is full of invectives against private property. Property is to be taken away from the individual. But why? Property is not bad. Would that every individual had more of it. The thing about which we need be concerned is not private property, but the method of its distribution and the uses to which it may be put. Private property used for speculation, private property used to suppress others, private property passed on to others to guarantee them against performing service, private property withheld from use to increase its value, private property owned by those who do not work but used by others in order to exist, private property held in excess of its need while others suffer for lack of it—these are some of the ill uses of private property.

When we examine closely the objections urged against private property, the objections are not against private property at all but against the private right to use private property in an unsocial way.

Co-operation favors ownership of private property. The co-operative method tends to bring about a combine of the property of many for its joint administration. In a society of co-operating neighbors, private property may become a blessing not only to the individual but to society.

Every individual wants property. It is a natural hunger. It not only makes him frugal, but it gives him a personal sense of satisfaction and freedom from care. The propertyless man is, indeed, a poor man. The man without property has consumed, or lost, all that he has made. A surplus of property is an anchor to windward. Property helps give the individual control of his life. With it he can purchase leisure. He can make individual things. He can invent. He can create beauty. He can establish high standards of living to serve as useful examples toward which society may level upward.

131

GOVERNMENT OWNERSHIP OR PRIVATE OWNERSHIP

One of the differences between the socialistic state and co-operative society is a difference between government ownership and private ownership. The demand of political ownership is that, with
the exception of intimate personal belongings, socially necessary
and useful property shall be owned by the state. The individual is
far away from ownership when the state is the owner. In the socialized state the property belongs to a great corporate body which permits the citizen to advise and guide it—provided he is one of the
majority. He may use it, it will serve him, but he has no sense of
personal ownership. He may be an owner of government bonds and
feel that this is tangible property. But a certificate of indebtedness
issued by a government is not a deed of ownership. Government
bonds are interest-bearing notes that tend to make the citizen
patriotic and desirous that the government shall be strong.

Ownership of necessities should be available to all. This is precisely what property should comprise. The sense of personal responsibility which comes with ownership is too precious a natural
heritage to be lost. The people are being led away from this personal responsibility. Government ownership does not promote responsibility nor thriftiness in the individual. Thriftiness creates the
ability to accumulate, protect, and conserve in the economic sense.
It may be said that if the government owned everything essential,
thriftiness on the part of the individual would no longer be necessary. Then so much the worse for the individual. The people are
not taking this matter seriously. They are being rushed pell-mell
into a doctrine that has the power to divest them not only of personal
property but also of thriftiness and individual responsibility. These
are ancient and salutary virtues.

Government ownership is coming, and it may be contemplated
with misgiving—the people reduced to a propertyless mass, dependent upon the benefactions of a great impersonal machine,
called the government. Stand by it, flatter it, wave its flag, serve it,
display a conspicuous patriotism, and it will yield much. But oppose
its dominant forces, and one will find himself in conflict with something which none can oppose with safety. The independent or strik-

ing worker in the socialized state finds himself not in conflict with economic forces alone but with political forces, and guilty of treason against the government; he is coerced, imprisoned, or shot. The rapidly moving tendency toward increasing the power and functions of the state leads to the creation of a great corporation within which the citizen must live and upon which his life must depend.

Still, the government ownership and operation of the essential industries, even under present conditions, has certain advantages over the prevalent system of private ownership and operation which cannot be disregarded. Every industry that is taken by the government removes from the field of competitive business one more factor which often spends money to influence politics and to drive hard bargains with labor. Money taken from the consumers for advertising and intensive salesmanship is keeping alive the disadvantages inherent in production and distribution for profit's sake. Government production is production essentially for service. The importance of this is seen in times of stress and emergency when neither the people nor the government can afford to remain at the mercy of profits; then the government takes over business.

The socializing tendency of the state is seen everywhere. As we look back over the past century we see the schools, libraries, highways, postal service, fire extinguishing, water supply, street cleaning, sewage and garbage disposal, and a hundred other functions pass from private hands into the hands of the state. Governments all over the world are moving in this direction. As an example of this tendency in the United States, the per capita cost of running the federal government in 1800 was $2.03; in 1850 it was $1.71; in 1900 it was $6.85; and in 1946 it was $471.15.

There may be advantages in complete state ownership which do not exist in partial state ownerships. Profit business is abolished by force of law and ceases to exist as a corrupting influence upon the state. Inasmuch as the chief corruption of the political government comes from the interests of privilege and profit, the truly socialistic state theoretically might be a cleaner institution than the state which exists in company with the above corrupting influences.

In the more highly developed countries there is seen a socializing tendency which lacks the bureaucracy and thwarting of democracy which stateism usually promotes. Sweden, Denmark, Norway, and other countries with much state ownership and control, succeed in protecting the consumers and moving toward democracy. The state functions in these countries have been promoted by socialists. It is significant, however, that in countries where expansion of state functions has brought the best results, the co-operative movement is a large factor in economic affairs. Government ownership then seems not wholly incompatible with progress in the direction of democracy, provided it is surrounded by co-operative influence.

But, however free of corrupting environment the socialistic state may be, in the absence of co-operative influence it takes on a quality which may be even more objectionable. That objection is bureaucracy, dominating and regulating the lives of the people. The socialistic qualities of the state may make for a more permanent state than the world has ever seen. Private business also, with its possibilities of competition as a spur and challenge, is removed. But by abolishing competition with itself, it denies itself the advantages which come from a hostile critic and competitor. It thus invites complacency or mediocrity.

On the other hand, co-operation at the most would only slowly and partially supplant but not necessarily displace profit business. The actual existence of profit business by the side of co-operation is highly desirable as a challenge to keep the co-operative movement up to its best.

Co-operation does not come into existence by edict, law or coercion, but only through the processes of experience. The great co-operative movement, the world over, has started small and experimentally and has grown in competition with profit business and state business. It can grow only as it actually demonstrates its superiority as a method of service. If profit business or the state can supply the needs of the people better, then co-operation will not grow. It must depend wholly upon its merits. No co-operative leader would want it otherwise. If it is not the best method, it cannot expand.

Furthermore, in co-operative associations a body of people must train themselves to control their own business. They must succeed in selecting from their numbers a competent board of directors. And this board must find able executives and administrators of the business; or the project fails. And this is all in the economic field.

The private ownership of property is an inherent quality of the co-operative movement. In co-operation, the people organize themselves not into a state but into a free society in which they are free to be members or not. Each member puts into the society something of his own. He is given a certificate of ownership which indicates the value of the property he has put in. This property, with that of all the other members, is united to carry on the functions of the society. It never even becomes communistic property. It is a union of private properties, put into a pool for a mutual purpose of more advantageous administration. The member puts into the society what it requires, or what he can; but outside of the society, and independent of it, he may still own more private property.

The member of the co-operative society begins by investing his capital with that of his fellow members—he may have put in property other than money to make himself a member. But presently, as the work of the society goes on, the amount of capital he has invested has increased. The additions are due to his patronage and his savings. The property which he gains is acquired by carrying on his economic affairs conjointly with his fellows rather than with an outside corporation or profit business. With his fellow members he becomes a part owner of goods, buildings, machinery, and everything his society possesses. But always he is a private owner. He remains an individual in an economic partnership.

The shareholding member of the co-operative society is the owner of private property. He can ask for his property and it is given to him. He may take his property and step out of the society with it. It is his. He may prove that it is his by going into private business with it; or by having it confiscated by the state.

The co-operative society to which I belong owns buildings, a bakery, a restaurant, and automobiles; and as a co-operator I know to a cent how much I own of that property. I can take it out. I can sell it and have the money in my hand whenever I want it. I have tested this fact.

When I was a citizen of a political corporation, the city of New York, as a citizen, I did not know how much I owned of the buildings, stores, and automobiles of the city of New York, nor could I sell my share. The reason was simple enough: I did not own any of the property of the city of New York. That property belonged to a great impersonal machine called the municipality, which taxed me severely, permitted me to use certain of its property, and was run entirely by a vast bureaucracy of officials not one of whom I ever voted for and not one of whom represented me. The same is true of the United States government. I should consequently say that this so-called public ownership is far removed from me as a citizen. It is, indeed, a very different property relationship from that which exists between my co-operative society and myself.

There is many a man in the British co-operative societies who became a member by putting in a shilling and who can now draw out a hundred pounds or more. He has put in no more money. The money that has been saved for him thus by this joint action with his fellows has accumulated. His society owns property; it also has a surplus. It will give him the hundred pounds whenever he wants it. He is free to end his citizenship in the co-operative community and withdraw his share of the property. Co-operation holds him only so long as it is to his interest to remain. His private property is not sacrificed in co-operative ownership. A large proportion of the membership of the more than 2,500 co-operative oil societies in the United States have not put in a cent of money; the accumulated savings of their patronage have paid for their shares and made them owners of expanding property.

The difference between these two forms of social organization is fundamental. The state is conducted in the interest of the state. The "commonwealth" is really state's wealth. On the other hand, co-operative society collectively administers the private property of its members. It is private business—free enterprise.

Some think of certain large operations as capable of execution only by the government. That is because the government is large and can undertake at once large things. Someday co-operation may be large, but the things it does are always arrived at by building up from small beginnings. Co-operation has traveled from the little store in Toad Lane to the British Wholesale Society on Balloon Street, and the British wholesale is the biggest productive and distributive undertaking in Great Britain. Large-scale enterprises are being developed and administered by co-operative societies in many parts of the world. Among these are enterprises of the type which many students of economics had heretofore assumed could be carried on only by governments if not by profit-making corporations.

Co-operative societies own ocean steamboats. Societies have engaged in road building and in organizing and conducting postal service. The farmers of the United States have organized co-operative telephone companies; they have erected poles, strung thousands of miles of lines, and conduct central exchanges. They are doing the same with electric power supply. When the Scottish Wholesale bought part of the towns of Calderwood, Maxwellton, and East Kilbride, when the Desborough society purchased the village of Harrington, and the Woolwich society bought from the government the garden city Well Hall with 1,200 homes, these societies were going into big business—the ownership of whole towns, houses, streets, churchyards, and all. The Scottish Wholesale maintains its own fire department to protect its many factories and buildings at Shieldhall, Glasgow; and this fire department often serves the municipality of Glasgow when the fire-extinguishing equipment of the city proves inadequate. The Cooperative Society of Basel, Switzerland, has so efficient a fire department that the expenses of its maintenance are paid by the reduction in fire insurance costs which it secures to the society. The Tennessee Valley Authority, a branch of the United States government, has a surplus of electricity of which to dispose. Experience has shown that the best results are had by encouraging the organization of co-operative consumer associations to distribute the current. These co-operatives represent something stable and are composed of people of all political parties. They are simple business organizations of consumers with interest only in one thing—electric supply. For the TVA to sell this electricity to public utility companies means that it is resold to consumers for the sake of profit and not service, with the concomitant hazards of this motive. To sell to political municipalities means that a change in the politics of the town disturbs the permanence of the service; a hostile board of aldermen or an adverse election may discontinue the service. But the co-operative is a nonpolitical business company set up to supply its members with electricity—one purpose only—and offers the best guarantees of permanence, without regard to what happens politically.

Many countries have co-operative societies which produce electricity for their members. The 1922 French Cooperative Congress passed a resolution calling for the establishment wherever possible of co-operative societies for the supply of gas, electricity, water, etc. The co-operative housing societies in Denmark, Sweden, and Holland have provided homes for the people cheaper and better than those provided by the political municipalities. Large-scale industries such as the state is supposed to undertake are within the scope of co-operative societies.

Some take the ground that co-operation must be limited to the intimate personal and household needs. They say that, "It can hardly be suggested that the millions of persons who send letters and telegrams or who travel or consign goods and parcels by a nationalized railway system could be marshaled into an effective democracy for controlling the management of the post office and the railway service." The same objection is cited in connection with municipal transportation, education, and medical treatment. One of the difficulties cited is that many of these municipal services "are actually used at any one time by only a small minority of any community, but are necessarily paid for by the community as a whole."

If these persons can be marshaled to control the management of the public utilities under the political state, why cannot the same persons do it in a co-operative society? As citizens, would they be more effective than as members? The fact that the citizen is compelled to be a citizen does not compel him to take any more intelligent or conscientious interest in the administration of public utilities than he would take as a voluntary member of the co-operative society. The effectiveness of the average citizen even in his municipal government is not superior to the effectiveness of the average member of the co-operative society in its affairs, even though both of them are inferior to what they should be. The same can be said of their control. There is no reason why expansion should be restricted in co-operative society and not in political society.

The fact that certain services are rarely used, or not used at all, by some citizens or members does not militate against their co-operative administration. The 35,000 acres of tea plantations of the British Wholesale Societies in India and Ceylon are a long way from the English co-operator who does not use tea, but they are as efficiently administered as any large enterprises under political control. The same applies to the medical service of the Holland co-operative societies, and to the administration of the Belgian co-operative brewery. Not all the members will require medical service, and some, I dare say, do not use beer; but these facts seem not to interfere with their democracy or efficiency.

Attention is called to the many municipal governmental services, all under a single political administration, as peculiarly advantageous. It may be an advantage that their administration is thus centralized, but co-operation does precisely the same thing. The directors of the British Wholesale conduct such widely diversified enterprises as a corset factory and flour mills, an automobile factory in England and an olive grove in Africa, a business office in New York and a soap factory in Manchester, a sawmill at Broughton and a hosiery factory at Leicester, steamboats and sanatoriums, and many other enterprises of such diversity and magnitude as no twenty-eight city fathers in any British municipality have yet attempted. From the standpoint of efficiency, democracy, and interest of the consumers, the co-operative administration is, perhaps, superior.

An obstacle to co-operative ownership is also seen in the "monopoly value" of certain factors, such as land or coal, and the "common enjoyment" of others, such as air and water. Does the citizen of the political state stand in a more advantageous position than the member of the co-operative society? As to land and coal, they can belong to a voluntary association quite as well as to a compulsory association. Most of the coal in such countries as the United States belongs to voluntary associations. But they are voluntary associations of capitalists. Perhaps, a wise preference is for the voluntary associations; but of consumers, rather than of profit-seeking capitalists.

There may be social value in the people having the most intimate possible control of public necessities. If co-operation can simplify the access to the things the people need, it is reasonable to ask, why interpose the complex state between the people and their wants?

Under stateism, co-operators may find themselves opposing the government. They may be called unpatriotic, for they may be planning to have the people take away from the state and take into their own hands the things which are the state's. If a group wants to buy out a private concern and make it exclusively its own and put the private firm out of business—that is proper—it is business. But if a group should want to do the same thing with the state, it might be viewed by the state as unsocial and unpatriotic. Such acts become treason and sedition.

Getting possession of industries is difficult. The best time to do it, however, is before the state comes into possession. There is always the probability that a government, which is strong and well established, will attempt to destroy the co-operative societies by taking them under the control of the state—as in Russia and Italy and Germany under the fascist regimes.

It may be easier for the people in their co-operative societies to get possession of the things they want when the prevalent method is private ownership, because co-operation is based on private ownership. A group of people co-operatively organized as consumers employ the same methods to obtain possession of things for themselves as any other private owners do who are organized in a corporation, company, or firm. They go in the market and buy what they want and make it their property. But getting things away from the state is different. The state is not to be bought out; it is not for sale; it tends to maintain its monopoly—its property is state property.

If this is correct, then it is imperative that co-operators get into their own hands the things they need, and organize themselves to own and administer those things co-operatively as fast as they can. Unless they do this, the socially necessary things may pass into the hands of the state from which their rescue will be difficult.

Spinoza said, "Each thing, in so far as it can, endeavors to preserve itself." For this reason the politician endeavors to stay in office—the state, in power. When a socialist minority has fought its way to a majority and has secured control of a government, or when a communist minority even remaining a minority has done the same thing, the satisfaction which comes from the possession of power will prompt them to keep their governments strong. This means that the governmental functions of owning property and administering the economic and social affairs of the citizens will not be relinquished. The political theory of liberty and democracy becomes only a previctory platform. For any officials, voluntarily, to give up power is difficult; for those in political control, it is, indeed, impossible. The state has never successfully been used to destroy the state.

The state is always found aggrandizing the state, except rarely where co-operative influence modifies this tendency.

This is the hazard in stateism—a hazard which its friends and its advocates do not sufficiently realize. It is toward the stateism here discussed, not freedom or democracy, that state ownership and control are moving—except in those situations where a decidedly influential proportion of the citizens and of the officeholders are sincere members of a substantial co-operative movement. Thus the Scandinavian countries, with their large degree of political socialization, are saved from the above calamities by their highly developed co-operative societies. They can move toward freedom and democracy under the influence of co-operation.

HOW THE CO-OPERATIVE DEMOCRACY DIFFERS FROM THE POLITICAL STATE

If all the people were organized in a co-operative democracy, how would this differ from a political state? Would such a society not be a state? To answer these questions we must distinguish between compulsory and voluntary organization of society.

A social club, union, scientific association, or any other voluntary society is fundamentally different from the state or local political government. People may join voluntary societies or not, as they see fit. They may resign when they disapprove of them. They need not belong to any at all if they so desire. Co-operative societies, like other voluntary associations of people, do not have governments. They do not have statute laws, but by-laws upon which the people have mutually agreed. These are simply rules of association which hold the members together upon the strength of their honor, mutual interest, and consent. If there are penalties for their violation, the penalties are approved of by the member when he joins the association. People are not born into the co-operative society. As mature adults they join a society of their own free will. In a voluntary society the extreme penalty for violation of the rules is to be dropped from the society. If the society does not like the member, it drops him; if the member does not like the society, he resigns.

The statute law of the state is not an agreement of mutual association. It is an ancient edict handed down from past rulers in the interest of a dominant class. It is backed by physical force, and has control over the life and property of the individual citizen.

May not the socialized state fulfill all the requirements that a co-operative democracy could fulfill? The answer is, No; for when a state fulfills all the requirements of a voluntary co-operative society it ceases to be a state.

The strength of co-operation rests on the fact that it is free and not coercive. If it possess greatness, beauty, and strength, they abide in its freedom. The existence of the state depends on coercion. As the world stands today, one must be a citizen of some state. He cannot escape. He may go up in a balloon or seek a desert isle, but some government will find him and claim him as its citizen. And it may coerce him into doing things he does not want to do. If he is one of those unusual people who does not believe in killing human beings, it may put a gun in his hand and send him forth to shoot other men as guiltless as himself. It may shoot him because he refuses to commit some great crime. Governments do all the great sins. There is no brutality to which governments do not stoop. Governments do crimes which wicked men shrink from doing.

Co-operation differs from the state in that it does not have to put people in jail for sedition nor hang them for trying to overthrow it. If the members of a co-operative society disagree with it or wish to overthrow it, they are free to do so. And they should be. It survives only upon its merit.

The state requires its citizen to say, "I love my country," whether it is lovable or not, whether he loves it or not. The co-operative society must deserve the loyalty of its members or it perishes. The state keeps its citizens by force; the co-operative society keeps its members by esteem, by justice, and by service.

The conflict between these two principles—the political state and the free individual—is now going on and can be seen in every part of the world. The differences between an organization built out of the old political, privilege-protecting state and one created anew for economic supply upon a voluntary basis are inescapable.

THE HAZARDS OF POLITICS

The co-operative movement in most countries is working out its destiny free from the political state. Individual co-operators belong to political parties, vote and participate in the administration of the affairs of the state. Indeed, they are prone to ally themselves with the political parties that are friendly to co-operation. This is natural and, perhaps, wise. The state exists; it affects co-operation; and it cannot be ignored by co-operators. But co-operative societies, as a rule, do not enter into alliance with political governments or parties. Political neutrality is a co-operative fundamental.

Co-operation belongs in the economic and social field. Suppose that it should violate this principle and ally itself with a political party; and suppose that party should win absolutely and dominate the country—which then of the two is greater? The business of a victorious political party is to administer the country. With the tendency toward stateism now everywhere ascendant, a victorious party would tend to administer industries which co-operation aims to administer. A conflict inevitably arises.

Political parties and the state also have their reverses. It would be an unhappy thing for co-operation to tie up to one of these and then to see it overthrown. The co-operative movement can ill afford to subject itself to the uncertainties of politics. Should the co-operative movement combine with a political state, the natural outcome would be that the state would take co-operation under its protection. This would be a calamity to an independent self-help enterprise.

The politically-minded suggest, for example, that the co-operative movement of the United States should ally itself with a political party. "The party of the workers" is suggested. But the workers of this country support the capitalist parties. Only a small percentage of the members of the co-operative societies are members of the so-called radical parties. Any part of the co-operative movement which affiliated itself with any of these parties would isolate itself from the neutral movement, and two sets of societies would exist. This is the situation in all those countries where one set of co-operatives is allied with the Socialist party.

There are other dangers in an alliance with governments and political parties; governments go to war and political parties promote cataclysmic changes. Co-operation need not kill people to win. Its enemies are not men, but special privilege. Its victories are won on the economic field, not on the field of battle. War does not settle economic questions.

These problems are new, and experience will do more toward

helping in their solution than can speculation. We may take its attitude toward co-operation as the index of the sincerity and radicalism of any political movement. Russia furnished such a test. The Soviet government by its edicts in 1919 and 1920 took over the co-operative societies and made them a part of the government. Their freedom was destroyed and they were run as adjuncts to the state. Government appointees were placed in charge of co-operative societies instead of the elected representatives of the members; and the societies became part of the political machine. Co-operation was emasculated.

The Soviet government appointed Communist patriots to occupy the positions which had been held by representatives elected by the co-operative societies. Administration of co-operatives became bureaucratic; membership was made compulsory and the societies lost their co-operative and voluntary character. Distribution failed. The plan did not work. Then the Soviet government, in the state decree of April 7, 1921, gave back the co-operatives their "freedom." But it has ever since remained a state-controlled "freedom." The government again in 1935 confiscated and destroyed the co-operatives of the towns and cities, leaving only those of the country villages. How soon the government will feel itself strong enough to confiscate these is a question.

There is no such thing as state-administered co-operation. When people are compelled to join societies, and when the machinery of government finances and conducts societies, they may serve the people, but they are not co-operative societies. Communism may succeed in Russia; co-operation may succeed; but not both at the same time.

WOULD CO-OPERATIVE SOCIETY DEVELOP BUREAUCRACY, AUTOCRACY, AND CORRUPTION?

The question is asked: After all, suppose the functions of the state are reduced to nil and the people carry on their social activities through a co-operative democracy, does it not amount to the same thing, and would not the same autocracy and dishonesty develop as are seen in the political state and in profit business? We cannot visualize a perfect society. The very nature of the state and of profit business makes for these things, whereas the nature of co-operation is to discourage them. Still, it cannot be said that an indifferent majority in any kind of society will not permit an aggressive minority to become dominant and even autocratic. Nor can it be assumed that any society will not become tinctured with dishonesty.

The nature of modern competitive industry is to get more than one gives. This leads to unfairness. We have seen that politics is corrupt, because the state is surrounded and dominated by corrupting business influences seeking privileges through its corruption. The very process by which the socialized state comes into existence is against it. It has a bad heredity. The state is found taking over industries which have broken down, or which have been watered and bled to death. In the end a great organization results, more complex and more powerful than before.

An increase of the functions of the state means an increased bureaucracy of officeholders. Officeholders breed officeholders. They possess an immense fecundity, reproducing their kind. With profit-making business out of the way, such a state is free to oppress society with its officialdom. There might be less real corruption in the wholly socialized state than in the present states, but not less autocracy. Bureaucracy multiplies autocrats. An autocracy carries with it the suppression of liberties. The communist and fascist governments prove this.

Co-operative society has an entirely different origin from that of the state. While the political state is descended from an organization, the purpose of which was to protect the interests of the dominant privileged class against the masses, co-operative society springs from an organization the purpose of which is to produce and distribute for use, to eliminate parasitism and to win democratic control for the people; it is decentralized; its organization begins out among the people; and most of the business and all the control should stay there. It has a foundation and traditions different from those of the state. It requires no patriotic history to make the people respect it. If it is respected, it is because it is respectable.

As co-operative society enlarges, a better state of justice should come upon the scene, the people should enjoy better conditions, the profit system should melt away before it. This is a theory, but it is one that is also borne out by the facts. In any co-operative society today, which has educated its membership in the simple requisites for success, will be found a high degree of loyalty to the society. Members are often willing to give their time and services gratuitously and with joy, as to a great cause. On the whole, they live up to the ordinary business obligations scrupulously and even generously. They constantly make personal sacrifices for it. There are variations from this rule; but such exceptions must be comparatively rare or the co-operative movement could not succeed. The observance of democracy and honesty is a part of its tenets, and essential to its success. As co-operative democracy expands, it is proved, the members must have been faithful. If there should develop in the co-operative movement a disposition to cheat it to a fraction of the degree that the average citizen is willing to cheat his government, co-operation will perish.

The unethical type and the defective intellect, wearing the physical exterior of the best, always provide exceptions to the rules. Co-operative society will have to reckon with these. They are not loyal, they form cliques, they secure privileges at the expense of others. Often officials who are doing a good job like to be free from control, and commonly the membership let them have their way. This leads to bureaucracy. Managers and executives of co-operative societies often tend to become autocratic. The members have the control and can prevent this, but indifference on the part of members is the common lot. Education of the members, literature which keeps them advised of the affairs of their society, frequent meetings with opportunities for discussion, prevent this indifference. But it is a world-wide complaint in the co-operative movement.

After the most perfect possible organization of society, there still remains the constituent unit—the individual. Those forces which make better individual men and women need to give full play to eugenics and education. Whether it is through science, art, or ethical culture, the influences which awaken in the individual a sense of his higher obligations to himself and to others have to be invoked. Co-operation will have to turn toward the attainment of better men at the same time that it aims to build a better society.

Peace after war is the supreme concern of the co-operatives, and to establish a world organization upon a co-operative basis instead

of expanding the political system is the great co-operative opportunity. The conflict of the future will be between compulsory stateism and voluntary co-operation. Democracy is the essential. The
expanded socialized state is incompatible with democracy, and
co-operation without democracy is impossible.

Chapter VIII

CO-OPERATION IN CONTACT WITH THE STATE

CO-OPERATIVE SERVICE IN TIME OF WAR

AT the last International Cooperative Congress before World War I (Glasgow, 1913) a strong resolution on international peace was adopted. The resolution contained the following statement:

"The Congress further desires to impress upon the public opinion of all nations the fact that the reasons for the continuance of armaments and the possibility of international conflicts will disappear as the social and economic life of every nation becomes organized according to cooperative principles, and that, therefore, the progress of Cooperation forms one of the most valuable guarantees for the preservation of the world's peace. The Congress, therefore, exhorts the people of every country to join our movement and strengthen their power. The International Congress of the Alliance declares itself in amity with all the Cooperators of the world, and welcomes any action they may take in this direction or in which they may participate."

This resolution was warmly supported by British, German, and French delegates, and was unanimously adopted by the congress.

At the start of World War I, the British societies provided care for German co-operators who were captured by the British government. They sent financial help to the Austrian societies. The *International Cooperative Bulletin*, the monthly organ of the International Cooperative Alliance, continued publication in English, German, and French, without interruption, throughout the war. When the German co-operators were forbidden by their government to print it, the German societies continued to issue the *Bulletin*. During the war the *Bulletin* published articles by Englishmen, Germans, Frenchmen, Austrians, Americans, Italians, and Russians. Each reported the progress of the movement in his own country. The Alliance was the only important international organization which did not break down during the war. It retained its internationalism. Its first congress held after the war was the first international meeting to bring together delegates from all the warring countries, including Germany, Austria, and Soviet Russia. They met upon the basis of equal fellowship.

Many examples of the principle of service in operation were seen during the war. When the Food Controller of the United States fixed a price on bread, the private bakers protested, saying they could not afford to sell bread for so low a price; the co-operatives protested to the government, saying that they had never charged so much for bread, and did not wish to do so. During the war the British Cooperative Wholesale Society (C.W.S.) often protested to the government against the high profits they were compelled to make by the price-fixing boards.

It is in times of national urgency, when profit-making business is taking all it can from the people, when government machinery does not protect the public, that the co-operative method stands out in contrast. Co-operation is then revealed as a kind of commerce which has the power to exclude from economic life a prime cause of human hostility. A French deputy, who saw what the co-operatives were doing to protect the people from the profiteers, exclaimed: "One stands in awe before such remarkable accomplishments. The co-operators demonstrate the finest qualities of intelligence and ingenuity of our race. With the critical spirit which characterizes us, it often happens that we decry the most beautiful things, which should gain and hold our admiration." This in 1917.

The people of Germany, Austria, Poland, and many other countries, as well as Russia, were protected by their co-operative societies. Professor Gide, of the University of Paris, quotes Professor Stein as follows: "Where would we be in this war, in this besieged fortress which is Germany, if we had not had the co-operatives?" (See *Internationalism*—1918, pages 62 and 255.)

During World War II the co-operatives were no longer able to express themselves as agencies of peace. They definitely took sides with their governments—among the United Nations voluntarily, and among the Axis nations by compulsion. They gave their governments the benefit of their productive and distributive facilities. Among the United Nations co-operation expanded. It served the people as a way of supply, and grew in public esteem as it was observed in contrast with profit business during the strenuous war years. The co-operatives in general refused to profiteer on the people or to practice black market methods. In the Axis countries, the co-operative method was quite subjugated as the autocratic governments destroyed its democracy and left only the material shell of its institutions to serve their desperate ends.

Immediately at the close of World War II, the co-operatives of the United Nations and the neutral nations, such as Sweden and Switzerland, raised funds of money and goods which were given to the damaged co-operatives of the invaded countries. The Freedom Fund was raised by the co-operatives of Great Britain, Sweden, Switzerland, Ireland, and America, and transmitted to the damaged co-operatives. In 1947, the Cooperative League of U.S.A. gave 28,000 gallons of kerosene and 2,600 gallons of motor oil to the Cooperative League of China. The Cooperative for American Remittances to Europe, up to January 1, 1947, had sent nearly $10,000,000 worth of goods in $10 packages to needy families. In many countries the relief provided by the United Nations Relief and Rehabilitation Administration was distributed through the consumer co-operatives. The co-operatives of Sweden gave direct assistance to those of Norway, Finland, and Holland.

In lands where the co-operatives had been damaged or destroyed, there was a rapid recovery of the co-operative spirit and then a reconstruction of the co-operatives upon a democratic basis. Fascism failed to capture the enduring support of the members of the co-operatives. The respect for democracy reasserted itself as soon as fascist dominance was destroyed, and the people went to work to rebuild their co-operative institutions with an extraordinary zeal.

GOVERNMENTAL ANTAGONISM TO CO-OPERATION

Governments, generally speaking, have been indifferent, or unfriendly; many actually have antagonized co-operation. The German government under Bismarck laid obstacles in its way. When the first Cooperative Congress was called in 1859, the King of Saxony dared not permit the meeting in his realm, because of orders from Berlin. When the co-operative credit movement was seen to be making steady progress, Schulze-Delitzsch, its promoter, was subjected to every conceivable form of official harassment and persecution. The Prussian Diet appointed a committee, in 1865, to draw up a law on co-operation. The one member of the house who knew anything about co-operation was excluded from the committee by direction of Bismarck. The German government persecuted Schulze-Delitzsch to the end of his days. The government opposed his propaganda because it taught the people self-reliance. It showed the people how to do things for themselves without the aid of political officials. It rejected the government's bounty. This was a heresy which the government opposed. The government wanted the people to believe that the people could not do things for themselves as well as the government could do things for them. Socialism at this time was making its greatest progress in Germany.

When Raiffeisen and Schulze-Delitzsch were making headway with their co-operative banks they shortly reached a point at which the powers of government took notice of them. They were not only teaching a doctrine dangerous to the state, but they were demonstrating that the people could organize to do things for themselves without praying the government to do things for them. It was then that Bismarck took up with Lassalle, the socialist leader, to find means to counteract this movement that threatened to make the people independent of the state. The political leader and the socialist leader proceeded to promote the idea of the socialist workshop—the self-governing, profit-sharing, co-operative producers' workshop—as an antidote against consumers' voluntary, nonpolitical action. Co-operative or "joint" marketing among the farmers also was approved. Bismarck introduced Lassalle to King William. His Majesty was induced by Lassalle to put some money into producer enterprises. The King went so far as to endow some collectivist workshops which were started in Berlin. After they had run for a little while they failed.

Lassalle was the great socialist propagandist and organizer of his day. He wanted the state to subsidize the workers and to help them organize as producers. He did not understand co-operation. He would have had the workers develop profit-sharing productive schemes. He would have had these promoted and assisted by the state.

The newer Germany, before World War I, had many laws against consumer co-operation. The movement was discriminated against by both federal and local governments, with the result that it drew to it the strong characters in the labor movement and gained strength by overcoming opposition. German societies were forbidden to sell to nonmembers; and government employees were forbidden, upon pain of dismissal, to join co-operative societies. Under the Nazi regime the societies were shorn of their self-governing independence and were administered by officials appointed by the government.

In Great Britain the government had been indifferent to co-operation until World War I. The co-operators had represented a conservative element. From the beginning of the war they had been patriotic and supported the government in every way. However, they kept down prices and in many instances showed that the prices fixed by the Food Controller were unnecessarily high and that the commodities could be produced and distributed for less money. This was their offense. Profit-making business, the trusts, the trade corporations, the landlords, and petty trade instructed the British government to attack the co-operatives. And the government did as it was bidden. The official committees on food control and distribution were made up of the elements which preyed upon the people. Food regulation was wholly in the hands of the interests which were making profit from the sale of food. And the world knows they made it. Only late in the war, after much protestation, were a few co-operators appointed.

The government neglected no possible means to cripple the co-operative movement. Espionage embarrassed the societies. Military tribunals throughout the country, dominated by private tradesmen, jeered at and insulted the co-operators. Men who were necessary to the life of co-operative stores were sent into the army by boards whose members desired the destruction of the co-operative stores. "We have had our shops closed, and the last man taken, on the ground advanced by the military representation that co-operators ought not to exist." Profit-making private shops were never so depleted of their man power.

The grievances became intolerable. These conservative folks had built an efficient organization, for the distribution of the necessities of life to the people, which could serve in time of stress without making profit. They were the largest distributors of food in Great Britain. They had the most capable and experienced men to meet such a crisis as the people faced. And they saw the government set to work its machinery to destroy them; they saw the government play the game with the profiteers against the people. They went to their co-operative congress in 1918 and voted to break down their conservatism. For the first time in the history of the movement, the chairman of the wholesale society made an unpatriotic speech. The temper of the people may be judged by this statement which appeared in boldface type on the first page of *The Cooperative News* immediately after the congress: "The true government is invisible. The true government of this country rests in the vested interests."

The Soviet government of Russia did not attack co-operation with a vindictive, destructive purpose; it sought to absorb it into the state. But the British government went at it differently. During the Irish war, in 1920 and 1921, the British state expressed itself in the destruction of the buildings and property of co-operative societies in Ireland. This work was done by the armed soldiers of the crown with the assistance of the police. Burning, looting, and smashing property was the method. The total destruction of thirty creameries meant a severe loss to the working people. In some cases co-operators were killed. A compensating fact is that actions like these help the masses to understand.

In many other countries the governments have at the behest of business acted against the co-operative movement. In the United States this antagonism has been chiefly local. The co-operative movement in the United States has not reached a size to cause the profit system great concern. The government is generally indifferent to it, excepting that when bills in the interest of consumer co-operation come before the federal authorities, the bills are usually not passed. Co-operation has fared much better since 1933.

In Italy the Fascists ruthlessly destroyed co-operative stores and killed co-operators, under the protection of the state authorities in some instances and with their help in others.

Persecution of co-operators has been committed also by the governments in the Balkan countries. It must be said that in these countries, with disturbed political conditions, governmental persecutions have been excited by the individual co-operators' connections with organizations that were hostile to the political parties in power. Under these conditions, profit business has united with the government in destroying the co-operatives. In many lands the dominant political regime, be it fascist, bolshevik, or what not, destroys co-operatives if co-operators officially are found in politics opposed to the dominant political party.

GOVERNMENTAL ASSISTANCE TO CO-OPERATION

The position of a government must be one of vacillation; it is pulled in many directions by many forces. When the people are poor or discontented or when profit business is so ruthless as to create a rebellious spirit or so inefficient that it fails, the government often turns to co-operation and favors its promotion. This has been the case in India where the British government has subsidized and promoted rural co-operative banking and credit societies among the poor farmers. The Japanese government has been likewise sympathetic. The Russia of the Czar did the same, but saw to it that a strict governmental control was maintained. State aid has been given in Austria, Hungary, France, Italy, and in many of the South American republics. In Germany, the Kaiser's government established a central bureau, the head of which was to guide and control the co-operative societies, which, "without such official head, might have become a danger to the state."

Nearly all instances of state aid have been confined to the agricultural population, who have never seriously threatened the state. Modern exceptions are found in the post-bellum aid given by European governments to consumer societies among the industrial population, and in some countries to housing societies. These were in critical times when the condition of the people was so distressing that co-operation was the only practical solution of their problems.

In the United States several states have fairly good co-operative laws. A few states have administrative departments which actually promote co-operation in a practical way. The Departments of Agriculture and of Labor of the federal government collect information and give advice on this subject. During the National Recovery Administration, 1933–1935, the economic conditions were so desperate that real consideration was shown the co-operatives. A co-operative official was appointed to the Consumers Board of the NRA; the President signed three special executive orders, governmental edicts, preferential to co-operation; a national credit union law was enacted; and many bureaus were created in the Department of Agriculture and in the several relief administrations for the promotion of consumer co-operation. As signs of better times appeared in 1935, these interests in co-operation were much curtailed. Still state funds are available for loans to farmer co-operatives for banking and for electric supply, and much co-operative literature is printed by the government. The government of the province of Saskatchewan in Canada in 1945 established a Department of Cooperation for the special promotion of this form of business.

Dutch and Danish cities, before World War II, made loans to co-operative housing societies up to 60 and even 80 per cent of the value of the property. Many German municipalities made these loans free of interest, and with an agreement that if, at the end of twenty years, the houses had not been rented or sold for profit purposes the loan was to be canceled.

During the session of the German Reichstag, 17 November, 1921, the Minister of Public Economy, Schmidt, speaking to the complaints against those who were exploiting the misery of the public, made the following remarks: "The consumer has within his grasp a weapon which is very powerful, with which to defend himself against the exactions of business; it is the co-operative organization. Let him make use of it. He can be sure that the little he gives to the co-operatives will not go toward the payment of tithes to commercial speculation. I see the position of the consumers reinforced by means of the consumer co-operatives and the network of their organization. I wish to call attention to the co-operatives, which, through their development, are competing against the commercial interests in cutting down high prices. This practice of self-help, this education of the consumer, is, in my opinion, worth infinitely more than all the laws and all the penal decrees." This from official Germany is noteworthy.

Shortly after the revolution following World War I which established the republic in Germany, a Socialization Commission was appointed with instructions to prepare a plan for putting German industry under the direct democratic control of the people. This commission after close study of the situation recommended that the most practical way of socializing the larger industries was to place them in the hands of the co-operative organizations: in other words, to encourage and assist the German Cooperative Wholesale Society to expand as rapidly as possible until it should absorb the big productive industries of the country. Here is an indication of the larger statesmanship, for if such a recommendation were carried to its conclusion, it would mean the gradual supplanting of profit business by the co-operative method and it would also mean the gradual diminution of the functions of the state. Had not the onerous conditions of the Versailles Treaty conduced to poverty and hopelessness in Germany, the disturbances that gave rise to national socialism would not have occurred, and Germany could have led the way to peace and civilization.

Before the Nazi regime, whole towns in Germany joined the co-operative consumer society by vote of the municipal political authorities, and thus obtained the advantages of more economic commodity supplies, banking, and insurance. This is not so much government aid of co-operation as it is co-operative aid of government. Over a hundred towns and cities took this action.

Whether co-operative societies should accept loans from the state must depend upon the circumstances of the loans. In those countries where co-operators constitute a large influence in the politics of the government such loans are, perhaps, not undesirable. In other countries it is a question. In the United States vast funds are held in trade-unions, insurance companies, banks, and trust companies, which could be made available on a strictly business basis. Loans from the government, however, are associated with bureaucracy, surveillance, political entanglements, and often corruption that might do harm. Swedish co-operators refuse any government aid whatever.

After World War I, poverty in Italy became severe. To relieve the situation, the Italian government, under socialist influence, made liberal loans and granted subsidies to co-operative societies. This gave the societies funds and apparent affluence. As a result, the political parties set out to capture the co-operatives. Co-operation became embroiled in a distressing political demoralization. Then, in the swing of the political pendulum, state aid was cut off. The co-operative societies, which had become accustomed to being kept alive by state credits, began to collapse; and the movement in Italy suffered a serious setback—as a result of having accepted government aid.

A noteworthy example of a government promoting co-operation was Denmark. It was influenced by co-operators. They were a power in parliament. This meant that the government did not attempt to govern overmuch and that the people worked out many of their vital problems in their co-operative societies.

During the Roosevelt regime, 1933–1945, the United States offered an outstanding example of the government promoting co-operation. Several of its departments and divisions not only gave instruction on co-operation, but went into the field to help people set up co-operatives. Up-to-date pamphlets were published by the Department of Labor on *Organization and Management of Consumers' Cooperatives, Cooperative Gasoline and Oil Associations, Cooperative Housing Associations, Cooperation in the United States,* and *Cooperative Statutes and Decisions.* The Department of the Interior issued a pamphlet on student co-operatives entitled *College Projects for Aiding Students.* The Farm Credit Administration published the following pamphlets: *Refrigerated Food Lockers—a New Cooperative Service, Managing Farmers' Cooperatives, Farm Credit Unions,* and *Sizing Up Your Cooperatives.* It also organized credit unions in both towns and country. The Department of Commerce issued several co-operative publications. The Consumers Counsel Division of the Department of Agriculture published much co-operative literature, including *Cooperative Bookshelf,* a bibliography of sixty-seven books and pamphlets on consumer co-operation published by the United States government.

Even though most departments of the government are addressed to the interests of the profit economy, the government has thus taken cognizance of this nonprofit form of business. The Rural Electrification and the Farm Security Administrations are setting up consumer co-operatives which in time may become wholly detached from government surveillance. The great opportunity of the government is educational, to teach people how to organize co-operatively, to administer for themselves the funds and facilities which the government provides for their relief, and to expand self-help instead of government help.

Chapter IX

THE FIELD OF POLITICS

CO-OPERATION IN POLITICS

THERE are certain things the people are not yet ready to under-take in their voluntary co-operative organizations. For this reason they often have to make the choice between the administration of some public utility for private profit and its administration by the government.

There are everywhere many well-run profit industries that are capable of going on for a long time. There are many other indus-tries in which the profit-making machinery is not capable of going on—it does not work. There stands the government, the most available organization, ready to take it over. Shall co-operators oppose state ownership because they believe they know a better method which they are not yet able to put into operation?

The answer must be different in each country and in each situ-ation. Even though big enterprises may often seem difficult for the co-operatively organized consumers to acquire, and government ownership of a public utility may seem the quickest way, still co-operators might be expected to say, "This is not the ideal method; the government may go ahead with it, but let us patiently prepare ourselves to make it co-operative in due time." We should expect them not to lose sight of their goal. Public ownership is often to be desired. In countries like Sweden, where the govern-ment owns 51 per cent of many public utilities, prices and services are improved for the consumers. In America the public owner-ship of water and electricity has on the whole been to the imme-diate advantage of the public, as have many other useful services. The ultimate results cannot be predicted.

Partial public ownership is seen in many progressive countries—Great Britain, Scandinavia, and the United States. But these are capitalistic countries where most of the business is still capitalistic profit business. Here public ownership is a reform measure. It smooths the way of capitalism. Where a useful business cannot be run successfully under capitalist auspices and is failing, or where the people are not satisfactorily supplied—as with coal mining in the United States—the government takes over the business. A problem is solved for the time, and the capitalist scene is not cluttered up with a bad mess. Then if the people are not satisfied with coal, the government, and not the capitalists, is to blame. By having the government take up the dead cats and dogs, the capitalist streets are always clean. This is going on everywhere. Government ownership represents reformative measures to sweeten the capitalist scene. But when the majority of industries, or all industries, are in the hands of the government, the situation is wholly different. Then most of the people are government employees, and a socialistic regime prevails. When government has ownership and control of most or all property, the inevitable result is control of the people. Control of things is naturally followed by control of men. Wishful-thinking theorists say this is not necessarily so; history proves it is so. The loss of freedom of the individual is the price he pays for the loss of his property. He suffers two supreme losses for the hope of a doubtful security.

Under some conditions, co-operation can make headway against a capitalistic government, which actually opposes it, better than it can against a government which claims to have the same object as co-operation. Such a government may hamper co-operation by transforming it into the tail of a political kite.

Co-operative education within a political party, converting the majority of members of the party to the view that the principles of voluntary co-operation are more important than their political principles, would be fatal to a political party. No party would do that unless it were permeated with more than a 50 per cent co-operative sentiment. This would mean that the party was no longer a party of the old political faith, but had virtually become a co-operative party. Educating statesmen to desire something above and beyond political action may be one of the tasks of co-operation.

A co-operative party is entirely consistent with co-operative principles provided that the party does not engage in political action. There is a place for a nonpolitical party. It would put up no candidates, it would endorse none, but it would spread information among its members as to how candidates stood on questions affecting co-operation and the consumers' interests. Such a party would be a real factor affecting politics without being in politics. The Woman Suffrage party was highly effective in this way, and ultimately won everything it wanted. The Prohibition party, which goes into politics and puts up candidates, elects none. A non-political co-operative party would find its value to be in educational work, which would be carried on especially at the times of the political agitation of the other parties. The opportunities of parties for education and for reaching the public in election campaigns are great. The co-operative party could appeal to the people as consumers. It could advocate organization and "class consciousness" among the one universal class in society. It could call into an economic and social brotherhood the great unorganized and inarticulate masses. It could adopt as its platform: For everybody, larger access to the good things of life.

In most countries, co-operators refrain from taking their co-operative societies into politics. There are many advantages in this course. To make a definite alliance with a political party means not only the endorsement of its political candidates, but also the adoption of a political platform. Such a step brings into the societies many conflicting and disturbing questions. Politics means compromising and trading with the other political parties that are opponents of the co-operative movement. A political party cannot devote itself to one single problem; it has to take a stand on all questions. Here is the trouble. Co-operators are united on the one question of co-operation; but in other fields they are of many minds. When they go into politics, the whole movement must support its political party and its officials. Co-operators have enough to do keeping together on the simple principles of co-operation; these principles furnish a program. As soon as affairs are complicated by adding a political or religious question, causes of disunion are introduced.

Organized co-operators in Denmark lay down certain conditions which shall be demanded of political representatives. Co-operators demand that any candidate of any party who receives their support shall support these conditions. It is not necessary to have their own political party to get their demands carried into parliament or into the municipal council. Plenty of politicians are going into these bodies who could not go without the votes of the co-operators. In many countries political parties understand that if they want the co-operative vote they must nominate persons who are sympathetic to co-operation. Often the people make united demand for action from their political representatives favorable to co-operation. Upon the co-operative principles, co-operators are agreed and united. The danger of splitting the movement, with the inevitable political discords, is avoided by keeping out of politics. Seductive political alliances, the trading of votes, and the evils in parliamentary action are thus obviated.

When two or more candidates for the same office give pre-election pledges to support the co-operative policies, so much the better. The more there are, the surer can the people be that one candidate standing for those policies will be elected. The co-operators can stand outside the political ring, and make the politicians dance to their tune.

Great Britain has a political Cooperative party, dating back to 1918. It has won an inconsiderable number of seats in Parliament. It has, however, elected many candidates to municipal councils. Besides being concerned with co-operative problems, it takes a position on political questions which are outside the co-operative field. In 1946, having failed to make satisfactory headway in Parliament, it entered into an alliance with the Labour Party (the Socialist party), and now commits itself to socialist candidates and the socialist program. The British movement is quite divided by this venture in politics.

The Labour Party in Great Britain stands for the usual socialist platform, which conflicts with the consumer co-operative movement. For example: the Cooperative Party demands "a State medical service to provide surgical, medical, dental, and optical aid for the people." Now it happens that in the countries in which the co-operative movement is neutral and not under socialist influence, co-operative medical service is being developed. In Great Britain the co-operators are working for political medical service. For the same reason, co-operative housing in that country is less prominent than municipal housing. Political milk supply is again being considered. Mines, banking, insurance, transportation, electric power and light and telephone service are regarded by British co-operators as state functions. The 1946 Congress of the British Cooperative Union adopted a resolution favoring public (political) ownership of basic industries. The directors of both the Scotch and English Cooperative Wholesales have passed resolutions favoring state ownership of the lands, mines, banking, and major industries. This despite the fact that British co-operatives are highly successful in all these fields.

This lack of confidence in co-operation as a direct means of solving economic problems can be traced to the Webbs and the other socialists who have influenced co-operative philosophy. Certainly it has not grown out of experience, for no people have proved more effectively their ability to administer large-scale industries co-operatively. It is not easy to understand why, in the presence of this proved efficiency, the British should hesitate before the greater opportunities. It is not difficult to believe that people who can so successfully carry on the largest businesses in Great Britain are more competent than the political officials in the administration of such affairs. Co-operation, if it represents a solution of the economic problem, has no economic limitations. If such limitations do exist, then co-operation is a palliative to mollify and support capitalism or stateism. It is possible to see co-operation not as a makeshift, but actually as a workable principle, capable of carrying through to the end.

Should the socialist program of turning over the major co-operative functions to the state be effected during a socialist regime, the predicament of co-operation would be a bad one in the event later of a Tory antisocialist victory. Such a turn in political fortunes is to be contemplated.

Industries that have been in the hands of profit business are passing over into co-operative ownership. Some are also passing into state ownership. Competition with profit business is the making of co-operation. But co-operation cannot easily compete with the state in business. Profit business must make profits or it closes up. The state can lose money in any business and still keep that business going, as witness the post office in the United States.

Profit industry and co-operative industry represent private ownership; in state industry the ownership has passed out of the hands of the people; and for the people to get back ownership again is involved in a complexity of difficulties. For these reasons, co-operation must beware of the prevalent expanding stateistic trend.

Chapter X

A DEMOCRATIC NONGOVERNMENTAL SUBSTITUTE
FOR THE POLITICAL STATE

WHAT DEMOCRACY IS

PERHAPS there are wise men who can tell the people what to do to be saved. There are undoubtedly many who know better what is good for the people than the majority of the people know. Many of these wise ones want to save the people. But there are also many stupid ones who would lead the people astray. A function of democracy is to save the people from being led to salvation by the wise and from being destroyed by the stupid. This is salvation by the law of averages. It provides for the people the satisfaction of saving themselves and the lessons of making their own mistakes.

Democracy is the people governing themselves. It means equal rights, duties, privileges, voice, and opportunities in the administration of public affairs.

It offers certain disadvantages. In the first place, an organization with all these conditions is bulky and unwieldy. Democracy moves slowly. Then, too, the public lacks creative power. It has wonderful sustaining power and appalling destructive power; but the mass of people cannot create much of anything—except noise. Creation is the act of the individual. Creation requires concentration of thought and action. The individual has that power. But society has not.

When the individual creates something, democracy looks upon it and shouts its approval; or democracy roars its disapproval and pulls it down. Democracy allows the individual to create and then sits as a court in judgment upon the product.

The democratic mass of people can use their destructive power as a constructive agency. This is the paradox of democracy. Whether the principle of democracy is right or wrong, what the people want they should have—even their own destruction.

The individual can break away from the mass if he wants to.

But he does not want to. The individual, who thinks he is better than the mass, always wants to have the mass do what he tells it to do. He should bear in mind that the fool and the knave have the same right as he has to impose their opinions upon the mass. And this is precisely what is going on. Democracy is an institution for the education of the mass through trial by right and error.

That is the reason why free speech and all other freedoms are good for the people. Democracy stands for the freedom of the individual. That is the only way the people can be sure that every new thing is given a chance to come forward for the trial. And that is the reason a political government cannot be a democracy: it cannot permit freedom. It is based on law and compulsion.

Democracy is the school of the people wherein they learn how to live together, to work and aspire together, to appoint together, and to recall together. It should be characterized by the maximum of control by the people and the minimum of regulation of the people. Its alternatives are autocracy and slavery. Democracy is the end to which civilized society must aspire.

Co-operative society is related to the democratic principle in that a democratic electorate chooses committees and directors who discover and appoint experts to do for the people the things which the people cannot do for themselves. "Who does a thing through another does it himself" is an old Roman motto. By means of this principle, democracy is made workable and efficient. The co-operative store manager and the factory superintendent are such experts.

In a members' meeting of a co-operative society, each member has one vote, but the member who can stand up and address the meeting convincingly is certainly a larger voting factor than the inarticulate member. The first exercises a greater franchise than the second because he influences the votes of others.

Democracy is relative. There is no absolute democracy in parliamentary usage. As soon as the people elect someone, then he becomes a superior person, not favored by the minority, and democracy is invalidated. The act of voting for candidates militates against democracy. The majority are satisfied, the minority are not. The will of the first is opposed against the will of the second, and the latter must yield against their wish and judgment. The will of the majority does not mean the best decision nor the wisest; it only means the will of the larger number.

The Greeks attempted to solve this problem in a truly democratic way. The cities of Greece, two thousand years ago, were so eager for democracy they selected the officials of government by drawing lots. This avoided the danger of a defeated minority party and ensured an equal chance for every citizen. The superstitious had also the satisfaction of feeling that this method left the matter wholly to the gods, who naturally are more competent than men in choosing candidates. The co-operative movement is rich in evidences of this hunger for democracy. For example, the St. Cuthbert's Cooperative Association, of Edinburgh, was started in 1859; but until 1881 it selected its directors by taking them in order from the roll of members.

This Greek and Scotch method has merit. We may look forward to the time when society may have so much confidence in each of its members that this method may be reestablished. Democracy cannot be had unless the gods can be trusted, or unless the society is composed of honest, competent, and socially minded members. In the Freidorf co-operative society, of Switzerland, practically all the members serve on the many special committees of the society. This is democracy come true.

The animal body is a society of cells. Each cell belongs to a special organ. Each organ is a committee of cells, serving in the interest of all—and of itself. This is the democracy of service. Indeed, this biological method is the ideal and most practical. The aim of democracy should be to divide into special groups, to perform special functions for the good of the whole community— just as the human body does. This is the committee method practiced by co-operative societies. Every member should serve and become expert in his particular field. The highly gifted and efficient individual would thus discover himself. Thus a genuine aristocracy of expertness and efficiency may constantly develop. In such a true democracy a universal aristocracy should arise. Co-operative democracy should breed toward co-operative aristocracy—the democracy of superior persons.

THE CO-OPERATIVE SUBSTITUTE FOR THE STATE

Evolution may substitute co-operative democracy for the state. This is now to be seen in many countries, coming about as a continuation of the growth of the co-operative method of organization and its encroachment upon the dominant system of society.

The beginning of this organization of society now exists in the co-operative associations. There are (1) the local societies. Next comes (2) the national society, which is a federation of the lesser organizations. Forty such national societies exist, and are united in (3) the International Cooperative Alliance. Here is the framework and the beginning of the co-operative society of the world.

The international union of co-operative societies in the International Cooperative Alliance has a constitution similar to that of the national bodies. Its purpose is to serve the interest of each unit—in England, Japan, Iceland, New Zealand, or any other corner of the earth; and it is controlled by these units.

These bodies already have their constitutions and their rules. They differ from political organizations; they do not make laws. Through the democratic franchise of the whole membership the co-operative society, with its monthly, quarterly, or yearly meetings of constituent members, is controlled by the people. This differs from the political society, in which the people elect their representative to parliament or congress, and control usually passes from the people's hands; in some countries the control is gone for many years after the election.

The co-operative organization of society, unlike the political organization, begins out among the people and not at the national center. Political organization exalts the central government; co-operative organization exalts the local society which is close to the individual. The national co-operative society is a union of a multitude of local units in the interest of the *members*. A national political state is a union of states or districts in the interest of the *state*. Co-operation seeks the good of the neighborhood in which it begins. This is one of the elements of its strength. Any democratic organization of society must focus its efforts on the neighborhood—the people who know one another and whose problems are similar. The neglect of this principle in political government has cost it its democracy, and left the people confused and bereft of control.

Where co-operative societies become large, they divide into districts to preserve local autonomy. Some divide into small block groups. The form of organization adopted by the whole tends to be an enlargement, a continuation, of the local organizations.

The co-operative movement is restoring the old "town meeting" principle of local government. It is doing this in many parts of the world. The meeting of the local co-operative society is a substitute for political action. The members' meetings of the co-operatives are schools in the local control and administration of the people's affairs. One may pass from a session of a municipal council to a meeting of the directors of a co-operative society with a profound impression of the fundamental difference between the two.

We have seen that the co-operative society in well-organized countries has to do with problems that are close to the lives of the people; that the methods of the meetings are democratic; that women as well as men participate.

Besides their local affairs, the societies have their national problems to discuss and national affairs to control. We have found that the national unions and leagues and the national wholesale societies are made up of local societies, and are controlled by them. The members elect the directors of these organizations and criticize their policies. It is a noteworthy fact that the directors of the wholesales usually are elected from the local administrative boards. They bring to their larger tasks experience with the people and the people's business. The local societies have served as the schools in which they got their administrative skill. We have seen that these wholesale directors are often full-time employees. They come from the masses of the people they represent. They have had the best possible experience to qualify them to serve their constituents efficiently and sympathetically.

Each local co-operative society, we have seen, is managed by a board of directors elected by the people. Experts to perform special functions are appointed or are developed among the members. Committees on financial control, education, recreation, arbitration, and other special functions are elected and appointed. The number and character of these special committees are limited only by the number and character of the enterprises in which the society engages. By this means is secured administration by trained experts. The centralized bodies, however, are always controlled by the local societies. It is its capacity to decentralize control that gives the co-operative idea its power for democracy.

This co-operative movement takes the existing machinery of industry, which is devoted to the purpose of making profits and creating classes that keep men asunder, and adapts it to the function of supplying the people's needs, creating friendships, and drawing men together. The economic basis of co-operation is its strength. The mainspring of man's social actions is his interest in the simple problems of his physical needs. The causes of great social changes in every age are to be found in production, distribution, and exchange. The union of people about their homes, the co-operation of neighbors working together to get the things they want, gives strength to society.

The more of the business of the people that can be carried on by local groups, the better it is. Instead of great central governments, to which the people look for help and guidance, we may hope for a world of nations each made up of thousands of little communities; and each of these little communities a self-governing society of neighbors, as self-sufficient as possible. Production and distribution should be kept close to the people concerned. The delegation of authority and the appointment of representatives to central bodies should only be for purposes which are beyond the capacity of the local community. Co-operation is moving in this direction.

But there are larger purposes, and national federation of the communities is essential. For purposes of efficiency, centralized administration is adopted. Decentralized control and centralized administration are the co-operative rule. The important provision of administration is that control shall never be permitted to escape from the hands of the people.

By this practical means of building from the ground upward, as the co-operative societies are now doing, a nongovernmental society is in process of creation in the place of the political state.

The present structure of co-operative societies is well adapted to an all-embracing expansion. Kooperativa Förbundet, for example, which is the national federation of Swedish societies, carries on a huge business in the interest of its constituent societies. Its headquarters are in its own building in Stockholm. It has a Commercial Department and an Education Department. Its annual congresses are composed of elected delegates. Its central body is in operation every day throughout the year. But it cannot control or coerce its constituent societies; they control it absolutely.

This central union is not a legislative body. It is in every sense a union in which the individual members of co-operative societies, acting through their local societies, promote and protect their interests. Its wholesale department purchases, imports, processes, and manufactures goods for the constituent societies. The union makes surveys, it collects and publishes informative reports, it shows societies how they may meet their problems, it takes steps to protect them from the political state and from profit-making business, and it makes available the lessons to be learned from the mistakes and successes of its many member societies. Its supreme function is to do the things that are for the good of the members of the constituent societies. This motive and method stand in contrast against the motive and method of the centralized national government of a political state.

The national co-operative federations are organized, owned, and controlled by the member societies. They have to do with the material and the substance of the movement, and also with the spiritual and intellectual affairs. In most countries the educational and commercial functions are combined in one national organization. In all countries the two work in close harmony. The annual reports and the transactions of the congresses of these organizations in the many countries of the world are piling up an accumulation of history and facts which society may some day cherish as jealously as it now esteems the voluminous traditions and laws of its centralized legislative bodies.

As the co-operative democracy evolves, decentralization of social affairs is seen. The serious work of the people is carried on out among the homes where the people are. The central national federation is an efficiency undertaking for better group action. At present the citizens of the political state turn their eyes toward the national capital for relief in their distress; in the co-operative society the people look to their own local group to solve their problems themselves.

Already the national bodies exist which might take the place of the political government. These are: (1) the national co-operative unions, leagues, and wholesales and (2) the national labor bodies. If we adopt some of the language of the state, one would be called (1) the Co-operative Assembly, the other (2) the Industrial Assembly. The two would unite to form the national Congress, which would be the substitute for the political parliament. The first would represent the consumer societies from geographic sections; the second would represent the co-operative workers from each major industry, trade, and occupation. In Switzerland, the Cooperative Union would constitute the Co-operative Assembly; and the Swiss Trades Union Congress with the national farmers' organization would constitute the Industrial Assembly. This is the substitute for the Houses of Parliament. A similar setup is applicable to the United States. The national co-operative league, with its educational work, on one side, and its commercial business and manufacturing, on the other side, represents the consumers. Organized labor and the farmers' productive associations of all kinds represent the producers.

As a matter of fact, this would not be so great a change from the present political system of representation as it might seem. In many countries the "lower house" theoretically is supposed to represent the consumers in all the geographical sections of the country in proportion to their number, and its deliberations are supposed to be in the interest of the consumers of each constituency. The senate, or "upper house," is really an industrial assembly. Its members in general represent the industries such as railroads, coal, steel, lumber, oil, land, cotton, banking, etc. The representatives in this central body are, however, not workers in these various crafts but are often lawyers and agents of business, representing chiefly owners. The confusing aspect of this present political organization is that the owners are a comparatively small and privileged class and their representatives in the industrial assembly are required to promote the fiction that their concern is for all the people.

As profit-making business, with its possibilities of war, labor disorders, depressions, and its need for police, courts, jails, and legislation declines, the political functions would be curtailed. As civilization proceeds, the useful functions now performed continue to devolve more and more upon the co-operative society. In the course of time, it may be possible, the relic of the political state would remain as the Bureau of Extrasocial Affairs, having to do largely with the vagrant nonco-operative souls who do not fit into the co-operative society. I trust that existing governments take no offense at this prophecy of their fate. The consolation is offered that worse things than this happen to governments.

The successor of the national political government would then consist of a national congress composed of the two groups, the representatives of the consumers and the representatives of the workers. These would be closely harmonized as individuals for the reason that the workers, first, would be employed in co-operative industries owned by the consumers; and, second, they would as individuals be members of the consumer societies which own the industries and which give them employment.

Already the workers and the employers in co-operative industry would have come close together. Here at last we see them meet as representatives of the people who are in the enterprise of doing with their brains and their hands the useful services needed by society. When this point in the social evolution is reached, the interests of industry, housekeeping, the family, and the supply and enjoyment of things will have at last risen to the importance now occupied by the state. The government, the police power, the political regulating authority, and the profit-making system will have receded to a minor position.

The political state is occupied with governing people; the co-operative democracy is concerned not with the government of men, but with the administration of things.

There are usually three departments in a state government: the legislative, executive, and judiciary. The useful features of these three departments can be assumed by the co-operative democracy.

The Congress of the consumers and workers can take the place of the present legislative department of government. Instead of the legislative functions of governments, the local co-operative societies and the national Congress would adopt rules and regulations for mutual good. Lawmaking as such would not prevail. The functions would be those of collecting information, the promotion of ways and means for supplying needs, the formulation of policies, and the framing of mutual agreements.

The centralized federal functions of the societies would be reduced as much as possible and would have to do only with those affairs which can be treated best by a body of representatives covering a large geographical area and representing many people. They would be largely advisory and administrative. The collection and collation of facts and information would receive especial attention as the foundation for action. The chief conference, advisory, and administrative functions would be carried on by the local societies, leaving for the national organization as little as possible. Its function would be, as is that of national co-operative congresses, largely fact finding, educational, inspirational, and dealing with international affairs.

The Executive Department in a co-operative democracy would grow out of boards of directors of national organizations. Such an Executive Department would serve as a national body for quick action and administration. It would appoint the various technical administrative boards. These technical boards would be comparable to what now constitutes the various departments and ministries of the governments such as have heads called "secretaries" and "ministers."

Foreign relations and other special functions would naturally call for experts. A Finance Department would employ experts to administer fiscal affairs. The Dispatch Department would have to do with highways, railroads, air traffic, transportation, mails, telegraph, and express. The Science Department would have to do with the promotion of discovery and invention, the rewards and protection of inventors, weather prognostication, geological surveys, statistics, standardization, and everything in the province of science. The Health Department would have to do, not only with regulating health administration, but with providing the people with information. It should also indicate the steps which local societies may take to protect the health of their members. The Departments of Foreign Affairs, Peace, Education, Domestic Life, Aesthetics, Recreation, Arts, and Vocational Training would organize these respective interests. The Department of Police would perform those social services of direction and assistance which represent the useful police functions. Each of these technical departments would have its necessary experts appointed because of fitness, precisely as the board of directors of a co-operative society now appoints managers and other experts.

The judiciary, as represented in the Supreme Court, would disappear. In its stead would be the National Board of Arbitration. This body would arbitrate questions of national scope. It would be governed by rules of procedure similar to those governing the Boards of Arbitration of local and district societies. Civil cases, representing differences between individuals which constitute much of court practice, would come before a Board of Arbitration. The Board for Delinquents would be a local body.

These are some of the more important departments. The Congress would have the power to recommend the establishment of others according to the needs. Elections as a rule would be for short terms. Proportional representation, as well as the referendum and recall of elected or appointed officials, would be provided for.

The national bodies would perform the functions of central administration such as are now thought of in connection with a national government. A similar organization would exist in districts, states, counties, or townships as the population and needs of the people indicate. The national organization, thus created by the local societies, would derive its authority from them and be controlled by them. There would be nothing comparable to the present centralized government or control. The control would be from without toward the center.

CO-OPERATION AND THE SOCIAL OFFENDER

The governmental department which, perhaps, is most closely incorporated in the state is the judiciary. Let us take this branch of government, with reference to its most difficult side, dealing with the social offender, and apply to it the tests of co-operation. It is assumed by statesmen that the state is necessary especially for the purpose of the "administration of justice." For this reason, let us examine this matter in the light of its nonpolitical possibilities.

The law court and the jail stand as high symbols of political society. These are the ultimate answer to the social offender. How could co-operative democracy administer these "bulwarks of civilization"? The answer is: The co-operative democracy would abolish them.

Even now in the present state of co-operation the need of a substitute for these ancient institutions is felt. The "grievance committee" and the "board of arbitration" are the beginning expressions of this need. The co-operative society that has such a body, before which members may bring their differences and submit them to their peers, is holding aloft a light, which in the end may penetrate even to the high courts of justice and put to flight the dark forms of legalistic usage. One successful American society has such an organization called the "trial committee." The last annual report of the society says: "There has never been any occasion to call this committee together but a 'fair trial' is assured anyone who comes before it." Some European societies have such a body.

When my neighbor and I, who are fellow members of the same co-operative society, have a difference over the matter of his cow eating my clover, and we take the case to the "arbitration board" of our society instead of to the political court, we are acting as neighbors, indeed. If we agree to abide by the decision of the "board," we have entered into an arrangement whose universal adoption would spell elimination of barristers, robed judges, and their trappings. The hope of simplifying and humanizing judicial procedure begins right here.

May we not look for the day when each community co-operative society shall have its board of arbitration, or trial committee, with simple rules of procedure, before which any two members as plaintiff and defendant may bring their differences for judgment? So fair and so disinterested should such a tribunal be that my neighbor and I will have greater confidence in it than in the court of law. The expense should be much less. With such a body in each community, and with these organizations all integrated into district, national, and international bodies, the questions of district jurisdiction should be simple.

The idea of the nonpolitical court is not new. In China, right-minded persons do not go to court with their disputes—at least not until they have tried arbitration. America had trial boards, which were practically nonpolitical, following the revolution of the colonies against England and before the adoption of the Constitution of the United States. Many private and friendly societies have such courts. Ireland used them successfully in 1921 when at war with Great Britain. Frontier people have always had them as they worked out their civilization. The "vigilance committee" of the frontier towns in the West of the United States sat as courts, made decisions, and issued decrees. Such committees functioned in Macedonia when the people were in revolt against the Turkish government. The whole of Macedonia at that time (1906) was organized into such village, district, and national committees. They sat as courts, heard evidence, and rendered decisions, which the people respected.

In the state of New York a "lay court" has been created, which hears all sorts of civil cases except for divorce. There are no judges nor lawyers. The two litigants choose their own judge. Each party conducts his own case and tells his own story. The purpose is to avoid legal delay, promote arbitration, and release justice from the bonds of technicalities. An association called the Arbitration Society of America is promoting these nonpolitical courts.

The people of India in preference to the British system have developed such nonpolitical courts. In order to understand the methods which co-operation applies in solving this problem, the co-operative courts of India may be examined.

In the Punjab are such courts organized specifically "for the equitable settlement of disputes by arbitration." There is a steadily increasing number of these societies. This type of organization has as its main object to save members the trouble, expense, and waste involved in false, frivolous, vexatious, and unnecessary litigation, by resorting to arbitration. An arbitration society is formed upon co-operative lines with a committee to hear and act on cases in dispute. Each person on becoming a member signs an agreement to pay compensation to the society if he fails to refer to the committee for arbitration any civil dispute or offense under the Criminal Procedure Code in which he is involved with a member of the same society, or if he obstructs the execution of an award granted under the society's by-laws.[1]

The rules of these societies provide that the awards of the non-governmental courts cannot be called in question by any civil or governmental court except on the proof of corrupt practices on the part of the arbitrators.

The successful party may enforce the award or it may be enforced through the committee upon the payment of the expenses. The main power for securing submission of members to the awards is the moral force and the pressure of public opinion in the village as focused in the society. Societies have the power to raise special funds to defend the rights and interests of members in any case and to bring to bear measures of settlement in case a member fails to secure settlement of his claim or is subjected to needless litigation. They have power also to institute, conduct, and defend suits. These societies have been started mainly at the headquarters of co-operative banking unions, and operate over the same area as the unions.

No compulsion is used to induce co-operators to join, nor is there any ill-feeling shown toward those who do not join. The results are reported as being highly satisfactory. The real backbone of these institutions is the moral influence of a healthy public opinion in the villages.

[1] When a dispute is referred to the committee, the latter is required to settle it within a reasonable period; and if no settlement is reached within a month, the parties involved appoint a single arbitrator to decide the dispute. In case the parties do not agree to a single arbitrator, the dispute is referred to a commission of three arbitrators, one nominated by each of the parties, and the third by the committee. These selections are made from a panel of five to twelve trustworthy persons, selected at the annual general meeting of the society. If all the members of the panel are challenged, one arbitrator is selected by the committee. The arbitrator is given the power to call witnesses, to administer oaths, to require the production of documents, and to issue orders regarding the payment of costs. There is a provision for the federation of the arbitration societies of a district to form a union to hear and dispose of appeals. This is the Provincial Court of Arbitration.

Thus co-operative societies show that it is possible for the people to have courts of justice for the settlement of disputes, which are independent of the state and of the political government.

The modern judiciary has been evolved to a high degree of refinement. Its principles have had applied to their elaboration some of the best minds of the world. Co-operative democracy can adopt its essential principles of equity and procedure and make them free from the coercive power of the state's statute law. Two co-operators would come before the tribunal of arbitration, not forcibly bound to abide by rules and laws imposed upon them from above, but they would voluntarily agree to accept the rules and decisions as a condition of having their case heard and judged; and if they jointly cared to modify the rules of procedure it should be their privilege to do so.

As to the criminal who has offended against the individual or against society, he is either sick or he is a creation of the political state. Co-operative democracy should not recognize him. There is no criminal. Of all the crimes committed by the political society, among the greatest are its crimes against its criminals. As the political society multiplies laws, it multiplies criminals. The number of criminals is increased while the human character remains unchanged. This is a political paradox. The state makes criminals and then proceeds to commit crimes against them.

The man who has done a cruel, unjust, or unsocial act naturally falls within one of two classes: he is mentally defective, sick; or he is the victim of social injustice. Sending him to jail as a punishment, or killing him, is the remedy for neither of these.

The sick were once supposed to be possessed of devils, and they were exorcised, avoided, and punished. It is only within the past century that the insane—the mentally diseased—have been treated as sick people. Before that they were chained and cast into prisons, where they were at the mercy of keepers just as the "criminal" now is. The execution, and even burning alive, of the insane, after a trial, was not an uncommon practice in Europe over a period of several hundred years preceding the eighteenth century. But better scientific knowledge presently classified the insane with the sick, and now they are so treated. The "criminal"

is a sick man and entitled to every sympathetic and humane consideration. A just society cannot make distinctions between ab-
normal conduct due to disorder above or below the base of the
skull.

If the "criminal" is not a sick man, then society is sick. If a
man is driven to do unsocial acts, and his mind is normal, then
society has denied him education, or food, or housing, or has
tempted him with drugs, alcohol, conspicuous waste or debauch-
ery, or has sent him into its industries too tender to withstand its
shocks, or has deprived him of parental guidance too soon. Society has done something wrong to him, and it is the business of
society to find out what is wrong with itself, make amends to the
victim of its wrong, and set about to remedy itself. At present it
does none of these things—it just punishes its victim.

The present criminal court is presided over by a judge, who is
learned in the law and is expert in knowing just what punishment to prescribe for each offense. He presides over a machinery
for inflicting punishment. It is based on the ancient idea that
punishment protects society from crime. It is a relic of the ancient
religious idea of vengeance.

How can diagnosis be substituted for prosecution, and treatment for punishment? Instead of the court, co-operative democracy would have a Board for Delinquents. This would be a
diagnostic institute—diagnosticians, instead of judges. The diagnosticians would be of two classes, the physicians, alienists, and
psychologists, and the sociologists; each would have advisory experts. The first of these would be learned in problems of action
of the human mind with special reference to its abnormalities; the
second would know the relations of society to human conduct.
These are, indeed, different from the judge, whose qualifications
consist in his knowledge of the fixed laws of the state, with especial reference to their relation to punishments, while his knowledge of humanity and his sympathies may be negligible.

The diagnostic work having been done and the decision made,
the remedy would then be in the hands of still another tribunal,
precisely as in medicine the departments of diagnosis and treatment are best administered separately.

The mentally disordered person who has done an unsocial act

would be placed under treatment for his disorder. The medical sciences have extensive information on the effects of bodily conditions upon conduct and character. The eyes, the teeth, the tonsils, the nerves, and the glandular organs of the body, as well as the brain, have great power to influence conduct. The treatment of abnormalities would be undertaken. A curable tumor of the brain has often been the cause of symptoms called "crime" and punished as "crime."

Here enters the rare condition in which co-operative democracy may use force. The social delinquent who is a danger to his fellow men, and who will not accept the treatment which might cure him, or whose disease is incurable, must be restrained. This is as proper and as natural as the restraint of a delirious sick man; it should be done with as kindly a spirit.

Not only in dealing with those whom disease renders unsocial and dangerous, but also in the matter of maintaining quarantine and protecting people from infection, in the enforcement of the prohibition against creating vicious habits by use of habit-forming drugs, and in a thousand other matters in which society is justified in protecting itself by restraints, force is the last resort. The insane, and the delirious sick, must be restrained; and the man whose mind prompts him to do damage or unsocial acts falls in the same category. Whatever our theories may be, if men had no organized protective force, they would soon get one. The danger that such force might be used aggressively and unjustly does not prevent society's having it. It is natural and inevitable. The individual uses it; and society will use it.

The co-operative democracy, where it has reached a sufficient development, could properly undertake some use of force. The important fact is that as the autocratic and coercive state has less to do, the need of force becomes less. A community with a fading political government, and with a voluntary co-operative association in its stead, would have less need of force than is found in the political state. This can now be seen as a fact in thousands of areas occupied by expanding co-operative societies, organized by people to promote their own good.

Punitive vengeance has been of doubtful value. Its effect has been to embitter the punished and brutalize the punisher. The principle of (1) restitution, (2) forgiveness, and (3) cure may be substituted for punishment.

In the event that a delinquent has done an unsocial act because of the influences of society upon him, the important step is that society shall publicly be advised of its deficiency and that the proper body shall be charged with carrying out constructive remedies in the interest of both the offender and the offended against. Scientific and humane examination of offenses tends to wipe out the "offense" and leave little to forgive. "To know all is to forgive all." Should there remain a moral sense of guilt, forgiveness is the treatment to heal the last vestige of the wound. This is an old principle that has come down to us from the East through at least five thousand years. It has an enduring virtue. The doctrine of punishment, which has been promoted by the zeal for autocratic power, for privilege, and for the suppression of democracy, has nothing comparable to offer.

While these social reforms may be carried out in other forms of society, three facts remain: they are not carried out in the present capitalistic society; the present society is not organized nor qualified to carry them out; and the co-operative democracy is adapted to their evolution.

It is entirely possible that, as co-operative democracy grows, the world may shake off the complex and brutalizing web of procedures in which it has become enmeshed, and introduce the principles of science, kindness, and justice in their stead.

PART III
CO-OPERATION AND PROFIT-MAKING BUSINESS

Chapter XI

THE NATURE OF THE PROFIT MOTIVE AND ITS EFFECT UPON SOCIETY

THE CHARACTER OF PROFIT-MAKING

As machines came into use which could produce more than the workers could consume, the owners of the machines sought markets for their products. And then the quest for markets and the competition with other producers were followed naturally by an intensifying of industry. Presently the machinery and the tools of the trade were in the hands of an owning class and the work was done by a working class. Now no clear-cut dividing line separates these two classes, but their overlapping is not sufficient to justify the denial of their existence.

The owners of the machinery of industry purchase raw material and labor. The two are mixed together and the finished product sold at a profit. The profits of industry develop as surplus capital in the hands of the owners of the machinery. All this is comparable to the fisherman who was able to catch five fish a day, but who increased his catching power by making a net which would catch twenty fish a day. The net owner was then justified in renting out his net to a neighboring fisherman, who would catch twenty fish with it in a day, and in charging him ten fish as a rental price. Thus the user of the net by working got for himself twice as many fish as before, and the owner without working got twice as many as before. This hypothesis is used to illustrate the profit principle and to display its value. But there are some features which it does not reveal.

In the first place, the owner got twice as many fish as he could use, therefore he had to sell them. The capital which he accumulated he employed to make more nets, with the result that his capital was more and more increased. He died and his heirs were born with capital and absolved from the necessity of performing service. Others worked and fed them. Presently as a result of expansion of the system and separating ownership of the tools from the users of the tools, the two classes developed; and the machinery of society became so changed that the worker who attempted to use his own tools could not compete with the more intensive and complex tools which had been evolved and which were owned by people who did not use them.

Out of this system has grown up an unbalanced complex of business. Most people are occupied in working for wages, and spending their wages for the things they need to maintain life. But there is the strange fact that they cannot buy back with what they earn the things they have made. They buy with what they are paid. If workers create four dollars a day of wealth, and receive for their labor only three dollars, they can spend only three dollars a day. With that they cannot buy what they have created. The surplus wealth, the one dollar's worth of every four, remains in the possession of the employer, or of the trader. He cannot use it all himself. He must try to sell it. But he cannot sell it in his own country because labor is not paid enough to buy it. Labor can buy only three-fourths. This surplus can no longer be sold in foreign lands because there also the same conditions are developing. A time has come when the people of the world cannot get the capital to buy the total products of labor.

All this creates the one peculiar condition that upsets the modern economic system. The condition is the lowered purchasing power of the consumer. Warehouses become filled with goods, merchants fail, empty ships lie at anchor—all for lack of markets. The consumer cannot buy. Unemployment, lockouts, poverty, and hunger are the results. Imperialism develops. Governments want colonies occupied by millions who do not have industries, who produce raw materials at low cost, and who buy the products of the dominating country's machines. These people must be kept in ignorance and subjection or they will develop industries of their own.

When the people cannot buy, governments can buy. The people cannot make credit and money out of nothing, but governments can. Accordingly, governments go into business—socialization—or into war. These justify large-scale spending, and money and wages again freely flow.

War comes also as the result of the quest for foreign markets or lands for imperialistic expansion. To keep the present system alive, temporary schemes may be resorted to in order to equalize an unbalanced economic organization. These expedients may give relief for a time; but recurrence of distress comes. A vessel from which the contents are escaping faster than replenishment is coming in, will sooner or later become empty; and a vessel in which the inflow is faster than the outflow sooner or later will overflow or burst. The present profit economic system is in defiance of the laws of nature. It works toward its own destruction.

The portion of the products of labor which is unpurchasable by the working masses remains in the hands of those who underpay labor. Everything conceivable is done to induce people to buy beyond their means. This follows as a necessary result. Thus we have on the one hand the advertising business and on the other hand the banking business with its mortgages. Property constantly changes hands. The purchasing power of the consumers is also depressed by the cost of commercial warfare. In the United States, of every 100 cents spent by the consumer 49 cents pays for the cost of producing what he buys; 51 cents goes to pay for commercial competition and distribution.

Although the inadequate purchasing power of the consumer is the primary result, every effort is made by the holders of the surplus wealth to depress still more the consumer's purchasing power by depressing wages. Energy is exercised in schemes to give the people less purchasing power, on the one hand, and in creating more unpurchasable surplus goods, on the other.

The delusion persists that the excess wealth in surplus goods can be sold and converted into money or exchangeable capital. It cannot. Attempts to sell it pile up a reckoning which mankind must settle. Outbursts, such as the World Wars, are only minor expressions of the unbalance of things. The profit motive in industry grinds away, adding more and more to the unbalance of society. The great reckoning is yet to come. The consuming masses simply have not the money with which to buy. What they lack is the difference between the cost of producing and the retail price. Profit is the burden that is breaking the back of the world.

One of the striking events that has come about during the evolution of profit-making industry has been the change of ownership. The time was when the owner of the industry was a man. Now the owner is a corporation which is interested in getting out of the industry dividends and salaries and perquisites for officials. Instead of the workers being answerable to human beings like themselves, they are employed by a corporation and are answerable to a corporation—a legal entity without a heart.

Freed from the restraints of personal conscience and the humane considerations which spring from human beings, impersonal profit-making business is able to move forward faster than business under personal control. The profit motive starts industries. Invention for profit, production for profit, and service for profit have been the motives which have set going the great economic machinery as it exists today. There is no doubt that it has made use of the acquisitive hunger to urge men on to useful performance. The great combinations of capital have been bold and willing to take risks, before the people demanded such developments. When no society would have ventured such a project, when no individual alone had the courage to promote it, railroads were pushed into the wilderness and across the plains. Investments in new enterprises involve risk. It would seem hardly fair to expect an individual to take financial risks in the case of enterprises of social value only. Capitalism was capable of taking these risks. It was impersonal; it ventured with other people's money; it made great accomplishments.

During the century of capitalistic dominance of the world, the human race has made greater progress in science and industrial art than ever before. The lot of the working people is generally better than it was at the beginning of the capitalistic era when the steam-driven machine came into use. Things have been produced and distributed and the people have been better fed. Labor-saving devices have been promoted, engineering feats have been accomplished, such as the world had never dreamed of. The telegraph, telephone, automobile, airplane, radio, atomic energy, and the wonderful distribution of electricity have been evolved under the stimulus of the profit motive. There are everywhere noteworthy examples of the highly valuable services capitalistic business has performed. Publishing houses which put out good literature at a low cost, instrument and utensil makers who have perfected and sell valuable instruments at low prices, banks which effectively serve the people, transportation lines which are well conducted, useful public utilities, and many similar enterprises are to be found as results of the much-criticized capitalist system.

It is also noteworthy that the amount of wealth has been greatly increased. There is so much wealth and such great possibilities for accumulating wealth that people of meager intellectual powers and often with slight industry acquire much property. Every industrial country has examples of men and women who were born in poverty, and often with discouraging physical handicaps, rising to positions of affluence. Where wealth is, there is opportunity.

While these opportunities are partly due to the speculative possibilities offered by the profit system, they are fundamentally due to natural resources and to inventions which have made excessive wealth production possible, although the inventors have often received little pecuniary reward.

Capitalism has made it possible for people to be rich. Among these have been some who have used their wealth to promote art, museums, libraries, parks, endowments for schools and universities, health foundations, scientific research, and to create the beautiful and cultural things which individuals but not communities can create. An important service that wealth has performed has been the creation of beautiful homes. These expressions of wealth have provided examples of the possibility of surrounding the family life with architectural beauty and art.

Compensations are naturally to be found in so complex a condition. Surplus wealth may serve good ends. Frugality and industry are promoted by the efforts to secure it. Possessors of surplus wealth are protected in old age and in times of incapacity. The helpless have it bestowed upon them and life is guaranteed. To widows and to orphans it may become a beneficent, life-giving agency. It wins leisure for the artist, inventor, poet, and humanitarian. There are those who say that its power for good is greater than its power for injustice. The questions which press are: Would it be possible for these advantages to be available in a society without the injustices upon which they now rest? Could not the widows, the orphans, the old, and the infirm be guaranteed protection at less cost? Is it necessary that the great mass of mankind shall live and die in poverty and that most widows, or-phans, aged, and infirm shall suffer in order that a minority may be protected?

Under capitalism, humanity has advanced; it has come into possession of much new knowledge. The fact that knowledge is often turned to bad purposes does not condemn it forever. The test of civilization is the degree to which it develops and employs knowledge and invention to promote the happiness and well-being of the largest proportion of the people.

Many engaged in capitalistic business are socially minded. They believe capitalism to be best for society. Social-mindedness is not a peculiar possession of the poor. There are also many who be-lieve in the profit motive, who want to see the world good and beautiful, and who are willing to make efforts to make it so in the interest of all mankind. No class can arrogate to itself the assumption of all the social virtues.

There are those who are occupied successfully in the struggle for profits who believe the profit system is unsound and unjust. There is, also, the rich man who would gladly join with the many to bring about the utopia or the different sort of civilization for which dreamers hope. But he believes that the mass of people do not want a different civilization earnestly enough or intelligently enough to be able to get it, and if they should get it they would soon lose it again. He has seen them try it, and they have dis-couraged him. For this reason, we find such men giving their thoughts to the promotion of science and art, as things which are substantial and will endure, no matter what may be the political and economic fate of the people.

One quality runs through this situation. The majority of men desire to act in terms of justice to their fellow men. For this reason, fair dealing within the limitations of the laws of business is the rule. Business in general is based on confidence in others, and this confidence is generally to be depended upon. Honesty is, indeed, the best policy. Furthermore, there are many men in the field of successful profit business who would not take advantage of the customer. They give good values. They strive to be of real service to their clients. They would not stoop to cheat. They are taking a profit which constitutes their wages for services rendered, and on the whole these wages are not high and the services are good. It is especially in those fields of business, still dominated by individual men, that this high sense of personal responsibility is seen. A large amount of the distributive business and the services of the world is performed on this basis. And the majority of the people still desire that it shall not be replaced by any other method.

THE EFFECT OF PROFIT-GETTING

The prevalent economic system establishes money as the supreme object of human endeavor and calls the attention of the people away from the real things of life. With the winning of profits as the main motive of industry, it is natural that devices for the purpose of increasing profits should be resorted to, which are to the disadvantage of the consumers. Earning money, as the motive of industry, is highly hazardous to any civilization. Money-getting, as the object of social activity, may in the end prove the most disastrous undertaking of the ages. The danger is not only in the unsocial immediate results, but in the misuse of the money itself. It has a commodity power which, in the hands of the unsocial, the unwise, or the vicious, expresses itself in harmful ways.

If a savage king controlled the nut trees and the olive groves and the fish in the lake, all of which were abundant, and if he would not permit the hungry people to eat until they gathered hummingbirds' feathers; then nuts and olives and fish would be scarce for these people. The struggle of life would be turned away from the real things such as nuts, olives, and fish, and directed to hummingbirds' feathers The people would even fall to fighting among themselves to gather feathers, while they were hungry and the fruit was rotting. This is precisely what occurs in the quest for money instead of the quest for things and services needed by society.

Academic economics promote the theory that "money is stored-up wealth." It is more than that. It is a writ of attachment, sealed and signed by the government with police power behind it, entitling the holder to the products of the labor of others and to things which will be produced by men and women yet unborn. With money one is given control over the lives of others and may place himself in the position of master as effectively as slaveowner ever could.

The modern profit-making control of commodities has largely set aside the law of supply and demand. The price the American farmer could get for his wheat did not pay him to raise it at a time when the people of Europe were starving for want of bread. The lumber mills shut down when the people needed houses. Eggs were being shipped from China to the United States during the Chinese famine of 1921. During the winter of 1921–22, the electric light and power companies of a number of Western towns in the United States used corn for fuel. At the same time there were five million people in the valley of the Volga dying of starvation, empty ships were gathering barnacles in every port, and the unemployed were praying for work. The supply goes where there is the money to pay for it at the most profit; or where imperialistic diplomacy says it may be permitted to go. That is what is left of the ancient law of supply and demand.

Money is invested to start such industries as pay the best. The question that decides whether a flour mill or a cigarette factory shall be started is, which will pay the more dividends; not whether the people need flour or cigarettes. And with the fortunes made in industry the rich invest in luxuries which require still more industries, even while the simple physical needs of millions are unsatisfied. Price is not controlled solely by supply, demand, or even by the value of commodities.

The present organization of the world's fiscal system naturally tends to promote scarcity for the consumers. No business in the profit system succeeds in the presence of abundance of its product. If the people can get easy access to the commodity, the business fails.

The high wages that labor wants, and sometimes gets, depend principally upon the scarcity of labor under the present system. It is said that labor is a commodity. The price is governed by the same market and profit conditions that govern the price of chattel slaves. Plutarch narrates the fact that in Sparta when slave laborers became too plentiful, and consequently cheap, the young men of the rich families were permitted to indulge in the sport of killing unarmed laborers until they became scarce enough to sell at a higher price.

The restrictions of apprenticeships, the limitations of union membership, and the exclusion of immigrants are among the present-day methods of the Spartans of labor. These acts, to promote scarcity and thus to raise the price of the commodity, are performed by the workers on their side for the same reason that they are performed by the capitalists on theirs. Both are in the grasp of the same economic forces.

Capitalists recommended that the workers should produce more as a means to cure the economic ills, while at that same time bananas, oranges, potatoes, coffee, fish, and other commodities were being destroyed by speculators in order to make the price go up. The American farmer has been encouraged by his government to destroy commodities and to produce less while other departments of that same government were spending millions to show the farmers how to produce more.

Access to things must be made difficult if profit business is to succeed. There might be enough for all, but the people cannot buy it. The price puts it beyond their reach. If we produce more we shall have that capitalistic calamity—overproduction. That means closing down of mills, lockouts, and the train of disasters which naturally follows.

The failure to use human resourcefulness and inventions is one of the expensive results of the profit motive. Invention is misused. The refrigerating plant has departed from its social use—the preserving of food from decay and the storage of foods in time of plenty for use in time of scarcity. Modern refrigeration, instead of being used for the public good, too often is turned as an instrument against the people and serves to corner markets, to promote monopolies, to take things out of use and create scarcity. This invention which could serve wholly for the public good has become part of a gambling paraphernalia.

Wastage of human life transfers the prevalent profit system from the field of economics into the realm of tragedy. Accidents and disease in industry, where these industries are run for profit, are more than tragic because most of these casualties are preventable with a slight sacrifice of profits. If it is cheaper for an industry to damage human beings than to introduce changes that would materially diminish casualties, the directors, as businessmen entrusted by the stockholders with the task of making the business pay, too often are found rejecting plans for safety.

Disaster becomes a source of profit. Epidemics bring profit to the doctor and to the apothecary. The liquor manufacturers profit by the craving for drink. The newspapers profit by scandal. The detective agency profits by crime. Employers profit by unemployment. Patent-medicine makers profit by the ignorance of the public and the incompetence of doctors. But none of these disasters is of benefit to the consumers. Can a civilization be built upon methods which get rewards from suffering and wrong, or which make hunger, accident, disease, and war profitable to a large and influential class of its citizens?

Of the four hundred and fifty thousand adults who die each year in Great Britain, five-sixths of them die in poverty. They leave no property. They have had income enough only to maintain an existence always on the verge of starvation and want. In the United States a small number of financiers, among the 2 per cent of the population who own most of the wealth, virtually control the fiscal situation. Before World War II, 12,000,000 workers who wanted work were unemployed; 20,000,000 people were so destitute as to be in need of public relief. This in a land capable of abundance for all.

Many students of economic history and an increasing number of business people believe that the end of an economic epoch is approaching. It is obvious that as capitalistic business fails to serve and breaks down, the socializing state attempts to assuage the damage and gather up the wreckage. This was the function of the National Recovery Administration in the United States in the 1930's. As this inevitable socialization expands, profit business grows fearful of the loss of its opportunities, and becomes timid and panicky at the presence of the socialism which it itself has created. It then resorts to autocratic methods, the suppression of democracy and of civil liberties, and the use of physical power. With force, it attempts the suppression of its own symptoms. Its ownership of the property, of the food, and of the machinery of wealth production, and its control of the police power attempt the destruction of every agency that threatens profits. This is fascism, now growing in the United States and in many other countries. It is the last stand of the capitalist regime, and destined itself to follow the fate of all autocracy and end in collapse.

As its political machinery weakens, fascism itself, like capitalism, moves toward socialism. It first controls and then takes over business with the hope of saving itself and saving business. This is what transpired in Italy, where the government "nationalized" the essential corporations. In Germany, the Nazi regime from the beginning called itself socialistic, and steadily tended in the direction of more and more governmental control and ownership. The co-operatives had to lie low, quietly compromise with the dominant powers, and preserve as much as possible of their co-operative character. But deeper than this in both these countries has been the co-operative spirit, which has remained undestroyed in the hearts of the people. This is something which fascism has neither been able to reach nor eradicate.

Fascism represents the stage of desperation of capitalism. Aggravated by the socializing tendency of the state, by the rise of socialistic movements, and by the growing power of labor, capitalists and middle-class businessmen accept the dictatorship of an autocratic leader who promises to "unite the people" and restore the ancient glories of a fading capitalist regime. Because of economic and moral collapse, they can be restored only by force and the abnegation of democracy. Unity is accomplished by destroying every element that does not "unite" under the fascist banner. Only profit business and the state are permitted to engage in industry, and forces not in harmony are assaulted. This brings co-operation under the ban. Its destruction is attempted. Inefficiency results from attempts at autocratic administration of voluntary and democratic co-operative institutions. The co-operatives are given as much freedom as will placate the co-operative consciousness. They function under duress, the same as in countries controlled by the Communists. Since autocracy has always fallen because of corruption or inefficiency, this same historic fate awaits the fascist regimes. And out of the wreckage the co-operatives may be expected to emerge, to become dominant or to play a minor role in social reorganization as the genius of the people inclines.

Business, in the more civilized countries, is quietly making the transition from the profit method to the co-operative method, and thus circumventing both communism and fascism. These two forces threaten those countries the least which have the largest co-operative development. And those also are the countries least disturbed by the tragedies of economic collapse.

Co-operation is not opposed to the profit system. At the present time most members of co-operative societies earn their spending power in profit business. Farmers' marketing organizations are profit businesses. The trade-unions are based upon the profit principle. Co-operators cannot favor laws or edicts that would make profit business illegal, or even that would discriminate against profit business. If co-operation enjoyed a monopoly and were the only kind of business permitted, it would suffer deterioration. The co-operative way has made its progress for a hundred years in competition with profit business. It needs the challenge and the threat of other kinds of business to compete with it lest it drop into complacency and mediocrity. It is disadvantaged by any privilege which profit business does not also enjoy. In these respects co-operation differs from profit business, fascism, and the various other forms of stateism, all eager for the exclusive establishment of their particular methods.

Since consumer co-operation is not concerned with profit-getting, but has as its purpose the direct getting of things and services, it is peculiarly free from the deficiencies of the profit economy. Whether we think of adulteration and shoddy goods, of overproduction and underproduction, of slums and inadequate medical service; or whether we think of crime, courts, punishments, and war, the difference between business to get money and business to supply human needs is strikingly obvious.

Chapter XII

PROFIT BUSINESS IN RELATION TO CO-OPERATION

THE TREND OF DISTRIBUTIVE BUSINESS

INDUSTRY was once carried on in the home and in the small shop by the individual worker who sold his product or his labor directly to the consumer; and trade developed from the individual trader. As the self-governing worker has disappeared, so is the independent tradesman disappearing. The trend is toward combinations of trade. This tendency is prompted by the interests of profits. The trusts and the great combines are indications of the change.

While the worker has been at the mercy of the employer in earning his wages he has been at the mercy of the merchant in spending his wages. Competition among merchants has been a temporary source of relief. But now the great combines are replacing competitive merchants by monopolies all their own.

Capitalist industry is combining for the sake of efficiency, and is tending to unite under centralized control both production and distribution. Chain stores, owned by producing organizations, are distributing directly to the consumers. The co-operative consumers originated this system. But the capitalist in using it can resort to methods which co-operators cannot use. The capitalist can introduce inferior material, and when the public finds it out he can discontinue it and change to another. The many devices of competitive business to increase profits at the expense of the consumers are excluded from co-operative practice. People who own business do not use that business to take advantage of themselves. Co-operative business attempts to excel in quality and in lowness of price. In some countries it fixes many prices.

Co-operators carry on education which promotes loyalty. They develop efficiency in business administration. Their wholesales are supported by distributive societies which from the business standpoint compete with the chain stores. They feel that they are guaranteed against inferior goods and the common hazards of buying. Furthermore, the urge for profits on the part of the chain stores—the dividends demanded by their stockholders, the salaries demanded by their officials, and the perquisites demanded by their creditor banks—keeps up prices to a point which makes possible co-operative competition. These conditions, which are inherent in the nature of profit business, lead to the development of new competing chains of stores, to the introduction of new competitive methods of business, and to other devices which business uses to the disadvantage of the consumers.

The profit chain stores in some countries are putting out of business the small private tradesmen. As these chain stores develop their own wholesales, an approach to monopoly is made. In many countries where the co-operatives have developed their wholesale establishments, their position is stronger. In countries like the United States, where the co-operatives are not so far advanced and where the chain store business has every circumstance to promote it, the situation is different. Here is every indication that the co-operatives have a serious struggle against this competition. It is possible for a chain store to open near an isolated co-operative store and to undersell it until the co-operative store is compelled to close. One policy that helps co-operatives under these circumstances is education of the members so that they understand the purpose and methods of profit business and patronize their own store even at a temporary loss to themselves in order to realize the future advantages of co-operation. But consumers cannot maintain a persistent loyalty if they can buy cheaper elsewhere. Nor should it be expected.

Their own co-operative wholesale is their best resort. Such wholesales develop where enough retail societies with enough purchasing power unite. Isolated store societies in northern Wisconsin and adjacent states suffered many failures until there were enough to unite and form a wholesale.[1] This wholesale, since 1929, has witnessed the failure of most of its competitors, and the success of its constituent societies is practically guaranteed. A number of such wholesales in other parts of the country are making

[1] Central Cooperative Wholesale, composed of over 150 societies, with its head warehouse at Superior, Wisconsin.

possible the competition of their member societies with profit business chains.

Another help enjoyed by co-operatives is that neighboring co-operative wholesales, the wholesales of other countries, and the international wholesale render aid. American societies are being supplied with commodities by the British C.W.S. Carrying on this international assistance, exchange is one of the large functions of international co-operative wholesaling which distributes commodities among some twenty-two countries.

An American project, for transforming a profit business into co-operative business, has been much discussed and surveyed. A national corporation vested in a board of trustees has planned to buy department stores. The customers were to be educated in co-operation and to buy the stock. As soon as they showed the ability to assume the responsibility the control was to be given to them on a strictly Rochdale basis. The plan has not yet gone into operation, but it cannot be declared impractical.

In the United States a peculiar employee psychology operates to the advantage of the co-operative stores. There is available a supply of managers of profit chain stores who want to become managers of co-operative stores. They grow tired of the mechanical routine of getting profits, and desire the human contacts, outlook, and sincerity which exist in the co-operative store. "I want to work for human beings," such a manager has said.

If the co-operative stores find they cannot make headway in the face of the great forces arrayed against them, then co-operation tends to enter the scene by other channels. The bakery, oil, coal, farm supplies, milk distribution, housing, insurance, and banking are fields in which the people of highly capitalistic countries succeed in driving in their co-operative wedge. Profit business has exploited these fields, and co-operative societies are succeeding in them. When people organize to serve themselves in any field, and when their organization has grown large enough and efficient enough, they are ready to move into other fields of service.

There should be no antagonism against co-operation on the part of business people. Its motives are honorable and its methods are open. The wider distribution of stock ownership is highly approved by business corporations. The co-operatives move in this direction. Their aim is the ownership of stock, distributed among all the patrons of a business. If it is proper for a private individual or company or corporation to come to a town and start a store, who would oppose a company composed of the people of the town itself doing the same thing? They do not propose to steal, nor to confiscate anything. They wish to buy and to pay for everything they get. As to damaging private business, the co-operators aim not to damage business but to improve business. They generally sell at the same prices asked by the other tradesmen. In small towns, the people, when they start their co-operative store, often discuss the matter with the local merchant, and then employ him to take charge of their store—provided that he is capable of getting the co-operative idea and functioning co-operatively. Co-operators generally have been animated by a friendly spirit.

Co-operation does appeal to the intelligent businessman. He is aware of the deficiencies and hazards of profit commerce. He sees the failure of the prevalent distributive method to supply the people's needs. It is a common experience to hear businessmen say: "I wish my customers owned my business and employed me as manager." Over a long period the author of this book has seen this attitude toward co-operation increase, until today it can be said to be fairly prevalent.

PROFIT BUSINESS ATTACKS UPON CO-OPERATION

In Great Britain, ninety years ago, the common expression repeated by economists and tradesmen was: a co-operative association is contrary to the principles of economy. This assertion was the answer to anyone who mentioned the subject. But still co-operation grew. Usually where profit-making business comes in competition with co-operative business, more or less hostility from the former toward the latter develops. Boards of trade, chambers of commerce, merchants' and manufacturers' associations launch attacks. The history of co-operative societies is a story of repeated attacks by profit business and the press. Skillfully concocted misrepresentations to destroy credit, to alarm the members, and to induce them to draw out their capital have been a common resort. These attacks have sometimes caused serious trouble; and always annoyance.

The co-operators of England had their conflict with the big soap business and won. A well-financed propaganda backed by chains of newspapers attacked the co-operatives. The movement continued to grow. The Swedish co-operators beat the sugar trust, the margarine trust, the flour trust, the rubber trust, and last the electric lamp trust, in attempts at monopoly. In Switzerland the conflict was with the beef trust; the co-operatives won. From these national conflicts down to the affairs of the village store, attacks upon the movement have resulted in better loyalty and solidarity, and have demonstrated the ability of the co-operators to protect their interests.

Local experiences in the United States, close to the people, furnish the following instructive examples. When a chamber of commerce rented all the available buildings in a town to shut out the co-operative, the carpenters called a strike and put up a building for them. When a bank refused a society credit, the working people of the town withdrew their deposits from the bank and joined the society. When the merchants offered a bribe to a member to circulate the report that the society was failing, the society published a report of the scheme, and its membership and capital were increased. When the merchants of Sweden sent a lecturer to a town to explain that a co-operative store would be a bad thing for the people, the audience at the close of the lecture proceeded to organize a co-operative store society.

The efforts of American bankers to restrict the development of co-operative banking have resulted in limitation of this form of service. Bankers have succeeded in having restrictions placed upon the amount of deposits and the capital of co-operative banks, no checking accounts allowed, and loans outside the state not permitted. Still methods are being discovered by co-operators to circumvent these disabilities. All this in the face of the fact that the failures of 10,000 capitalistic banks during the past twenty years lost the depositors many millions of dollars, while failures among co-operative banks were practically nil.

In all countries attempts have been made to tax surplus-savings and loan-capital of co-operatives as though they were profit. Tory governments in Great Britain have penalized co-operators for their efficiency and prudence in supplying their needs, while they have given doles to the unemployed and the less efficient. American business took action which prevented the self-help co-operatives, among the unemployed, from making things for their own use. This was apparently in ignorance of the fact that business had to feed them when they were not permitted to feed themselves.

It is not profit capitalism that threatens co-operation. Co-operation can beat the profit system on its own ground, and is steadily doing so. The great threat to co-operation is the socialized state, for the growth of which capitalism is largely responsible. The tragedy is that there are those who do not see this situation and who would have co-operation absorbed to enrich a socialistic state. Profit business, in its attacks upon co-operation, does not realize it is promoting political socialization of industry.[2]

SOME DEFICIENCIES OF CO-OPERATION

Co-operation is as imperfect as human beings are imperfect. This cannot be said of profit-making business; it is less personal. Profit buiness possesses inherent qualities which make for the development of acquisitiveness and selfishness in men; co-operation tends to make men less selfish and, therefore, less competent in terms of the modern competitive economic struggle.

The hunger for privilege and advantage is bound to appear in any organization of human beings. Likewise there are in the co-operative movement individuals who seek self-advancement. In these societies, as in all others, there are certain individuals who do most of the thinking and initiate most of the actions. Natural incompetence, or indifference, prompts most of the membership to remain inarticulate. This means that the articulate minority have the most influence, and if so disposed are sometimes in a position to promote their own selfish ends.

I once asked a secretary how many of the 7,000 members of his

[2] See Author's pamphlet, *The Socialistic Trend* and chapter on "Cooperation in Relation to Government," p. 61, in the Author's book, *The Cooperative Way*.

society attended the last members' meeting. He replied, "About four hundred . . and that was about four hundred too many," he said in an aside to the president of the society. Indifference among the members makes autocracy possible among officials.

As societies grow large and old, and even in smaller societies, the control tends to go into the hands of a few officials and paid employees. Often the manager is the autocrat. He sometimes actually selects and controls the directors. Often this bureaucracy is for the selfish financial interest of one or more officials; sometimes it is promoted by a few enthusiastic, intelligent, and willing members who believe they can get better results for the good of the society without democratic control. In many societies this sort of official autocracy is prevalent to a large degree. It exists, to a greater or lesser extent, in all countries. The leaders of co-operation are aware of it; and the educators are making efforts to find remedies. One method, now coming into general use, consists in dividing the large societies into small district groups with local autonomy. There is, perhaps, no economic field in which less advantage is taken of the indifferent majority for personal ends than in co-operation. The principle of mutual aid which pervades the membership discourages unfair egoism. And the democratic rules of co-operative societies protect in a large measure the common good against the possible encroachments of the selfish individual.

Co-operation means work. Most people are not willing to enter into a business project if they see only a small saving. They prefer to pay the capitalist his 5 or 10 per cent profit, and let him do the work, have the responsibility, and sustain the risks. It is his pay.

Another difficulty confronting co-operation is that it represents the economically weaker and inexperienced elements of society competing against the stronger and experienced elements. The conditions of the competition are controlled largely by the strong and the experienced. The people are accustomed to the profit system, and laws and usages are in its favor. It has the traditions and the support of the government, as well as the wealth of the nation.

The co-operative movement labors under the disadvantage, in its competition with profit business, that the latter can act more quickly and is more promptly responsive to its directing force.

The restricted number in control give profit business an advantage in these times of large affairs, unexpected opportunities, and emergencies. The co-operative association has a large personnel of owners and controllers; and profit business has comparatively few in control. Co-operation attempts to meet this by concentrating administrative authority in a few expert hands, and by still maintaining decentralized control among the members.

Profit business is concentrated upon making profits; that is the main thing it has to think about. Co-operation has to make a commercial success as only one of its several important functions. It is a social movement, operating in the field of business; it has many and complex relations to consider, not the least of which is its concern for labor. It cannot drive its employees as does profit business. Labor in many countries deliberately demands more from co-operatives in order to create a standard upon which to base demands from profit business. Sometimes the membership meeting of a society overrules action of the directors and increases the pay of labor. This does not occur in profit business, which has only one purpose—to make profits and keep going—and in which questions of justice and ethics have to be secondary to this main purpose. With co-operatives, action taken by delegated or appointed authority must be such as will be approved by the majority of the members. The officials of profit business are not much concerned for the social, ethical, or economic opinions of any considerable body of people. They are free to act quickly.

The position of co-operation in combating the attacks which can be made upon it by profit business and by government has already been discussed. Profit business can increase sales by advertising spurious values. It is always seeking things that appear to be better than they are. The boycott of co-operatives by manufacturers, dealers, and transportation companies; the bribing of co-operative employees; misrepresentation—all these are expedients to which profit business resorts, but which co-operation cannot use. It is a peculiar if not difficult fight in which one side may use every killing device and the other side must abstain from unethical methods. It is veritably a warfare between force and virtue. Virtue may win; but it must first suffer some hard knocks.

The co-operative society, unlike profit business, has never yet successfully begun as a big enterprise; it must grow up from a comparatively small beginning, creating much of its executive talent as it grows. Moreover, as it develops people of executive talent, profit business sometimes hires them away by offering larger wages. In compensation for this is the fact that new co-operative executives with enthusiasm, interest, and talent are always coming up from the ranks of the people, and also from profit business. There is also the feeling that the co-operator who is willing to be hired away by competitors is not a real co-operator and the movement is better to be rid of him. Profit business often pays big salaries. Co-operation does not do this, and consequently does not attract executives hungry for large incomes.

Co-operative societies often suffer for want of proper guidance and education when they are not connected with a federation of other societies. Such isolated societies commonly are negligent in bookkeeping and accounting. Managers may be inefficient or dishonest. It sometimes happens that education and propaganda are used to stimulate loyalty in the members when better efficiency in the management is the need. To keep on patronizing an inefficient business when better values could be had in profit business is one of the results of misdirected loyalty.

Autopsies on dead societies in the United States show the following causes of death: starting with too little capital; giving credit; buying on credit; defective bookkeeping, auditing, and accounting; paying savings-returns before developing reserve; too low prices; members unfamiliar with co-operation; neglect of education and social work; factions in the society; business in wrong location; stock unwisely selected; incompetent management; indifference on the part of members; failure to meet a need; underselling by competing business; being content to just keep going, with no program of progress; and violation of one or more Rochdale principles. But the lack of competent executives, leadership, organizing ability, and educators sums up the pressing need. The co-operative movement is in want of superior people, who are now attracted to profit business, the arts, and the professions.

Co-operation does not much attract the academic intellectuals. They are found patronizing profit business while they occupy themselves talking and writing about its wickedness and about other schemes of social betterment which are not so near. To go into co-operation means to put up some money, to be concerned for goods on the shelves and delivering the milk and bread on time, to wrap up packages, to make change at the cash register, to keep things clean, and to carry on business. These are all vulgar and material duties. Many well-meaning people prefer to think of such things as functions for a future utopia; but they do not want to be bothered with them now—talking and voting are easier. There is also the danger of a co-operative business failing. There is the reproach that goes with failure. It is more comfortable not to take such chances, but to work instead for some noble scheme that cannot fail—because it does not exist. The stubborn facts of everyday life are less romantic than the dreams.

Co-operatives have to develop in a society that is adjusted to the profit motive. People have been taught to prefer the profit idea to service. They are in sympathy with gambling. And the initial savings in co-operation are too small to be attractive.

Perhaps the greatest deficiencies are sheer inefficiency and bungling on the part of employees and indifference on the part of members of co-operative societies. These, at least, are the most common causes of failure. Man bungles in business and in politics and also in co-operation. Though the co-operative method were the best way conceivable to supply human needs, though it were capable of bringing peace and justice to all men, there is no assurance that these would be the reasons for its acceptance.[3]

[3] See *Problems of Cooperation*, 1942, by the Author. This book is a study of the deficiencies of the cooperative method and the difficulties in the way of its expansion.

Chapter XIII

CO-OPERATION AS A BUSINESS PRINCIPLE

HOW CO-OPERATION CAN SUCCEED

I HAVE visited a little co-operative society which has been running a store. It started with a capital of $2,800. One hundred and forty people put in $20 each. They did a business exclusively among themselves of $28,000 during the year. At the end of the year, the society had a net surplus-saving, or "profit," of over $1,400. If these people had invested the same amount of capital in an ordinary enterprise, such as a savings bank, and bought goods only from profit retail stores, they would have accumulated an aggregate surplus at the rate of 3 per cent. That would have given them a total of $84. Had they invested in a precarious enterprise at 7 per cent, they would have accumulated a surplus of $196. Instead of this, they invested in a social-economic enterprise and had a return on their capital investment at the rate of 50 per cent.

But this 50 per cent return is not all. They were not investing in a precarious undertaking. It was as safe as they cared to make it. They had absolute democratic control over their property and their funds; if they had lost, it would have been because they threw them away. They paid the usual price for their commodities. They were guaranteed against adulteration and short weight.

The total average purchase of each member at the store for the year was $200, and the average budget of each family was $1,400. This means that the members bought only one-seventh of their necessities at their store, and that altogether they spent $168,000 elsewhere. There are communities in Europe in which the co-operative society provides everything the people need. Had co-operation reached that point in this little society, then these members would have spent $196,000 to at least as good an advantage as they spent $28,000, and the returns would have been commensurately larger.

It is instructive to compare a profit business corporation with a co-operative corporation. In the profit business, a number of people decide to form a corporation to run a store on a profit basis. The shares are, say, $10 each. Mr. Smith is a man with seven children and little money; he buys one share. Mr. Rich had inherited money and has no children; he buys ten shares. The corporation starts a profit-making store. Rich has ten votes at the stockholders' meeting to Smith's one; it is not worth while for Smith to attend. During the year, Smith buys $500 worth of goods at the store. Rich has no family, and he buys nothing. The concern made profits out of which it pays a dividend of 14 per cent to its stockholders. Smith gets 14 per cent on his $10, which is $1.40. Rich gets the same percentage on his $100, which is $14. Smith wanted to reduce the cost of living for the sake of his children and he patronized the store faithfully; his efforts saved for him 20 cents for each of his children in the course of the year. Rich did not buy anything. But Rich got ten times more than Smith. This is capitalistic business.

From the private business standpoint, Rich was entitled to, say, 6 per cent, which is the wages paid for the use of his capital. But from what standpoint was he entitled to 8 per cent more which he did not earn? When Smith put his money on the counter and got his goods, the amount above net cost that went into the cash drawer was his by every right except by the law of profit-making business. Rich was given 14 per cent for the use of his money, which should have made him guilty of usury. In most states there is a law against usury. However, dividends are privileged, and money invested in a profit-making corporation is at liberty to make all it can out of other people.

But suppose these two men had joined in organizing a co-operative corporation, how differently would they have fared if the business and savings had been the same? Smith would have got his 6 per cent interest on his $10, amounting to 60 cents. And he would have got 8 per cent additional, not on his $10 but on his $500 of patronage, making his returns $40.60; but Rich would have got interest on his $100 capital, or $6, and nothing more.

In the profit-making corporation Rich, the investor, would have received ten times more than Smith; in the co-operative corporation Smith, the patron, would have received nearly seven times more than Rich.

The consumer societies connected with the British Cooperative Union in 1938, the year before World War II, did a business which shows a net return of nearly 20 per cent on the total share-capital invested, and 12½ per cent return calculated on the turn-over. There are societies in many countries which show 50 per cent returns on the invested capital. This means that, having made his investment, the member of the co-operative society has only to patronize his society, where he buys at fully as good advantage as in profit business, and his capital earns this large return, which is really a donation from the movement.

The co-operative movement, we thus see, has the power to do for its members at least four times more than capitalistic invest-ment does for the capitalist.

Let us now turn to the capital owned by the British working class. If the working people invested this capital co-operatively, on the same basis of return as their present co-operative invest-ment, and gave their patronage to their societies instead of to profit business, they would, at least theoretically, move toward the position of competence of the middle and upper classes.

The total of wages and salaries paid in 1938 in Great Britain was £2,327,000,000. The total trade of the co-operative societies was less than one-tenth of that amount. The economic picture in Great Britain would be quite different should the people spend this other nine-tenths of their earnings with themselves. More-over, it should be borne in mind that the majority of people are wage workers. In the United States, for example, all the money in the country passes through the hands of the workers more than three times a year: they earn it and spend it all every four months. It is the spending of this money with profit business that produces the profits that make it possible for the nonworkers to live with-out performing service. Where consumers organize and spend their wages with their own business enterprises and keep the profit for themselves, they accumulate the surplus for expansion of their own industry. They organize and administer the co-operative sluiceway which shunts off the golden current from the pockets of profit traders into their own pockets. The consumer occupies the strategic position; he might win by organizing his spending power.

When capital is needed the people have it. The working people in the United States have over $15,000,000,000 lying in the banks drawing less than 2 per cent interest. This money is capable of financing a co-operative movement bigger than has been attained in any land. Large amounts of money are not always necessary to start and develop industries. There is a prevalent idea that industries must be started with borrowed money. This is the modern method. This method is used in the promotion of industries in which the promoters desire to risk nothing but other people's money, and in which the purpose is to make profits as promptly as possible for the promoters. American industry has been built up by this method. It is quick. If service, on the other hand, is the underlying principle, much money need not be necessary. There are postal services, farms, mines, banks, parks, insurance societies, cathedrals, hospitals, and universities which have been started in a small way and have grown to great size without large initial capital.

The £28 with which the Rochdale Society began was indeed small capital. A co-operative society in Pennsylvania began with a bag of meal. What was put into these societies to create their larger capital later was just the extra money that otherwise would have been paid to profit business for its goods. Some societies are started without share-capital. In some the members pay for goods in advance; in others the goods are obtained on credit and paid for by the members when they take the goods from the store. Many co-operative insurance societies need capital only when losses are to be paid, and then an assessment is made. Societies which provide only service, such as educational societies, often need no capital. There are societies in the United States, the buildings of which were put up by the members of the society without receiving pay. Capital is usually needed and should be used. These facts are mentioned simply to show the possibilities of noncapital enterprises.

We have seen in the discussion of co-operative wholesaling (page 85) that, in the United States, during and after World War II, there was so much money in the banks and the taxes upon profits were so high, that co-operatives acquired many properties for nothing. Bankers and factory owners came to the co-operative societies with offers to sell manufacturing plants. The banks and the government loaned the money at low interest rates. Farmers' consumer co-operatives bought factories, gasoline refineries, oil wells, pipe lines and other industries without the members being asked to put up a cent. The profits from these businesses were so large that in from eighteen months to three years the surplus-savings equaled the total cost. Within these short periods the co-operatives had paid off the principal and owned the properties free and clear without cost to themselves. This is a way by which the great industries of a country may be co-operatized. The technical experts are left in their positions. The control and ownership pass to the people who consume the product or use the service.

The people gradually can acquire industries, if they organize to do so. The actual movement in that direction proves the theory. Co-operation is demonstrating that there is a way to permanent control of big industries. It is not by capturing the political state and taking over the industries, nor by confiscation, nor by the syndicalist method. The people can get control just as the private owners get control, by beginning at the bottom and developing the ownership and the ability to carry on the business. The slow way is often the quick way. With enough capital to begin a business or equipment to perform a service, however small, the constant patronage creates the surplus savings with which the business expands.

The consumer society does not attempt production until it has developed experience in distribution, and succeeded, and then added to that a successful experience in wholesaling. The consumer co-operative organization that starts manufacturing is a group of people experienced in the business administration of distribution. The new principle they have to learn is in the field of obtaining raw material and machinery. The more difficult side they have not only mastered but they control: the distribution of their product. The capital which the organized consumers need to start a producing industry is created usually in their distributive business by converting into savings that fertilizer of the capitalist field, called "profits." The consuming public creates it. It is multiplied over and over as commodities pass along from the point of production to the point of consumption. The wages the workers spend go to create it.

When we look upon the great industries of the co-operative consumers, representing billions of dollars of capital, we behold an answer to the industrial riddle—how can the people secure control? Cease paying profit to profit business, keep that surplus for themselves, and with it, the world can be bought.

A society of people producing for themselves is a balanced organism. There is an equipoise between production and consumption. To have things scarce, to keep the prices high, is incompatible with the interests of the consumers. To produce too much because of uncertainty of markets is incompatible with the interests of the workers. The co-operative system makes for a planned estimation of the amount of products needed and the amount of labor required.

The regulation of supply by the co-operative customers can now be effected. At the meetings of their societies one finds the members expressing desires for certain products. These desires are transmitted through the manager and he gets what the members want. In countries with manufacturing co-operative wholesales, demands come from the membership of the constituent societies for certain articles. If the demand represents a capacity to consume a sufficient amount of a given article, the wholesale secures it or establishes a factory to make it. This is going on every day in the co-operative movement. The demands of the consumers are being met. In co-operative organization, the people have a machinery for registering their wants in channels which give promise of fulfillment. The co-operative wholesale societies are constantly soliciting and receiving information as to the desires of the masses of individual members of their constituent societies. These matters are the subject of constant interchange of information.

The co-operative society produces for a known clientele of consumers. The hazards of overproduction and underproduction do not prevail as in profit business in which distribution is a problem of salesmanship, competition, and ability of the consumers to buy.

Dominated by the philosophy of abundance instead of scarcity, the co-operative aim is to keep prices down. Dominated by the interests of the consumers, the aim is to keep quality up.

If members of a co-operative democracy should want something which is unusual and expensive, the decision rests finally with the consumers. Every new function that is added to the labors of the people in the co-operative society adds to the total length of the hours of labor. Here we have a balanced system. If the consumers desire a thing strongly enough, all they have to do is to make it. Theirs is the want; theirs is the toil, for they also are the producers. The enjoyment is theirs; the labor is theirs. The merit of the co-operative society is that in it the workers get what they make, and the consumers make what they get. In the profit system every possible method is employed to get things without giving an equal return; and the people who do the labor get but a part of what they produce.

"Factories are free" is a thesis proved by many co-operative societies which have gone into production. The consumer co-operative oil business, feed business, and fertilizer business, in the United States, with their many factories and their appurtenances, running into many millions of dollars, are owned by an aggregation of farmers, the great majority of whom never put in one cent of capital. Co-operative practice permits a nonmember to patronize the business; and when the surplus saving which accrues from his patronage reaches the value of a share of stock, he is given the privilege of becoming a member and receiving his stock certificate free of cost. These businesses have been started by a few pioneers with small resources. The rest have patronized themselves into ownership of shares. The capital for expansion grows out of savings. The co-operative consumer, once the business is started, spends himself into ownership.

PART IV

CO-OPERATION IN RELATION TO THE VARIOUS LABOR MOVEMENTS

Chapter XIV

THE ORGANIZED LABOR MOVEMENT

SUPPORT OF THE PROFIT MOTIVE BY THE WORKERS

NEARLY all great social events associated with cataclysmic changes, which have been called revolutions, have only been political downfalls resulting in substituting one dominant class for another. By a real revolution we should understand the revolutionary reorganization of the political, social, and economic life of the people after an existing system has fallen into inefficiency. Revolution comes from decay.

When a political system has promoted the interests of a property-privileged class until much wealth has developed on one side and much poverty on the other, when business fails to yield profits, when the purchasing power of the masses slumps, and a general discontent arises, the political and economic regime breaks down. A chaotic condition prevails and the people try to establish a new organism in place of the old. Revolution is more an upper-class than a lower-class phenomenon. The fall of the Roman Empire and the French Revolution bear testimony. The whole world is on the verge of such a breakdown now.

Often one political regime overthrows another by the use of force. This is called revolution, but usually it is only a superficial change of one group of rulers for another without radical difference and without fundamentally involving the interests of the masses.

When the quest for profits and privilege has brought things to such a pass that the government falls and the people attempt some drastic change, democracy is often the alleged desire. But it is doubtful if the people have ever yet attained political democracy on a national scale. The workers, as a class, have always failed to give supreme consideration to all the people, the consumers. Instead, they have been concerned with attempts to promote the interests of their own special class and the interests of production instead of the interests of consumption. There is little possibility of an effective revolutionary uprising of workers to destroy the capitalist system. If the capitalist system does not destroy itself, the workers will not destroy it by revolution; for while the capitalist system is moving along smoothly the workers are satisfied to leave it undisturbed. The masses of workers with capitalistic jobs favor capitalism. The workers themselves, selling their labor, are engaged in profit business.

Most wage workers want the old relation of master and servant preserved. They do not want to change the methods and purposes of industry. They want to get better conditions for the workers as employees of capitalist employers. The attitude of labor on the whole is not revolutionary. Furthermore, most of the workers, who do want a reorganization of industry upon a different basis, have in mind industrial organization of producers at the point of production, or they want state ownership and control.

In the Russian Revolution the leaders did not organize a society in the primary interest of all the people. Nearly half the population of Russia in 1918 was already organized in consumer co-operative societies. A great co-operative movement was on the road toward democracy. But the bolshevist leaders, being academic Marxists and desiring control, proceeded at the opposite end of the industrial order and attempted to organize a government largely in the interest of the industrial producers—a small part of the population in an agricultural country. The Russians, instead of building upon their existing co-operative societies, made the choice to build a civilization upon the factory and production, instead of upon the home and consumption. And they attempted to build something new, to which the people were strangers. Forceful liquidation of all opposition was necessary to do such a thing. Labor, the servant side of man's nature, was exalted; and consumption, the master side, was neglected. A permanent economic change promoted by this means is scarcely thinkable. Uncertainty, autocracy, coercion, and compromise with capitalistic methods have been the results.

Most workers protest against long hours of work with inadequate pay and against the fact that people who do not work are getting what seem unjust profits. But they do not protest because things are not made for use, or because the things they make are of poor quality and unbeautiful, or because the people who need them are not getting the things the workers make. They are not so much concerned about the use of things produced, but rather for the producer and his wages.

There is a class struggle going on. It is the struggle of the workers to climb out of the working class and into the capitalist class.

Let the workers in any industry get all they are asking—shorter hours and more wages; let them secure control and ownership of the industry; let them control the marketing of the product; let them be in a position to have "the full value of the wealth they produce"; let them be absolute masters of the situation—and they tend to become monopolistic, and proceed to exploit the rest of society. A different set of masters at the factory is not revolution.

This matter is of vital importance to the working people. It is imperative to understand that the work the man does for wages is not the supremely important thing from the social standpoint. What is produced becomes important when it reaches the place where it is to be consumed. Then it becomes all-important. Therefore the use function of the article, its capacity to do good to the consumer, is the vital matter; and not what the producer can make out of it in the form of money reward for himself. The time when the worker has got his pay for producing an article is not the time to test its social value. The true social test comes when the consumer uses it. Civilization cannot be built around the workshop and the factory. Civilization must be built around the home, the school, the theater, the studio, the laboratory, the social center, the playground, and the free society—the places where things are consumed and enjoyed, and where people do the things they like most to do. It is more important for a man to read, to listen to music, to eat, to look at flowers, to write poetry, to hoe his garden, to play with children, to walk with his wife, to dance, to sing, to paint a picture for the joy of it, to experiment in his laboratory, to talk with his friends, to play his flute, and to rest, than it is to stand by a machine to make something which has no intimate relation to him—something in which he is interested only for the wages he can get out of it.

The ambition of labor should be to win a living—a good living—and to shorten working hours more and more with the view of securing more and more leisure. Leisure is the great ideal. Its other name is freedom. Leisure means opportunity to do what one wants to do when he wants to do it. Not more work, but more leisure should be the aim. The more man is liberated from the compulsions of earning a living, the more he can enjoy the freedom of living a life.

TRADE-UNIONISM

Whatever may be the ideals of trade-unionism, one thing is certain: its chief concern under the present economic profit system must be for wages. Since the employer must get as much service as possible for the smallest pay, the worker must bring to bear all the powers he can to maintain wages. It is an inexorable force of circumstances that grips these two sides.

The trade-union movement arose in response to the need of relief for the underpaid working people. It was begotten of the hardships and suffering arising from the exploitation of labor and its aim was to secure better wages and conditions for the workers in shop, field, and mine. To achieve these, it adopted joint action. Collective bargaining was substituted for the weak position of the lone worker.

The trade-union movement began in Great Britain in the early nineteenth century. At first it was legislated against by Parliament because it threatened the profits of the business class. When the steam-driven machine was introduced, and the workers ceased to work with their own tools, the new machine form of industry made the worker a part of the machine. With his own hand tools he could no longer compete with the machine; he had no alternative but to sell his labor to the owner of the machine. The worker's ownership of his tools had given rise to the guild; the worker's loss of his tools gave rise to the trade-union. The trade-union movement became necessary when labor became a commodity to be bought along with raw material at the lowest possible price.

Had it not been for trade-unionism the workers today, probably, would be laboring fourteen hours a day, women and children would be found in industry in greater numbers than now, the workers would be receiving wages just sufficient to maintain an animal existence, and the wealth of the owning class would have accumulated to an amount to stagger imagination. On the one hand would exist a great class of workers, denied schooling and the common decencies of life; on the other, a great class of the owners of property, greater and wealthier than the present owning class, and supporting arrays of police and soldiers "to maintain order." Labor without organization works in peonage. It was out of this condition that unionism lifted the world. There was no other effective force at work to save labor from degradation.

We have to thank trade-unionism for saving humanity from slavery. The world owes a debt of gratitude to those pioneers who advocated organization among workmen. Brave men with vision broke the laws of their country to advocate unionism. Sometimes they were bold enough to go out on strike. They went to prison. They were deported to the penal colonies. They died like rats in the filthy vessels that bore them overseas. England persecuted and deported an army of the best men in the kingdom. This "criminal class," which was sent to Australia and to other penal colonies to get them out of the way because they were "dangerous agitators," soon built up a civilization in distant lands which has astonished the world. Trade-unionism has been a civilizing influence.

Labor needs the right to organize. The "antiunion" campaign which is promoted by the great financial groups is a dangerously reactionary enterprise. Abolition of joint bargaining, carried to its conclusion, would deny labor the right of collective agreement and place the lone working man, woman, and child at the mercy of the aggregations of organized employers owning the means of subsistence.

So keenly is the need of unionism felt among thoughtful workers that a strong feeling exists that membership should be obligatory. To attempt to enforce this violates the principles of liberty. The state compels citizenship. The trade-union cannot afford to pattern after the state; but it can stand with the co-operative society in making membership voluntary. Such organization may be made so valuable that the craftsman cannot afford to be a nonunionist. The advantages of membership in associations of brain workers, such as doctors and lawyers, are so great they practically draw nonmembers of these particular crafts into compulsory membership. Labor might do the same.

The co-operative movement is naturally close to the trade-union movement. When the workers by bitter struggle secured the right to organize and then by bitter struggle again when they won the right to strike, they made a significant discovery. After the state had been compelled to permit these two steps, some workers observed that the problem of labor still was not solved. Although the employer at first resisted paying increase of wages or granting shorter hours or making any concession to the workers, still, when the concession was made, the workers found that the employer did not pay for it. He added the increased cost of producing the commodity to the selling price, and passed it along to be paid by the consumers. And since most of the consumers are working people, it was the workers themselves who paid much of the increase in their wages. In the early part of the nineteenth century, when the working people realized this fact, the modern co-operative movement was born.

Trade-unionism is incomplete without organization at the point of consumption to supplement organization at the point of production. So while the trade-union movement was established to secure for the worker the best returns for his labor, the co-operative movement was established to secure for the worker the best returns for the fruits of his labor. The first gives the worker more means with which to purchase, the second gives him more purchasing power with his means. The two movements are complementary.

Most workers at the present time, who are members of co-operative societies, earn their livelihood in profit industries. Trade-unionism helps them to increase the amount of capital they are able to bring to their co-operative societies to spend. Also, it gives the worker experience and understanding of craft and business methods. The organized workers especially are able to translate the valuable lessons learned in profit industry over into co-operative industry. Moreover, organized labor collects information concerning labor costs and gives the co-operative societies the benefits of this knowledge. On the other hand, the information on costs of production in co-operative industry is given to the organized workers in profit industry. Co-operation also makes standards. The co-operative factories in several countries set the standards which the government and the trade-unions require profit industry to follow.

Co-operative industry is a constant lesson to the working people that labor can be organized on an incorruptible basis. Big capitalistic employers bribe labor leaders to sell out strikes and to betray labor. Co-operative societies cannot use bribery in case of strikes because the costs of the business are accessible to the members, who are mostly workers, and the members would dismiss in disgrace any official who resorted to this practice. The sympathies of co-operation are with labor. Consumers Cooperative Services, of New York, went to Washington and insisted on a minimum wage for restaurant workers 43 per cent higher than that fixed by the Labor Board. Here is a consumer co-operative employer of labor, conducting restaurants and other activities, demanding higher wages for labor than labor demanded for itself.

THE RELATION OF EMPLOYERS TO EMPLOYEES IN THE CO-OPERATIVE SOCIETY

In addition to the fact that the co-operative movement is in sympathy with the spirit of trade-unionism, there is the fact that co-operative societies have been of real assistance to labor in its struggles for better conditions. Every co-operative country shows instances in which the consumer co-operatives have come to the help of labor in times of unemployment, lockout, and strike, as well as in improving the general conditions of labor.

There will always be a conflict of interests at some point between producers and consumers, so long as one person consumes what another produces under a price and wage system. But the consumer co-operative movement is a ground upon which these differences are being best worked out.

The worker in profit business is in a different position from the co-operative employee. The worker in consumer co-operative industry realizes that he is engaged in a social undertaking. He is a member of the organization that employs him. No one has any more votes or voice than he in its control. He knows that his industry is benefiting all the consumer members of the society who own it. He may also easily learn that, while it is maintaining just wages for its employees, it is keeping down prices not only for members but also for nonmembers who patronize profit business.[1] The thoughtful co-operative employee wants his industry to succeed and knows that if he asks too much for himself his industry cannot compete with capitalistic business and will be destroyed. As a patron, he also gets back his savings-returns. Trade-unionists by becoming members of consumer co-operative societies secure a voice in determining the conditions under which the workers employed by their societies shall work. If there is a majority of wage earners in each co-operative society, as is usually the case, the balance of power is in the hands of labor. Workers, as members of co-operatives, may bring about an approach to reconciliation of the interests of producers and consumers.

The organization of the workers in consumer co-operative industries in each country looks toward the time when the majority of consumers will be employed in these consumer industries. This is already the case in many communities, such as Freidorf, Switzerland, and Desborough, England. Should this become general, the majority of organized consumers will be also organized working people. Then the interests of the consumers, who are not only the workers but the homemakers as well, will dominate. In the last analysis, the consumer interest, as the greater interest, must be supreme.

There must always be in industry a central managing authority who makes the decisions and the plans. The final authority cannot be evenly divided. A committee composed of an equal number of workers and employers comes to a deadlock. There must be one odd deciding vote. Wherever decisions are to be made promptly in the interest of efficiency, authority must be centralized. Thus, in industry there will always be the workers and the employers or directors of work. They may both come from the same class and be responsible to the same; but there must be those

[1] By keeping down prices in profit business, co-operation tends also to keep down wages in profit business among workers who may be members of co-operative societies. On the whole, the co-operative redounds to the advantage of these same workers by making their wages go farther, whatever they are.

who supervise and direct the work of others. Unless they have authority their function comes to naught. And, if production is to be for use and not profit, the controlling voice must be in the interest of the users.

In some countries employees, who are members, are eligible to minority membership on boards of directors of consumer societies. They may be elected by the general membership. In some cases they are appointed by the employees. Employees have the right to membership in the society, and as members of the society to attend members' meetings, vote, and criticize or interrogate the management. The general tendency is to give employees every facility to have a voice in the administration and control, except that there is no disposition to grant employees, as employees, a controlling majority. This would be fatal to co-operation. In the "shop steward movement," whereby the workers have their chosen representatives in each industry and a large voice in the shop where they work, labor-union organization improves the status of the workers. In some countries employees are not permitted on the board of directors of consumer co-operatives.

Methods of harmonizing the employers and the employees have been brought to a higher state of development in consumer co-operative industries than in capitalistic business, private service, or state employment. The Joint Industrial Board, consisting of employers and employees, is coming more and more into action. The Works Committee, consisting of employees, listens to grievances of the workers and formulates their demands. It makes suggestions to the management not only in matters pertaining to the employees, but also for the general good of the industry. Such harmonizing machinery as this serves with efficiency in European co-operatives.

There it is often obligatory for the co-operative employee to belong to the trade-union of his craft. This practice is now becoming universal. A growing tendency prevails to grant to the employees every possible condition of self-government which is consistent with the integrity of the co-operative institution. The Central Wage Board in many countries enforces agreements between employer and employee. This board is composed of an equal number of members of the central federation of consumer societies and of the trade-unions. Individual employees of societies also have the right to appeal directly to this board. In the larger societies, the employees elect a Workshop Committee or a committee from each of the various departments. They not only have the right to take any question directly to the directors, but in some cases they must be consulted before any changes in the conditions of labor are made.

Factory workers' councils exist in many industries. The wage-worker members constitute a Workers' Council and the salaried employees constitute an Employees' Council. Each of these two groups must be represented in the Factory Committee. A Factory Assembly is composed of all the employees. These Workers' Councils are largely deliberative and advisory. They have not power to enforce decisions against the will of the employer. But they have access to the records of the business, and they are dominated by the trade-unions. District and national Economic Councils also exist. The national council for each industry consists of an equal number of representatives of employers and employees. Co-operative societies effectively use this machinery.

In Great Britain there is a Joint Committee of the Cooperative Union and the Trades Union Congress. The rules of these two bodies provide that all disputes shall be submitted to this committee. Since these two bodies represent practically the whole of the co-operative movement and of the trade-union movement, this means that arbitration instead of the strike shall be used to settle differences. Here is the plan of an admirable machinery which has not yet come wholly into operation.

The National Congress of Workingmen's Cooperative Societies of Spain agreed that co-operative societies shall employ none but trade-unionists, and comply with the maximum trade-union requirements; but the societies hold the right to withdraw any advantages to the employees if the workers' unions do not exact the same requirements from profit-making employers.

In these plans are seen the possibilities for harmonizing the two ever-conflicting elements. Theoretically they are the best yet devised. Practically they have been in operation scarcely long enough to be tested, but all the indications are that they can be made effective.

The General Survey Committee of the Cooperative Union of Great Britain has expressed the opinion, which has been approved by a cooperative congress, that the co-operative movement should take the lead in regard to labor conditions. The use of the strike, in a movement which is established to give the people control of industry, is deplored. Friendly relations exist between the British Cooperative Union and the trade-unions. The co-operative societies commonly pay the recognized trade-union district rate for all occupations, "plus an agreed percentage," which keeps the co-operative standard higher than the standard in profit business. The societies also grant shorter hours in general than prevail in the district. The trade-unions in return should agree not to strike against such co-operative societies. Such a plan transfers the struggle for better rewards for labor to the capitalistic field.

Strikes among the employees in co-operative industries are a negligible matter. The workers tend to be loyal to co-operation because of their understanding of its meaning and because of the advantages which they enjoy as workers in the co-operative society.

Strikes, however, do occur. The conditions of labor in many co-operative industries are not good. The wages often are small. But these facts do not reflect upon the co-operative movement. The conditions in similar profit-making industries are worse. Co-operation must compete with these. If the co-operatives had to charge more for the same commodities than the profit stores, the workers would not buy at the co-operatives. They would patronize the products which were the cheaper—i.e., which were produced by the lower paid workers. Many inexperienced co-operative businesses in the past have failed and closed up because they overpaid labor, and as a result their prices were high and working people would not patronize them but in preference gave their patronage to the businesses that paid labor lower wages.

The worker in the co-operative movement who strikes for higher wages than are paid in the same competing profit industry is sabotaging his labor movement. He is striking against himself. So long as the majority of workers are selling their labor to profit business, they are the ones who set the standards of labor and wages. Anything better than those standards, anything better that is bestowed by the co-operatives, is philanthropy from the hands of the consumers. The benefits which the co-operative consumers enjoy make it possible to bestow some bounties, but they cannot go far because the vast majority of them are still poorly paid workers, earning their wages in capitalistic industries.

In many countries, the strike is prevented by the joint committee and the labor boards which automatically fix wages for all industries. The co-operatives, like the capitalists, are bound by these conditions; and wages are the same with both. But the co-operative employee enjoys a better position because of additional insurance benefits, provided by the co-operative, which place him in an advantageous position with reference to sickness, unemployment, and old age. His working conditions also are usually better—light, air, recreations, shop conveniences, holidays, and superintendence.

It was a practice among some of the early consumer societies to divide the "profits" of the society not only among the consumers, in proportion to their patronage, but also among the employees in proportion to their wages. This latter method was introduced as a concession to the early impulses to regard the worker, rather than the consumer, as the special object of co-operative concern. Experience has demonstrated the unwisdom of this policy. It is a form of "profit sharing" which fails to recognize the fundamental fact that a co-operative society does not make profits from its members. The overcharge which the consumer pays is his money.

As co-operators become more familiar with the working and meaning of these compromises they tend to abandon them. It is impossible to fix in any industry what is labor's share, for the sharing begins with the raw material and ends after transportation to the consumer. Neither co-operative nor capitalistic profits can be isolated. Labor, of course, needs to go after something better and more tangible than profits. It should go directly for the things it wants to consume. Practical experience shows that it is neither logical nor expedient for the employees of the co-operative society to claim a share of the surplus-saving ("profits") of the organized consumers. They are consumer loans. If it is possible for labor to have more wages, labor should have them in a straightforward way—by giving labor more wages.

Paying employees "dividends" on wages creates a preferred class of workers who in their co-operative industry receive higher pay than their employers who work in the same trade in profit industry. The bonus on business, paid to executives and workers as a reward for efficiency, may have something to recommend it.

It is dangerous to co-operation for the trade-union to squeeze from the co-operative society all that the society can be compelled to yield. Many societies have been destroyed in this way. Communist influence, with its exaltation of labor and its lack of understanding of consumer economics, has done the co-operatives much damage. The important function of the trade-union, in its relation to the co-operative society, is the fixing and maintenance of high standards—of right conditions of labor, first for the trade-unionists and then for the whole industry.

Trade-union activity in the co-operative society serves to improve the working conditions in profit industry as a result of improving them in co-operative industry. The co-operative consumers can work in close alliance and harmony with the general trade-union movement to improve the condition of the working class as a whole; and the co-operative employees can do the same. By such combinations wage standards can consistently be maintained.

Examination of co-operative societies shows the organized consumers taking the lead in giving better conditions to employees. "Speeding up" is not much found in co-operative industries. In Great Britain, the co-operative stores were the first shops to introduce the half holiday per week for the benefit of the employees. This was done many years before "early closing" was made legally compulsory. The eight-hour day for women was introduced in the Crumpsall biscuit factory of the English C.W.S. twenty years before it became a law. As a whole, co-operative stores are open for shorter hours than other stores. Co-operative industries have taken the lead in abolishing night work and in improving the sanitation of shops.

It was the British co-operative wholesale that fixed a minimum wage for women at a rate four shillings per week higher than the legal minimum wage. The consumers, who own the British wholesale, voted to do this against the advice of their board of directors. The stockholders of a capitalistic corporation would not do such a thing. But the general membership which acted in this way had information and understanding of their business which the stockholders of a profit corporation do not possess. There are many examples of the members of co-operative societies voting for better conditions for their employees than they themselves enjoy.

Continuous employment has usually characterized co-operative industries. Unemployment is prevented by the standardized nature of co-operation and by the more sympathetic attitude toward the employees. But the greatest advantage of co-operative employment is the fact that the worker is engaged in a social movement to supply the people with the things they need. The pity is that so few of the workers have yet been educated to this feeling. There is abundant experience to show that co-operative industry suffers much less from over- and underproduction than does profit industry, and that unemployment and labor turnover are strikingly less than in similar profit business.

The factories of many co-operatives are equal to the best in the world. Shower baths and dining rooms in factories are not peculiar to co-operative industries, but are there as a right of the workers and not installed in lieu of wages, or as a palliative, or by legal compulsion.

When the shoe factory of the Swiss co-operative union at Basel was running full time, making more shoes than the societies could use because of prevalent unemployment, and storing them in its warehouses in order not to throw its workers out of jobs, the superintendent's reply to my question was illuminating: "This is not a profit-making business; it is a social enterprise." Here is the truth in a nutshell. The owners of that factory represent nearly half the families of Switzerland. The loss of a few pennies to the owners, if there should be any loss from overproduction, would amount to little compared with the loss of employment to the workers if the factory closed.

In general, the world over, co-operative employees receive somewhat higher wages than are paid in similar competing industries. Executives are paid comparatively smaller salaries than are paid in profit business, although their salaries are adequate and the positions are esteemed and much sought.

The problem of workers' compensation and participation in

control in co-operative industries is working out as an evolution-ary program. Competition between co-operation and the profit system makes this necessary. The matter is chiefly in the hands of the working people. But there are certain ideals that can be in-sistently striven for and, indeed, certain labor conditions which even now can be insisted upon.

First: the workers can have trade-union organization and all the rights of joint bargaining that go with it, be they industrial workers or farmers.

Second: they can have self-government in their industry so far as pertains to the relations of the workers among themselves.

Third: they can have conditions and wages as good, and better if possible, than are prevalent in similar profit businesses.

Fourth: as members of their co-operative society they can have equal rights with the other consumers in the control of the society which employs them.

When more than half the consumer members are employed in the co-operative industry, it is evident that the voice of the work-ers becomes the majority voice. By this evolutionary method, what begins as consumers' control moves slowly on till it becomes workers' control of industry—but workers' control in the interest of the worker as a consumer.

Still, there is more the consumer co-operative movement can aim to do for its employees. Better pay, shorter hours, better working conditions, entertainment, education, insurance, and other protection can all be striven for. In many societies these advan-tages for the workers have been developed to a high degree. Food, clothing, housing, education, recreation, insurance, and health protection ought to be guaranteed to the co-operative worker at all times, if co-operation is to fulfill its obligation to labor. All the above benefits may be expanded until the workers get the best possible conditions of life.

ORGANIZED LABOR AND CO-OPERATION

In the evolution of the union between labor and co-operation each makes its contribution by helping the other. The co-operative movement not only performs services for its members in distress, but it is found rendering aid to the working people in times of unemployment. There is the story of the Belgian workers who would not join the co-operatives: they were on strike and were about to acknowledge defeat on account of hunger; a truckload of food drove up in front of their union headquarters and proceeded to unload; it was from the neighboring co-operative society; they won their strike and joined the co-operative society.

The strike of the Irish dockers of Dublin is an example of the possibilities of helping the workers. Thirty thousand unskilled workers had entered upon a long-drawn-out strike for better conditions. They were in need of food. The British Trades Union Congress investigated and decided to give £5,000 toward food for the Irish workers. They were refused a loan from the English bankers. They then asked the British C.W.S. if it would supply 30,000 hungry Irish workers with food on the guarantee of their note. The reply was a prompt affirmative, with the assurance that, "within 48 hours 60,000 packages of foodstuffs will be on board in the harbor."

During a coal strike, the Northumberland Miners' Association asked one of the great commercial banks for a loan and were refused. They then applied to the British Cooperative Wholesale Society for £70,000, and were promptly given the money. In the same year a substantial sum was loaned to the striking cotton operatives in Lancashire. As a result of assistance which the C.W.S. has given to the unions in times of stress, the latter are more and more drawing out their funds from commercial banks and placing them in the banking department of the C.W.S.

During a strike in England of the National Union of Railwaymen, the union was prevented by the bankers from getting at its funds for the immediate payment of strike benefits. The Cooperative Wholesale Society's printing department got out the necessary supply of checks payable at the co-operative societies. The societies honored the vouchers issued by the local strike committee.[2] In the struggle for profits, food will often be found casting the deciding vote. When labor is locked out or when it folds

---

[2] *The Producer* (London) says: "This prevented the Government from putting in operation a project to starve out the railwaymen's families by withdrawing their ration cards or withholding the food supplies under Government control."

its arms and the wheels cease to turn, a deadlock is established. In this deadlock, the side which has the food wins.

The truck drivers' strike in Wisconsin tied up trucking in 1945. But the drivers' union permitted oil to be delivered to the co-operative society in Racine, which had the only oil station in the city that kept open during the strike. In a similar strike in New York in 1946, the co-operatives were the only retail food stores that continued to receive loads of goods during the strike.

These examples are typical of what is going on in many countries. The trade-unionists of Great Britain have reciprocated in the help received from the co-operators. The Port Talbot co-operative society had been meeting with such signal success that the wrath of profiteering business descended upon it. It was conducting its own bakery, and lowering the price of bread. Under pressure of the business interests, a flour milling firm from which it got its flour refused to supply the society. Then the transport workers notified the Food Controller that unless the millers let the co-operative society have flour all the men of his union would come out on strike. Inside of two hours the co-operators had flour.

In the United States, the consumer co-operatives are in general in sympathy with the trade-union idea, but there is distinct disapproval of the racketeering that prevails among the leadership of some unions.

Co-operation gives trade-unionism an opportunity to lift itself above the status of a class movement. Through co-operation the unions can demand and secure the public confidence and sympathy. When the unions unite to insist on the prevention of inflation and better economic conditions for every worker, they can find common ground for all. A certain amount of public sympathy is always lost to the trade-unionists because the public is easily persuaded that the demands of labor spell higher prices. Labor can reach common ground with the rest of society by laying emphasis not on its special needs but upon everybody's needs. The workers may come to see that high wages are not as important as low cost of living, and that the good of the whole community is in the end more important than profits for a class.

When organized labor becomes wise enough to renounce participation in a class warfare, to join with the co-operators in promoting the common good, and in making labor's demands always in terms of public social demands, the status of labor will be improved. Much is said of "class consciousness" and "solidarity," but their weakness is that these slogans are in the interest of a class of individuals. Accordingly their meaning is narrow. The world is ready to give its approval always to a cause; but not to a class.

Labor has learned that it can tie up industry through the trade-union and the use of the strike. It can paralyze the machine. It can stop things. This is not constructive. Labor might take the next step, and learn how to start things. Co-operation is playing its part in the training of the workers to start something new and constructive.

But beyond all this, there is still another side to this relation. In many countries, although friendliness is expressed, there exists a certain trade-union coolness toward the co-operative movement. Some trade-union leaders are jealous lest co-operation attract the interest of the workers away from the trade-unions. In the so-called "workers' political movement," this same undercurrent is seen. This hostility is not the rule; it is exceptional, and not always easy of discovery. It is found in some officials and academic theorists. However, it is a real force and operates to hamper the advancement of co-operation among the organized workers, although the rank and file of workers themselves are scarcely conscious of it and do not approve of it where they know it exists. The United States is the country in which this attitude is most conspicuous. As a result, labor is comparatively backward in co-operative organization.

The rank and file of trade-unionists are sympathetic to co-operation, when they learn its meaning; and although the co-operative movement in the United States is predominantly agrarian, many consumer co-operatives have been started by industrial workers. The societies of Fitchburg and Quincy, Massachusetts; of Superior, Kenosha, and Racine, Wisconsin; of Waukegan, Illinois; of Dillonvale, Ohio; and of many more industrial centers are of trade-union origin. An older society at Maynard, Massachusetts, started by trade-unionists, employs fifty-five trade-union members.

The mistake sometimes made by trade-unionists in starting a co-operative is to have it controlled by the trade-union. This is fatal to co-operation. It cost the United Mine Workers $750,000 in Illinois to try this experiment. A consumer co-operative must be controlled by the consumer members as consumers. To permit control to pass into the hands of any other organization, no matter how worthy, violates co-operative neutrality. A co-operative cannot be run in the interest of any political party, trade-union, or other special group and remain a co-operative. Co-operation is of the consumers and by the consumers acting for the consumers.

Chapter XV

PRODUCERS' PROFIT-SHARING INDUSTRIES

THEIR POSSIBILITIES AND LIMITATIONS

FOR many years before the modern co-operative consumer movement was established, the working people had experimented with the profit-sharing copartnership shop. It was also called "co-operative" and "self-governing." This was the ideal of the early co-operators. The idealists of the time wrote, preached, and organized from the standpoint of the shopworker. The first half of the past century in Great Britain was a laboratory period in which every possible experiment in profit-sharing production was made. And not only workers' money was lost, but millions of the capital of sincere philanthropists. Out of the great price that was paid, few shops survived.

The fate of these shops, generally speaking, has been to follow one of three courses: (1) they fail; or, if they succeed, (2) they become distinctly capitalistic enterprises and the workers acquire the capitalistic psychology; or, if they do not fail and do not develop the capitalistic spirit, (3) consumer societies and other organizations buy the majority of the shares and the workers lose control, or they are bought out completely by the co-operative consumer societies.

A few producers' profit-sharing workshops, often called "co-operative productive societies," are still making some progress in European countries. In Great Britain, in 1913, there were 108 of these societies, with 34,662 members. In 1935 there were 90 societies, with 33,264 members. In 1939 there were 89 societies, with 18,811 members.

How nearly these shops are controlled by the workers may be seen from the fact that there are more workers than there are shareholders. The workers have not been able to finance these undertakings. The shareholding membership is largely outside the shops. These nonworking shareholders put in their money for either investment or philanthropy. The co-operative consumer societies are putting more and more money into these enterprises, and securing more and more control. Most of them have long ago ceased to be shopworkers' productive enterprises.

These British so-called producer societies in the last few years have not increased their membership. The total sales have slightly increased. The number of employees in 1940 was 21,814. In contrast, the total employees of the consumer societies in Great Britain in 1940 were 333,355.

The wages earned in these producers' factories are on the whole slightly better than in capitalistic factories. The pay is no better than in consumer factories. Many of the employees are girls. As is the case in all industries, they are there only until they can get married or find a better job. This fact prevents them from developing a permanent interest in the shop. Their eyes and hearts are turned toward the home—the place where things are consumed.

In the middle of the last century, when many copartnership producer industries were failing, the British Cooperative Wholesale was persuaded to finance some of them in order to save them. The advocates of "producers' co-operation" succeeded in influencing the wholesale to invest its surplus in these enterprises. The first experiment resulted in a failure which lost the wholesale £8,000. A second time, the advocates of "producers' co-operation" urged the wholesale on, and it loaned more of its savings to the Bugle Horn colliery. When this coal mine, worked in the interest of the organized producers, failed, the wholesale lost £25,000. The co-operative consumers slowly learned their lesson, and the British Wholesale thenceforth proceeded with production strictly as a consumer enterprise, with consumer control and an assured and organized membership to consume its products.

The United States has a hundred-year history of workers' copartnerships. Since there was at first no co-operative wholesale society in this country to buy them out and take them over, two alternatives have awaited them: they have either failed, or, if they survived, they became capitalistic, profit-making businesses. The Knights of Labor organized several boot and shoe factories in New England between 1875 and 1885. Printing societies, iron foundries, cloth mills, glass factories, laundries, clothing factories, and box factories have passed into history. Other producer copartnership enterprises in the United States have produced furniture, underwear, brooms, coal, nails, pipes, lumber, pottery, soap, stoves, tobacco, and almost every other American product. At the organization of each of these, the same language was used and the same plans were made as we find in the case of groups of workers now planning producers' industries. The Cooperative Stove Works of Troy, New York, founded as the result of a strike, developed a capital of $106,000 in twenty-five years, but by that time there were only ten of the original workers in the concern, and six men owned more than half the stock. The same happened in the Co-operative Foundry of Rochester, New York; it grew till it had a capital of $200,000 and was doing a business of $350,000 a year; yet it ended by becoming a capitalistic stock company owned by thirty-five nonworker stockholders. A similar history follows several cigar, hat, and glove factories. The clothing workers in America have organized many profit-sharing factories, which have always failed or become capitalistic businesses. However, many of these capitalistic businesses are highly successful as profit-making enterprises.

Those companies which provide in their constitution that only workers can be stockholders are changed into corporations owned by nonworkers by the simple passing of a resolution. Owners can do with their business what they please.

Both Germany and France exceed Great Britain in the number of producer societies. Some of them are of many years' standing. But in all these countries the number of members and the rapidity of growth of the consumer societies are much greater and from every standpoint more vigorous. It has become rather obvious that in France the industrial producer societies have only been kept alive by subsidies from the government and apparently have no future.

These industries are carried on for profits. It is confusing to call them "co-operative"; they should be classed with the efforts of the workers in the trade-union movement for better rewards for their labor.

The factories of the profit-sharing producers at first often aim to sell their products preferably to the co-operative consumers. This purpose has been carried out in many instances; but as prosperity, or adversity, tinctured with age, visits them, they are found selling their products where they can get the most money for them. This is the lesson experience teaches. The organized producers often prefer to sell to the unorganized consumers, because they can get better prices.

The self-governing workshop, the syndicalized industry, the producers' profit-sharing enterprise, and the copartnership soon discover that the smaller their membership, the greater is the proportion of the profits which each may have. This tends to make them exclusive. They hire outside labor while the ownership remains in few hands.

In the case of some of these copartnership workshops which have succeeded, when the owners of the stock died, the stock has passed into the hands of their heirs. If the shop was producing much profits, the owners of the stock have been found employing others to do the work while the owners lived upon the income. Thus most of these industries, which the syndicalists had hoped would solve the problem of industry, have tended to defeat their very syndicalistic purpose. They have either lost the workers' money or converted the workers into profit-making capitalists.

Producer control has always meant man control, because the male is the majority sex in industry; a large proportion of women must remain out of industry and stay in the home to bear and nurture children. On the other hand, the consumer co-operative movement organizes the control of industry, not from the standpoint of the shop, but of the home, where women are an important factor.

The consumer co-operative movement is building up a service system in industry, but it is a slow and arduous process, because it must go on within the atmosphere and under the conditions which the dominant capitalistic society imposes. It is impossible to begin with the ideal, and start right off by giving the worker "the full value of the wealth he produces." This is the goal at which co-operation aims; the syndicalist and the profit-sharing producer would adopt it as a method. Attempts to begin at once by bestowing full social justice upon a small group of workers at the expense of all the other consumers fail. They make for a defective philosophy as well as a defective practice when attempted in a capitalistic society. What is an *end* cannot be constituted as a *means* in this field.

The idea that all the workers should combine to own and run industry originated back in the days when each man owned his own tools. The idea of the producer copartnership has been the craft idea. But now, as we view the complexity of machinery and the enormous capital involved, we appreciate the difficulties. Huge factories costing millions of dollars, in which often one machine operated by one man costs many thousands of dollars, characterize modern industry. It is difficult for the workers to get the necessary capital.

Some "revolutionists," knowing that the workers cannot get gradual control of productive industries, hope for a wide-reaching and cataclysmic invasion of the shops by the workers. They hope that when capitalist industry becomes weak or goes to pieces, the workers will take possession of the shops and stay there. We have the Italian experience, in the 1920's, to teach the difficulties of this course. Neither the markets, the raw material, nor the trained executives are ready for a sudden industrial revolution. Many difficulties faced the Italian workers when they took possession of the factories. They operated them for a few weeks. Then they gave them up. They found that two of the most important factors in the industry were still in the control of the capitalists. These were the supply of raw material and the marketing of their products.

The organized producers do not control these factors. The product of every shop, except those owned and run by the co-operative consumers, or the socialized government shop, must be thrown into the market to find problematical purchasers. The selling business is as difficult a specialty, almost, as the producing business. On the other hand, the methods of the organized consumers solve each of these problems of industry. In many countries the co-operative consumers are gradually gaining more and more ownership and control of raw materials and natural resources. As to their markets, they are assured. The consumer owners set up industries adequate to supply their needs.

Producer copartnership brings about a change of personnel of control; it does not change the motive of industry; it still leaves the profit motive undisturbed. These organized producers are in the position of trade-unionists: no matter how successfully they are organized and operating, they still have not gained control over what their wages and profits will buy; and therefore they still must join a consumer co-operative society to attain that end. Finally, the women want to marry. If they marry, they usually leave the society. In the consumer co-operative society, on the other hand, if a woman member marries, the event strengthens the society.

To what extent are these profit-sharing productive industries changing for the better the motive, methods, and conditions of industries? The answer is: it is not so much the industries but the workers that are changed. They learn to carry on business, and their incomes are often improved. Such industries should have the approval and encouragement of the organized consumers.

The advantages of producer co-operatives are more positive where the workers use raw materials of their own production. This is the case, for example, among farmers and fishermen. These workers begin with nature and not with commerce. If they have the ability, they use the methods of producer organizations to win better rewards for their labor. Producer co-operatives are often essential to give workingmen better incomes so they may have more purchasing power. The farmers in many countries were in no condition to start consumer co-operatives until they had got themselves better incomes by means of marketing associations. The poor fishermen of Nova Scotia organized lobster-canning factories. They catch, can, and market their canned lobsters so successfully as greatly to improve their incomes. Then, having succeeded, they take the next step and organize as consumers. By these two means they are lifting themselves into a vastly improved social, as well as economic condition. Producer co-operation becomes the key that opens the door for them to better life.

Thus in a capitalistic society worker-controlled industry plays a part. The workers should know, however, that it is capitalistic profit industry and that it does not change the method or motive of business. But it does begin by giving the workers experience in business administration, and, when successful, it gives them funds which may be used to change the economic system by means of consumer co-operative organization.

THE WAY OUT FOR THE ORGANIZED PRODUCERS

Any organized craft of workers may adopt the methods of consumer co-operation. They may *begin* with the practical and *end* with the ideal. This is a collective method that is capable of success in the presence of competitive industry.

The hat makers, clothing makers, cigar makers, or other organized workers may begin by organizing a consumer distributive society. They consume hats and clothing and cigars as well as other commodities. They must permit other people, however, outside their craft to join their consumer society—open membership. They may start a store where the products of the shops in which they work, as well as other commodities, are sold. They may buy other goods for their store in the open market, and supply themselves. As their distributive business grows they may open more stores; when other groups open stores, they may federate to form a larger society with larger distributing capacity. When its distribution has reached a volume to justify such a step, the federation of consumer societies which run stores may start a factory to produce for it. Such a factory would produce the articles which the members know how to make. It should be the largest that is consistent with economy and efficiency. Such a federation with its retail stores and its factory must connect, if possible, with other co-operative societies to become a part of a federation in which other avenues of distribution of its product may be found. As the business increases, the factory output may be increased. The reverse of this is dangerous—factory output in excess of guaranteed sales is the speculative method and the method of the producer copartnership factory. By maintaining a distributive business with a membership of consumers, the product of the factory which the consumers own is disposed of by the co-operative method based on production for use by the owners of the industry.

Many consumer co-operative societies are pursuing this method. They start factories which give employment to their members who belong to certain manufacturing crafts—such as creamery workers, shoemakers, and tailors. In the United States are consumer co-operative societies which were started by unemployed bakers, who in the course of time established bakeries which gave employment to the baker members. The self-help co-operatives among the unemployed, in the United States, produced for their own consumption and then acquired other commodities by barter and purchase. They thus built up consumer co-operatives.

The same principles apply to any useful service. Socially minded physicians are showing patients how to form co-operative health societies, which are providing salaried positions for physicians. The members of farm marketing and political associations are organizing themselves into consumer societies.

No organization is truly co-operative, in the sense of moving toward a greater co-operative society and the curtailing of profit business and the state, which is limited to a craft or class. Nor is a productive industry really noncapitalistic which produces commodities to be sold to the public for profit. Any such organized producers can convert their society into a true co-operative society by opening the membership to all and engaging in distribution or service to the members as consumers. So long as membership is limited to the workers in a single craft or industry, and is wholly devoted to marketing their products for profit, they are best classified as a labor union, guild, syndicate, or marketing association.

Theoretically, it is natural to think of beginning with the organization of production, if industry is to be democratized. Why begin with the consumers? The British co-operative consumer movement, for example, is composed of nearly 10,000,000 families. It employs 333,000 people. Its productive industries employ 140,000 people. Is the interest of the 10,000,000 working-class consumer employers superior to that of the 140,000 working-class producer employees? The final object must be kept in view. The working people may organize themselves so strongly as consumers that they are all members of their consumer societies and give employment to themselves. They may be their own employees. And, finally, their own organization may produce the things they need, so that they will be independent of production and supply by others.

The majority of productive industries, which are operated either by capitalists or by copartnership workers, fail; this is their common destiny, at least in the United States. Not any of the productive industries operated by societies of co-operative consumers fails. Some have been discontinued but they do not fail. This is an important economic fact.

Now for three-quarters of a century a European consumer co-operative movement has been engaging more and more in production. At present, as we have seen, it carries on a multitude of industries. Certain factories, steamship lines, farms, and coal mines, at times, have been found not to pay; and in some instances productive industries have been discontinued. Some which are not paying, from the business standpoint, are continued because the society as a whole prefers to run them when they serve the needs of the consumers. Failure has taken place in none, any more than does the private garden of a solvent family fail even though similar products might be bought in the market at lower costs. Production and distribution for use are unique, and cannot be subjected to profit-business standards.

Chapter XVI

AGRICULTURAL PRODUCERS

THE POSITION OF THE AGRICULTURAL WORKER

THE farmer is in a different position from the industrial worker. The farmer usually works for himself; the income from his labor is determined by the price he gets for his produce. The industrial worker organizes to sell his labor power. The farmer organizes to sell the product of his labor and of the soil. Agricultural marketing organizations, for the joint selling of commodities which have not been produced by co-operative associations but by individuals, are essentially labor organizations. They do not tend to develop collective capital. A marketing association usually is a pooling business, in which each partner, after the produce is sold, takes his money as the pay for his labor and goes home. Pure marketing associations have not shown a tendency to develop reserves, set aside a percentage of the surplus funds for education and other social purposes, nor to develop a program which aims to embrace all classes of society, nor to change the method and motive of industry. Farmers' productive and processing organizations, in their relation to the consumer, respond to the same tests as other workers' industrial enterprises. The consumer is their market, and they desire to get the best price from him that they can.

Consumer societies the world over have commonly rendered aid to the working people. We have seen the philanthropies of the consumer societies, relief work, and the promotion of education, art, recreations, and even the care of the poor. Generally speaking, agricultural marketing associations have not lent their aid to such social undertakings. They are profit business organizations.

There is much theoretical interest in the idea of "getting the consumer and the producer together." This provides for two separate classes in society. The ultimate aim of the consumers is to produce for themselves, if they would find the way to production for use. But this in agriculture is a remote possibility. Consumer agricultural production, in general, has not proved to be as easily carried out as industrial production.

As a matter of good policy, trading between these two classes should be promoted. The organized farmer as a worker is reaching out for help, and there are many reasons why the organized consumer should give him his patronage as well as his support. In the present organization of society, this direct trading may receive encouragement from each side. Still it must be understood that the farmer seeks a good price for the products of his labor; and the consumer wants to get things at a low price for use. When the farmers secure a monopoly in any commodity, they exemplify profit-making business in full bloom; whereas, when the organized consumers get a monopoly, they solve a social problem for all the people, including the farmers. The price goes down. This is because the farmers represent a class and the consumers represent everybody. The consumer co-operatives of Sweden literally have a monopoly in margarine, flour, rubber galoshes, and electric lamp bulbs. As a result, the price of each of these commodities has been reduced to everybody in Sweden, including all the farmers.

The Swiss agricultural societies put the matter squarely when they said that they preferred to sell to unorganized consumers in the cities when they could get better prices from them than they could from organized consumers. And why should they not? Agricultural groups in other countries have taken the same position. The following from *Le Coopérateur Suisse* has behind it fifty years experience: "We do not hesitate to say that if the groups of agricultural producers should unite in large organizations and secure monopolies it is not outside the range of possibilities that all the rest of the nation would be as much at their mercy as it is under the domination of the trusts."

Those who were interested in the theoretical aspects of co-operation once looked upon the citrus fruit growers of California as having co-operative possibilities. This organization succeeded financially; and now, from every standpoint, it is a big capitalistic enterprise. It is interested in getting as much profit out of the public, including the farmers, as possible—and succeeding. Such organizations desire a monopoly and a tariff duty on their products in order to keep up prices. The raisin growers of California organized a "co-operative" producer association. It became highly successful, entered high finance in Wall Street, and ultimately became the property of the bankers. The milk dealers are doing the same thing in many places. It is possible that there are examples of organized farmers selling their products to organized consumers at a lower price than they could get elsewhere. I have not been able to find such cases. But there are many instances of consumer co-operative societies paying farmer marketing associations more for their products than the same products could be bought for from unorganized farmers. And there are instances of farmer associations selling to capitalistic business at a lower price than they were charging co-operative consumers for the same commodities.

The Danish agricultural producers sell their products in the "best market." They do not sell to the Danish consumer societies if they can get better prices abroad. There is never any question of co-operative producers making concession to organized consumers; it is not expected.

This does not mean criticism of the farmer. There is no more useful worker than he. He has to get the best returns he can, the same as any other worker; and the way he can get good returns for his labor is by getting good prices. But these facts do not militate against the two trading together. When prices are equal and satisfactory, the organized consumer should prefer to buy from the organized farmer and the latter should prefer to sell to the former.

Co-operation cannot be especially concerned for the farmer. There are the shoemaker, the carpenter, the clothing worker, and every other worker—all entitled to consideration. Each is organized as producer to get the most possible from the others. Organization of workers at the point of production divides people into antagonistic groups. Each group desires high prices, and therefore scarcity, of the things they produce. But they want low prices, and therefore abundance, of the things produced by all the other groups. They all consume a greater variety of things than they produce. They are thwarted and cannot have what they want. Community of interest is found when they all unite in consumer co-operatives. Then they have common cause.

HARMONIZING CONSUMERS AND AGRICULTURAL PRODUCERS

In the exchange between producers and consumers there is a third element which is inimical to the interests of both. This third element, for convenience, is called the middleman; but it appears in many forms. The middleman is a complex thing. Merchants, speculators, exchanges, packing houses, refrigerating companies, grain elevators, railroads, and banks are some of the organizations which stand between producer and consumer and take tribute from each. These constitute the middleman. Both producers and consumers are contending against this common factor. Through agricultural producer associations better prices have accrued to the producer; and the saving usually has not been wholly at the expense of the consumer, but of the middleman.

It is found practical for the farmers to organize their consumer business, stores, etc., separately from their produce-selling associations. The Danish farmers found this the better method. Thus in Denmark the same farmer belongs to a produce-selling society, milk-testing society, a cattle-breeding society, and a consumer society which conducts a store. All these are separate organizations. In America, many farmer organizations perform both functions.

The farmer, like the industrial worker, owes it to himself to organize as a consumer as well as a producer. The farmer who spends as much as he receives is as much of a consumer as he is a producer. If he has been organized as a producer he has had the first lessons in organization. A farmer marketing association is even a better school for preparation for consumer co-operation than is the trade-union.

Many farmer organizations have opened stores where their products may be sold directly to the consumers. In those societies, in which not only farmers but any consumers may join in the ownership of the stores, the agricultural producer movement assumes a larger social significance.

The farmer often finds the same organization that serves him in selling his produce co-operatively can be used to buy co-operatively. Thus the managers, who sell the produce for the farmer exchange, buy fertilizer, feed, seeds, oil, and farm machinery. The next step naturally follows: they buy other necessities co-operatively—coal, sugar, coffee, clothing, dry goods, and hardware. These latter goods require a store. And there is the consumer society, grown out of the farmer trade-union organization. The store grows and adds more departments, and the society has all the possibilities of growth and development which any consumer society possesses. Such a farmer organization is a complete unit because the machinery for getting better rewards for his labor is closely combined with that for getting more with the rewards. The industrial worker's trade-union can seldom be brought as close to his consumer co-operative society as this farmer organization. It was tried in Illinois by the United Mine Workers, in the early part of this century, and failed. The farmer-consumer society is in the strategic position to develop a co-operative wholesale; it has learned organization on a large scale early in its experience. It can also sell commodities at wholesale which its members produce. In many countries are consumer co-operative wholesales which have thus grown from farmer marketing associations.

This is natural because all marketing associations engage also in purchasing. It begins with the buying of office stationery, and never stops. The citrus fruit growers once bought boxes for shipping fruit; now they manufacture their boxes and own the mills that produce the lumber. This is consumer co-operative production.

In some countries the organized farmers and the organized consumers have set up a joint marketing board. The farmer societies sell produce to this board. The consumer societies buy from it at the current market price. The board pays the producers the current price. Between the two prices is the difference which would otherwise go to the middlemen. This surplus-saving, or "profit," is distributed to members upon the basis of patronage. The consuming purchaser and the producing seller both get savings-returns—one on the amount he has bought from the board, and the other on the amount he has sold to the board.

A central co-operative banking association is highly effective in harmonizing these two interests. The organization which serves as the joint board to protect both producer and consumer is often the co-operative bank. Co-operative banking may be a means to make the agricultural producers independent of their worst ex-

ploiters, and harmonize them still more with the consumer societies. In India and Japan co-operative banking has proved a
great help to the impoverished farmers. It is the money that the
farmer owes to the private banks that oppresses him. If he did not
have to make himself beholden to outsiders for financial aid his
lot would be easier. When the German and Danish farmers got
their own banks their lives took on a different color. These banks
perform a consumer function.

The agricultural producer movement and the consumer movement can be co-ordinated. The latter are buying from the former,
and the members of the former are becoming members of the
latter. This practice is increasing in many countries. It is seen in
the consumer societies which are composed largely of farmers
such as the Hangya in Hungary and the S.O.K. in Finland. These
organizations eliminate a horde of traders until the agricultural
producer and the consumer do much business directly with each
other. Thus the farmer prepares himself for consumer action. In
the United States, the farmers, who got their first lessons in
mutual service in their marketing associations, are now the dominant element in the consumer co-operative movement of this
country.

THE EVOLUTION OF CONSUMER CONTROL IN AGRICULTURE

The trend of industry is toward combines. This is natural. The
farmers are acting according to this tendency. They sell and buy
together. They must perfect their selling organization as a trade-
union expedient. On the other hand, to enlarge their purchasing
power, they buy agricultural materials co-operatively. Out of this
grows the consumer society, which, in agricultural countries, develops as a natural companion of the producing and selling society. The next step in the line of economy is the common use of
machinery. Movable agricultural machinery is often owned by
many farmers in common; also high-class male breeding animals.
The co-operative principle enables the little farmer to enjoy the
advantages of the big farmer. In some countries the next natural
result that follows is to treat their farms as though they were a
community of farm lands, to cultivate as a unit a combination of
farms, and plant, harvest, and sell the product together.

When the evolution of agriculture has reached that point, the line fences have disappeared, and it is immaterial to the farmer just which particular plot of ground is his personal possession. There is an exception to this latter assertion: it is material to him if he desires ownership for real estate speculative purposes.

Since we are dealing with the philosophy of co-operation, we might theoretically pursue the consumer ideology in agriculture, to discover where it might lead. If the farmers apply the co-operative principle up to this point, and if they desire to be agriculturists and not real estate speculators, the pooling of their land is a natural sequence to the pooling of their labor and their produce. Thus has come about the corporation of farmers, each of whom is a joint shareholder in the corporation farm. Theoretically, many little farms may be converted into one farm with many shareholders. Modern industry is moving in this direction because it is the most efficient and economical way. The big farm corporation has its manager and its experts in the various departments of the industry.

We have thus visualized common ownership of the land, and the farmer has become a salaried employee and shareholder of the corporation which owns the land. In the United States big capitalistic corporations are getting possession of the farms. If the political socialization trend prevails, the lands will become the property of the state, as in Russia. American farmers are not for this program any more than were the Russian farmers; but it happened in Russia. If the prevalent trend in farm ownership in the United States continues, in another generation the government will own the farm lands of this country, and the farmer will either be an employee of the government or he will rent a piece of land from the government. This condition is being brought about by "the American way" of speculative business, of which the majority of American farmers approve. Only the co-operative way can save for the farmer the farmer ownership of farm lands.

If the farmer were to accept the idea of a corporate farm, and be a shareholder and an employee of the corporation that owns it, there would remain but the final step to change the whole motive and manner of the undertaking from a profit-making business to a social enterprise. As to being an employee, the arguments against it are largely sentimental. Everybody who works for pay is essentially an employee. Men, especially experts, seek employment with corporations in preference to attempting to run a little business of their own. The guaranteed salary is becoming the desideratum of people who seek economic security as the reward for useful service.

If the farmer is a shareholder of a corporation that owns farm land and employs him, which should he prefer: that the shareholders be all farmers or that they be consumers irrespective of occupation; that the products of the land be sold in the speculative market at the highest possible price or be consumed by a known group of member stockholders; that the farms produce for the profit market or that they produce for use? The relative merits of these different motives have already been discussed.

We have considered, in this theoretical speculation, the evolution of farm land from individual to collective ownership. Let us now think of it as the property of the co-operative consumer society. The member of a co-operative society of consumers, who is employed by such a society in agricultural work, is a part owner of the agricultural lands of the society. He may have invested in the society capital equal to the value of his individual farm. He may have sold his farm and put the money in the bank of his co-operative society. Just what particular area of land is his, he cannot say; but he can say to a penny just how much equity he has in the society. He can prove that he is an owner of the property by taking out all his capital, if he wishes. He has a home. He can say that yonder house, which he rents from the society, is his home. It is his so long as he is an agriculturist, working for the society. And his chances are perhaps better for having a home than they were when he was at the mercy of the speculative profit and mortgage loan system. As a member of the society that owns the land, he has a vote in the administration of its affairs; and nobody has any more voice in it than he. He is working on his own lands.

The same methods of acquiring farm property, as are found in other industries, prevail in acquiring agricultural land. The consumers buy the farms with the surplus-savings accruing from co-operative business. They have thus acquired oil refineries, and the lands on which they stand. They are beginning to acquire oil-producing lands. As consumers they already own many thousands of acres of tea, coffee, and forest lands, to say nothing of farms and mines.

In a given agricultural district the local consumer co-operative societies would acquire the farms near the towns; farms which produce above the local needs would be bought by the national wholesale society; and farm areas which were not necessary to supply the needs of the country would be purchased by the International Cooperative Wholesale Society. This is the natural distribution for use of land, if we theoretically pursue the consumer co-operative principle to its end.

Countries with a land capacity to produce more than they consume would offer the field for international co-operation. This would be the case in the countries which produce the excess of grain, meat, cotton, wool, flax, tea, coffee, rice, tobacco, hides, furs, petroleum, metals, and coal. Such commodities handled by the International Cooperative Wholesale would be taken out of the field of international trade and exchange. Coffee would not be produced by Brazilians to be sold to English, French, and Swedes, but it would be produced by English, French, Swedes, and Brazilians, all united as members of the International Wholesale, on their own lands in Brazil for their own use. When we translate these four nationalities into all the nationalities of the world, and coffee into all the commodities, we have eliminated the flagrant cause of international hostilities and put human service in its place. The farmer may thus play a large part in a great social movement.

THE ULTIMATE IN AGRICULTURE

The theory of consumer ownership and control may be applied to agriculture the same as to other industries. The first step is to organize the farmers in order that they may get better returns for their labor, that their standard of living may be elevated, and that speculation in the products of their labor may be minimized. This is what the producer marketing association does. It is essential for the protection of every worker. But this purpose is external to the consumer co-operative movement. It is an organized labor function. The many agricultural producer societies all over the world that are catalogued as "co-operative" are essentially trade-union or labor organizations or manufacturing associations selling their products in the general market at the highest possible price for profit.

The theoretical end of consumer co-operation, it might be said, is to purchase the land from the farmer and employ the latter as an agricultural technician. Since the ultimate goal of co-operation is to provide employment for the members of all co-operative societies, the farmer is thus no exception. To the farmer who does not work but who hires others to do the work, this may not be agreeable. To the farmer who works and hires labor also, the consumer co-operative method might appeal. To the farmer whose family do all the work on their own farm, co-operative farming would at least give relief from worry about the mortgage and markets. To the farm laborer who works for wages and who suffers much from the uncertainties of unemployment, the co-operative method would seem to have something to offer.

The progress from the present system of private or tenant farming to that of consumer ownership, were it possible, would be slow and gradual. It would be upon a voluntary basis and in no sense confiscatory. No farmer would join it or sell his farm unless he saw it was to his advantage to do so. The farmer likes to have customers for his farm. This offers one more opportunity to the farmer which he may accept or reject, as he sees fit.

The gradual acquiring of ownership of farms by the organized consumers naturally depends upon the size and needs of the consumer co-operative societies. The local distributive societies begin by buying local farm lands for the production of vegetables, eggs, milk, and fruit. Wholesale societies have bought tracts of grain land, fruit land, and other general productive facilities. The English consumer societies own over fifty thousand acres of farm land in England. In 1946 they added 2,000 acres of apple orchards to their holdings. As such ownership progresses, cultivation and harvesting by intensive scientific methods naturally are practiced. Laborsaving devices shorten the hours of labor. Each farmer tends to become a member of his local society. The greater the saving in the cost of production and distribution, the greater the advantage to all the members.

This movement is so slow that it cannot properly be regarded as a tendency; but if it should expand, we should be concerned with several questions. How might co-operative consumers ultimately own farm lands and still give the farmer a sense of personal attachment to the land? How can the farmer under the consumer method think of his farm and home as the family "roof tree" and hope to hand it on to his children after he has gone? How can he think of himself as something more than a "hired hand"?

In the United States the tendency under the prevalent method is to make the farmer more and more of a "hired hand." The owners of farms are becoming fewer; the farms are going into the hands of those who do not work but who hire others to do the work. The "hired hand" and the tenant farmer are increasing and the owner farmer is decreasing. The "sharecropper" is the forerunner of farm peonage. The debts of the farmers are becoming greater and the farms are passing to the banks, insurance companies, and capitalists. Were the co-operative consumers to own the farms, farming might at least become a social undertaking rather than a disabled profit business which requires to be subsidized by the government. All this is so except in times of war when the farmer enjoys a boom for which he pays with the loss of his farm later.

In a co-operative system of farm administration, each farm of a convenient area, it might be assumed, should have a superintendent. He should be provided with a house which would be his and his family's in perpetuity. When he is retired because of incapacity or old age, the house should still be his, and his pension and insurance from the society should adequately provide for him. He should be succeeded by one of his children, if such could qualify for the position which he occupied, or by another of the workers on the farm. The house and grounds adjacent thereto should remain in the family so long as the family desire to continue upon the land and effectively function as farmers. A prolongation of tenure should be granted widows for their lifetime and to children. These conditions should be insisted upon. There should also be opportunities for the farmer to own and have personal title to a piece of land and a house if he wished. Capitalistic ownership should never be excluded by the co-operative method. It should be encouraged in all fields of ownership.

Each farm district should provide houses for all workers. Each worker and his family should have a house and grounds, in the same way as the farm manager. All workers should receive a guaranteed salary. This would be paid whether crops failed or not. A standardized yield would be calculated under scientific conditions; the wages might fluctuate with the yield, if it were found that this incentive were necessary; but there should be a minimum below which wages could not fall.

A transitional method may be conceived of, by which farm lands might be owned by the organized consumers but rented to members. The products from these farms would be bought by the society and paid for upon a standardized market basis. Properties might be leased thus in perpetuity, the leasehold to descend to the family of the lessee, so long as the lessee continued to produce from the farm. For sentimental reasons, the individual farmer may prefer to have a deed for a house and garden, to call his own; but as he would not be allowed to sell or rent the property for profit, a lease would be as good as a deed. The ninety-nine year lease is the common practice in co-operative housing, and provides a more secure claim to a property than does a deed. It is only objected to because it prevents real estate speculation and land gambling.

Against the above theoretical considerations is the fact that farming has made its best progress with the individual farmer in ownership of his own farm. And this private ownership is entirely consistent with consumer co-operative theory and practice. Indeed, it is co-operation that may be the instrument used by the farmer to save for himself the ownership of his farm. In the middle of the past century, 98 per cent of United States farmers farmed their own land. Today 48 per cent are tenant farmers. Fifty years ago 45 per cent of the farms of Denmark were the property of absentee owners, and were farmed by tenant farmers. Before the German invasion in 1939, 3 per cent were tenant farms, and 97 per cent were operated by the owners. Fifty years ago the Danish farmers were just finding their way into the co-operative movement. Now 90 per cent of the farmers are members of co-operative societies. They are united in the Federated Danish Cooperative Association. The most striking parallel in Denmark, and that should teach economists a lesson, is that the Danish farmer's gaining possession of his farm has gone on directly parallel with his entrance into the co-operative movement. And this means the consumer co-operative movement as well as the marketing associations which the farmers developed side by side. The farmer is a manufacturer, and as such he should buy his requirements at wholesale as other manufacturers do. Under the capitalist system he has been buying at retail prices and selling his product at wholesale prices. Co-operation is showing him how to reverse the process and improve his economy.

In terms of both ideals and expediency there is much in favor of the farmer being owner of his farm. Denmark and the other successful agricultural countries show the reasons. No one can be found who will take the personal interest in a farm, will apply himself more intensively to the solution of its problems, or will work harder and longer to make it succeed than the individual owner. There is no substitute for personal responsibility. The sick cow, the dry crop that needs to be hurried under cover before a threatening storm, the calf in the ditch, and the hundred emergencies to which the farmer responds day and night, all receive the best attention from the farmer owner to whom they make a personal appeal. This value can be preserved best with the farmer on his own land. The other methods here discussed are only in the light of the changing events of the world in which agriculture may have to share.

The farmer may be considered to be different from other workers. His land may be regarded as a part of his physical equipment and be to him as a worker the same as the carpenter's tools are to him, the fisherman's boat and tackle to him, the mason's trowel to him, or the unskilled worker's muscles are to him—a part of his labor equipment. And with this outfit of land, tools, stock, and buildings, the farmer augments his labor power and gets produce which he exchanges for money or the things he needs. If the farmer prefers to remain in this category, it should be for him to decide. Under these conditions he can function as a part of the co-operative movement just as any other worker with useful labor to sell. He may be attached to the consumer society which pays him for the products of his labor, to be used by the nonagricultural members, and which supplies his consumer needs. Or his marketing society may sell his produce for him.

The attempts of consumer societies to run farms have proved their most difficult problems in production. Many farms in many countries have been bought and then given up. The Scottish Co-operative Wholesale experimented with 10,000 acres of wheat land in Canada at large expense. It sold to the government the Calderwood estate after many years of farming losses. The Swiss union in 1920 bought eight farms with 350 head of cattle. In time they gave up most of them and worked in closer business co-operation with the Swiss farmers' marketing association. This is the experience in many countries. It is still a question, whether consumers can run farms as well as factories. Thus far they have not proved that they can.

Farming is something more than a manufacturing business; it is a way of life. The farmer and his family live and have their being in the midst of their industry. Their emotional as well as economic life is bound to it. It would be a serious change that disturbed these relations. The co-operative movement is not based on a predetermined philosophy; its philosophy is developing out of its facts. Co-operation is experimental. In what direction it will move, no one can predict. Only this is assured; it develops in the direction which at the time seems to give the best results. And we should at least examine all possibilities.

For farms to be owned generally by consumer societies is speculative and naturally remote. It will come only if it serves the farmer and consumer interests best and permits the farmer and the farm worker to possess an interest in the land. Such an interest should certainly be more secure than prevails under private ownership in agricultural countries where the farmer owner is exploited by the middlemen and moneylenders to such a degree that his tenure of the land is always doubtful. In such latter countries, the sons and daughters leave the farms if they can get away.

The speculative advantage of owning a farm, with the hope of selling it some time at a profit, may be alluring to farmers with the gambling spirit. This is a prevalent motive in the United States; but the more prevalent it becomes, the more clearly does it spell the decay of agriculture. Speculation is one thing and farming is another. The two are incompatible. Unfortunately the farmer is often more real estate dealer than agriculturist. The advantage which the individualistic speculative idea offers is the remote possibility of the farmer selling out and becoming richer than his neighbors; but the actual condition which it produces for them both is exploitation and disorganization of their industry. The business of farming is at least taken out of the realm of land gambling and made an agricultural pursuit by the co-operative method.

Under the consumer co-operative method the farmer is released from his most oppressive exploiters; those who gamble in his produce and those who sell him credit from crop to crop. He is released from the personal hazard of bearing alone the losses of crop failures due to drought or other natural causes. Losses from fire, hail, and insects are not his constant dread. No mortgage disturbs his sleep. Under the co-operative method he develops a personal attachment to his home. He can plant trees that in his old age will shelter him. The flowers which his wife cultivates in the garden will be there for their children and grandchildren if they so desire. Personal ownership, with its risks and responsibilities, is not found to be more secure than this.

The application of the co-operative principle may offer a moral and cultural advantage. The farmer who is acting for the organized consumers is producing food for the purpose of feeding people. His own living is guaranteed him before a seed has sprouted. The purpose which animates him is not to desire high prices nor to wish for scarcity of the commodities of which he has much. His shrewdness is not pitted against the needs of the consumer, with the purpose of getting as much and giving as little as possible. Any shrewdness that he possesses he may exercise in producing more and better for the consuming public of which he is a member.

Producing for use instead of for profit theoretically should make a better man of the agricultural producer. Farming may possibly be lifted to a higher position, which its importance demands, with the social purpose of service in agriculture realized. With the farmer's function liberated from the speculation of commerce, farming may be made to take on a different meaning.

It has been said that farming must always be an individualistic business because its success depends upon the personal interest of the farmer. There are, perhaps, certain sacrifices of quality that must be made under the social administration of things. Shoes are not made as well since the factory has taken the place of the old shoemaker. Travel is not as safe nor perhaps as healthful since the railroad, motorbus, and airplane have taken the place of the pedestrian. But these changes have all brought advantages and advancement.

The farmer, whose traditions have always prompted him to desire the personal and monopolistic ownership of his farm and the control of the sale of the products for profit, is in the same position as that occupied by the industrial worker who wants to own his shop and tools for the same purpose. The social use of these necessities may become essential to civilization. And production and distribution for use and service may demand that the consumers shall own and control the sources of their needs. Where the co-operative consumers own the farm and consume its product, the service motive in agriculture becomes supreme.

I have visited farms owned by the consumer societies in Scotland, England, Finland, Germany, and Switzerland, and have been impressed by the influence of production for use upon the character of agriculture. These farms producing milk, meat, eggs, butter, cheese, vegetables, fruit, and wood for the use of the members at least seem successful. The managers seem to be especially socially minded and useful citizens, and perhaps, happier in their work than the average of the neighbor farmers who are running their own farms—or what they call their own farms. There are consumer societies which conduct creameries and also own pasture lands and their own cows. The same societies that own the land and the cattle distribute and consume the milk. Such societies employ chemists and experts who analyze and study the milk in their interest. These farms, possibly, serve also in the interest of promoting a better state of civilization. The test can be found in any one of a hundred questions. Let us apply one test.

What is done in the case of a cow that is found to be diseased but that still gives milk? The manager of the co-operative farm is given every incentive to eliminate such milk and protect the consumers from every form of infection. The esteem in which he is held and his success as a manager depend upon doing just such things. He has one especial duty: doing what is in the interest of the consumers. Not producing good profits, but producing good milk, is his concern. He has no incentive to bribe an inspector to let him send diseased milk to the consumers. He needs no laws to regulate and control his conduct. Producing milk for use and producing milk for profit stand in strong contrast. Morals are more a matter of economics than is generally conceded.

The circumstances attendant upon the political regulation of foods are complex. The safe milk is from one's own farm, where the milk is pure because it is to the interest of everybody who touches it to keep it pure, and not because inspectors and officials with coercive powers are trying to compel purity. The best protection for the individual is that which is naturally effective and which does not have to depend upon a machinery of laws and penalties.

This is cited because it illustrates a great principle that runs through this whole matter of production and use. This principle applies to everything that concerns the health and the lives of the people. The farmers are as honest and as intelligent as other workers, and their functions are the most useful of any industry. But they are caught in the web of a system not of their own making.

In the evolution of agriculture, the voluntary principle must be preserved. There must be no confiscation—no coercion. Co-operation, if it continues to expand, must come about as the natural method. There should always be the individual farmer with his individual farm—making his experiments; working out individualistic problems; doing something better, perhaps, than the co-operative society; or living his individualistic life. Only if the co-operative method is best should it become the prevalent method.

The farmer of the present day need not be concerned as to an immediate consumer control of the farms. It is not for the eyes of this generation to see. The farmer may still hold on to his farm, and produce for the best price possible. But he needs to give consideration to the consumers of the future who will have among their members, not him, but his children's children. It is for them that he should ask himself this question: since we cannot have back the old pioneer days, what sort of organization of society will be best for the world? The farmer should be able to answer this question as wisely as anyone can.

Agriculture is an undeveloped industry. In the United States, it is operated on a basis of 11.3 per cent efficiency. That means that it could produce 88.7 per cent more than it does. If the knowledge and methods available were employed, 5 per cent of the population could raise all the farm products of this country. On the basis of the *known* maximum yield, an area of the size of the state of Oregon could grow the eight major crops. But this would be making use of the soil. In time, the production of foods, now an agricultural enterprise, is destined to become an industry, and much of it to be removed from the soil. Scientists in Germany, Denmark, and England have successfully raised cereals and vegetables on a large scale in artificial media. This chemically grown vegetation produces its own heat. The vitamin content is now in its experimental stage. Many crops a year, each vastly richer than crops raised from the soil, can be grown in almost any climate. Practical farmers are already successfully raising fodder artificially. It is being demonstrated that many of the vegetables for a family can be grown in the kitchen or cellar. Also much of the food essentials can now be produced synthetically. Food production is entering a new era.

The rapid expansion of chemical and botanical science seems destined, in a greater or lesser measure, to substitute the industrial technician for the farmer. The production of animal foods naturally follows the course of the vegetables. These are circumstances to which the future must adjust itself. It is possible that these changes may come faster than now seems conceivable.

CO-OPERATIVE FARM COLONIES

The dream of a communistic or co-operative commonwealth has found expression from remote time in the formation of colonies upon the land, with communal ownership, where the members live and earn their livelihood. The history of these enterprises is commonly that of idealism seeking a practical demonstration. They represent revolts against the existing order of society. But these colonies possess the deficiencies which are inherent in all enterprises in which production is not under consumer control.

Colonies have been promoted either by idealists or by selfseeking exploiters of the human hunger for justice. If such colonies succeed financially they then become profit-business enterprises. Idealism does not easily persist in the presence of great financial success.

History is replete with societies which have established communal interest in the land and attempted a co-operative life. A body of earnest souls put their capital into a common fund and start a new life upon a piece of land. They all perform service. They produce as far as possible all the things they need to consume. They work, and they are happy. But it is difficult to maintain a balance between consumption and production. Either they produce more or less than they consume. They either buy from the capitalistic world without or they sell to it. If they buy more than they sell, their fate is shortly sealed by exhaustion of their resources. If they sell more than they buy, they become a profitsharing productive industry. The successful colony becomes such a business. Production is speeded up. The more this is done, the more wealth can be got from the consumers in the outside world. The taste of this income provokes an appetite for more. Few have been able to resist it.

The "successful" colonies have become societies of producers interested in making profits from the outside world of consumers. If financial success is attained, then it is soon realized that those who are in the organization can best protect their prosperity by restricting their membership. Presently they become exclusive, and hire from the outside any additional help rather than add to their numbers. Or they divide up the property, each member takes his share and makes it his own private possession, and the colony as a commune ceases to exist. Sometimes a single individual or a small group of individuals have pocketed large profits for themselves in the end.

In the United States there is a continuous history of these colonies, beginning with the Shakers in 1787. These experiments include the purchase of 20,000 acres of land by Robert Owen in Indiana, and the establishment of his colony, "New Lanark." Other colonies were Brook Farm, Fourierist Phalanxes, Icarian Community, Nashoba, and the Oneida Community.

If production from the soil were concerned only with production the picture would be different. Production itself alone is pristine and pure. But as selling begins, the scene changes. Marketing in the capitalistic world is threatened with the hazards of the current profit system. The unsocial impulses are engendered at the market place.

There are colonies succeeding because they practice the simple co-operative methods of agriculture for consumer purposes. The members aim to create on the farm the things they need, food, housing, clothing, for their own use. This was the practice of the American farm two hundred years ago when the farm family was the co-operative society and when farming was highly successful. The substantial colonies today follow this primitive method. They are often built around some religious or ethical dogma or leadership. Their superstitions are of more harm than good, but their ethics constitute a cementing force that holds them together. They practice simplicity of living and rigid social standards. They are austere and seem not to have much fun, but they make a success of agriculture.

Much confusion still exists as to the relationship between producers and consumers. This confusion in theory has been responsible for much disappointment in practice, and has caused large financial losses in action. Producer marketing business is allied to capitalistic business, and suffers the ups and downs and the vicissitudes of profit enterprises. In a country as highly co-operative as Denmark, failure of the co-operative bank after World War I was due to loans made to marketing associations. These organizations were selling in the world market and were subject to the world market fluctuations. The most stable and secure business in Denmark was the consumer co-operative associations.

They gave Denmark its substantial co-operative character and profoundly affected Danish thinking. It is consumer-consciousness that most effectively directs the mind toward constructive social action both in the town and on the land.

What policy of action might win success for land colonies? Is success possible? The answer to these questions can be found in the study of the consumer societies that are gradually and steadily approaching this end through a program of evolution. By keeping the consuming function as the main purpose, making membership unlimited, and organizing in conformity with the Rochdale methods, a co-operative land colony can succeed. This is what is going on in the co-operative housing societies and land settlements. These organizations establish the members on co-operatively owned lands, in co-operatively constructed and owned houses; but they proceed to occupy the members in co-operative work only as fast as development of the organized consumer market will permit. Such are the colonies at Basel, Switzerland, the housing societies of Scandinavia, and the land settlements in Austria. They are practical because they take cognizance of the fact that as long as they are surrounded by a capitalistic society, they can take wages as individuals from that outside capitalistic society and spend it co-operatively with their own society. Success is won by the evolutionary method. That consists in, first, earning a living and taking wages from capitalistic business; second, establishing the society of consumers; third, learning to distribute capitalistic products to themselves as consumers; and fourth, creating their industries of land and shop to supply their known wants and thus finally making themselves independent of capitalism.

It is precisely this evolution from capitalistic society that the so-called "communistic co-operative colonies" have neglected. They have been composed of idealistic individuals who have been discontented with society and desired to flee from it wholly and at once with one jump. Having transported themselves into their utopia, they shortly come to realize that their colony is a small oasis in a large desert. Profit-making business surrounds them. They then proceed to produce things which they may sell in the capitalistic society from which they have fled. But the channels through which they open communications, the gates through which they take in the gold of the desert, permit the arid sands of the desert to enter also. The result is that the infection of profit-making enters with the profit. The quality of capitalism comes into their utopia with the profits. And presently the oasis has been transformed into the likeness of the desert. Such, at least, is the story that history tells.

Where individual farm ownership prevails, this whole program can be reversed. Let the farmer-owner, with his family farm, think of himself as a consumer engaged in farming for the purpose of producing directly every thing possible for his family needs, as his farmer ancestors did when they sold little and bought less. Then the farm was run to produce food, clothing, housing, recreation, and luxuries for the use of the family. Consumer farming succeeded, but producer farming is failing. Let this family farmer unite with his neighbors in a consumer retail society. Let every 100 or 1,000 of these retails unite in a consumer wholesale. What the farmer can not produce for the use of his family, he gets from his retail; his retail, from its wholesale; its wholesale, from its national wholesale; and that, from the International Cooperative Wholesale. The farmer gets the money to make these purchases from the sale of his produce or his labor to the co-operative. This is the evolution of consumer co-operation from the farm. As it moves on, it coordinates with the city consumer, moving in exactly the same direction from his end.

The ideal community is the small village in which most everybody is a member of the co-operative, where the farmers live, and which is surrounded by the farms. In time, these farms may be pooled in a community of farms, as the members of the co-operative pool their other resources, for joint administration.[1]

The retail co-operative should produce all it can. Some already have flour mills, shoe factories, and canning factories. The wholesale produces only what can be made more economically on a big scale—electric appliances, flour, feed, fertilizer. The national wholesale produces oil, gas, automobiles, tires, farm machinery. The international wholesale supplies tea, coffee, rice, petroleum products—things produced only locally but needed widely. At each stage of co-operative union, public utilities would be conducted

[1] See Author's pamphlet, *The Small Community, the Hope of Civilization*, 1945.

by the organization whose size and scope adapt it best to each service—telephones, electric power, water power, highways, parks, libraries, schools, universities, scientific research, rail, bus, and air transportation, postal service, international transport. This is the evolution of co-operative democracy from the farm.

PART V

THE LARGER POSSIBILITIES OF CO-OPERATION

Chapter XVII

THE ETHICS OF CO-OPERATION

HUMAN HUNGERS

CO-OPERATION rests on the simple principle that we human beings need one another. In our present state of society, in which competition for profit is the main economic force, this need is expressed in two ways. There is a negative and a positive way. The negative way means the contending of one force against another. The merchant needs customers, the manufacturer needs labor, the prosecuting attorney needs criminals, the soldier needs enemies. These are engaged in the balancing of accounts in the great game of give-and-take; and in this barter and matching of forces there arises a desire to gain more than one gives—to win, to succeed, to get ahead of the other, to defeat, to destroy. The positive expression of this human need is the co-operative way. We human beings need one another; we need not only to be helped by others but we need to help others in order that we ourselves may rise to the highest fulfillment of life.

Each creative mind takes from the past and gives to the future. Each generation stands upon the shoulders of the preceding generation. There is comparatively little new knowledge; we amplify the old knowledge. Human invention applies the climax to an old story. Human beings are presumptuous in adding a last touch—only temporarily final—to an agelong chain of knowledge and then laying claim to the whole thing and calling it their own.

The most learned modern chemist is himself not the genius. He is himself plus Scheele, Priestley, Lavoisier, Liebig, and Davy. If he had existed alone, he would still be a savage, hunting the forest for food to keep himself alive. Each mind supplements the other.

It is impossible to follow the light of high ideals without contact with others who have needs. The great inspirations come from our catching glimpses of the needs of others. Man is helped by his neighbors whom he helps. So long as his neighbors have

271

needs, his place is with them. Man belongs where mankind is, with its problems and its hungers. So long as one is hungry, others eat their full portion of bread in guilt. So long as one is persecuted by injustice, the shame is for all. The individual needs the challenge and assistance of fellowship with human beings who also are seeking the realization of full life. The consciousness of kinship draws men together and calls for co-operation.

There is an ancient falsehood, much used by the promoters of militarism, which declares that it is natural and good for men to fight one another; and that man has attained his high position by contest. This philosophy—that the thieving and brutal have survived and the honest and kind have perished—is in conformity with neither the facts of history nor the findings of biologic science.

These negative expressions—these antagonisms—have dragged man down. It has been by mutual aid that he has lifted himself. The precious heritage of the ages has been the things attained and preserved by co-operation. It is not true—as a human being I resent the slander—that man is hostile to man. A powerful natural tendency is to be co-operative and helpful. Were this not so, the human race long ago would have perished.

Co-operation stands in contrast to the antagonistic spirit. It rests upon natural human impulses. It is creative. It invites all the people of the world to join it—irrespective of occupation, race, religion, or social standing—and to enjoy equal rights in its administration. No new qualifications are necessary. The more who join, the greater is the success. This is the test of its humanity. It aims to create no privileged class. It is all-embracing. This is, at least, the theory of co-operation.

With what does co-operation deal? With food, clothing, housing, and all the material things that human beings want. And the most important material thing with which co-operation deals is the human being itself. To supply this human being with the things for which it hungers and to place human beings in more harmonious relations with one another is the purpose of co-operation.

In this endeavor men and women are seen working together with the material products of industry, and at the same time employing these substances to nurture in their own lives the flower of higher ideals. The aim is that life shall grow sweeter and character more fragrant in this field of mutual service.

The first impulse in the economic world is the acquisitive. The present industrial system has made it possible for people to live and have the best things by means of income from property. It has put into the hearts of the people the desire to have capital for capital's sake—because labor can be compelled to support the owner. Capital is a form of wealth that is capable of earning more wealth, with which one can live and purchase and command the service of others without oneself performing work.

There is a second impulse which expresses a primitive instinct found buried away in the soul of many individuals. It is the desire to serve others. It is a natural impulse. It is suppressed because it is expensive. Today this ideal breaks through the crust of economic determinism now and then to insist on expression. Usually it is people of religious zeal or high ethical impulse who dedicate themselves to this purpose, and give their lives to the service of their fellow men. They perform many services which should be performed by others. This altruism often prevents some from helping themselves. It promotes indolence and strengthens parasitism. While saving their own souls the philanthropists may make it easier for others to be lost. For the individual to do for others becomes a valid philosophy only in the presence of the philosophy that others should do for the individual.

Thus there are those who are served more than they serve and those who serve more than they are served. But there is a third ideal to animate humanity. It is the co-operative ideal—a democracy of servers served.

Co-operation tends to set people working together to give and to take in equal degree. Its purpose, it may be said, is to eliminate the parasitism and exploitation which make the two other purposes possible.

If I would live a fair and honest life, I must give back to society as much as society gives to me. The unbalancing of this relation one way or the other breeds injustice. In co-operative democracy the individual discovers that in working for the interest of the others he is working for himself. He discovers that the other members in working for themselves are working for him.

Everybody has a common interest. All are serving each. Each is serving all.

The co-operative idea represents self-interest made social; and self-interest is the greatest driving force in the world. The doctrine of the co-operator is that he should help himself, it is true, but in co-operation the best way he can do it is by helping others at the same time. He joins a co-operative society to improve his condition, to get more things and to get better things than he could get alone. But he can get no advantage out of his society unless everybody else in it gets advantage out of it also. He works to make it succeed so that he can get better things. And the harder he works and the better things he gets, the better are the things that the others get. And the more earnestly the others work to make it succeed so that they can get better things for themselves, the better things he gets. Then he discovers that he is working with his fellow men for the advantage of all, and he gets a new understanding in the light of this revelation of kinship and mutual interest. This is the theory; and, in practice, it is exemplified.

MORALITY

What the world needs today is not sacrifice, but rebuilding, to turn the forces already available into constructive channels.

The defect in modern business organization, from the ethical standpoint, is that men are divided into producer, trader, and distributor groups, all rivaling each other in the effort to get profits from the consumer. The consuming public is the great unorganized sea in which all may fish and take out what they can. The education that is behind most men prompts them to go into life not to do the service, but to get the gain. "Let the buyer beware" is a business principle recognized even in law.

Society is not organized to promote the best life so long as men find reward in acting selfishly for themselves alone against society. We may hope for the time when the individual shall ask himself the questions: "Am I producing good things? Do I plow and sow with the thought of the consumer to be fed? Do I teach well? Will these shoes give comfort and good service to the wearer? Do I find it to my interest to give consideration to the interest of others?" The individual needs to get away from the idea of producing in the interest of self alone; he must translate his interest into the good of his fellow men if he wants his fellow men to translate their interest into his good. This is the higher incentive of co-operation.

The finest sense of human devotion and loyalty is found in the institution called the family. This inherent sense of loyalty and obligation to the family may be expanded to embrace all mankind.

There are certain finite facts such as food, goods, and property. There are also certain infinite things such as truth, love, and kindness. The more one man has of truth, the more others have; but the more he has of property, the less others have.

Co-operation is a mechanism to translate the finite into the infinite, so that the more property one has the more property others will have. Two persons cannot occupy the same space at the same time, but two persons can enjoy the same music at the same time. I cannot afford to own an opera house. I know ten thousand people who cannot. But they all can enjoy music. Those people with me can all make their contribution toward the ownership of an opera house, and we can translate our little finite property into something infinite. The co-operative method makes the cost to the individual ten thousand times less and multiplies the joy ten thousand times—all with the same amount of space and effort—while the sole motive is the social and cultural enjoyment of the audience.

There is a theory that the competitive struggle for profits, for wages, for livelihood, has produced the great things. But examination shows that, while great works have been accomplished by the hungry, the struggling, and the suffering, still greater things have been done by those who were not so oppressed. The healthy and the happy—people with jobs and assured incomes—have made and are making the great contributions to science, invention, philosophy, art, music, and literature.

It is possible to have a standard of success different from the financial standard. An approach to this is seen in the sciences and arts. The biologist is thinking of his science, of discovering new facts concerning life, which may be useful to mankind. So long as his mind is in this realm he is living up to the ideals of service. Unfortunately he is often enmeshed in a system of profit-making from which he cannot escape, and the result is that his ideals often are subordinated to the economic urge to attain wealth and influence.

The physician and engineer, on a salary basis like the scientist, can be free from financial interruptions, free to devote their lives to their specific tasks. The president of a steamship company can have as his main concern the safe, expeditious, and economical transportation of passengers and freight, and not the winning of profits for officials and stockholders. The function of the merchant can be to distribute goods of good quality to the people who want them; he need not induce people to take goods which they do not need.

Through co-operation, we discover that it is possible for the people to change from self-centered aims to aims that are as broad and high as humanity. The co-operative method is slowly driving home, by demonstration, the idea of a new standard of success. People have better relations to one another and the hardness of human contacts is ameliorated in terms of mutual aid. Some religionists speak in terms of self-abnegation, but they cannot afford to act in those terms. Co-operation can be lived. It is capable of practical application today.

Chapter XVIII

THE PLACE OF SCIENCE AND ART IN CO-OPERATIVE SOCIETY

SCIENCE AND ART

As a better adjustment of the economic and social life is brought about, humanity must look to science and art to create the great values and carry it on to better things. The scientist, the inventor, and the artist should be free to create. They should have the disinterested mind. Competitive profit-making business has failed to provide the freedom under which they could best expand. And the totalitarian socialized governments have degraded science, art, and education by imposing restrictions and rewarding conformity to political "ideologies" which have been established by force. Those who could produce things or ideas of commercial value or political approval were sometimes rewarded, but the lot of the majority has often been failure of opportunity or, what is still worse, compulsion to conform to the propaganda patterns of a political power. Still these creative people are the consummate flower of every civilization. No obstacle should be put in their path. Society should make them free and exalt them as its most precious product.

When the co-operative society of Ghent used its surplus-savings to employ Van Biesbroeck, the Flemish artist, and told him to create beautiful things, it did an important service. This significant act was an historic event in the emancipation of art. The beautiful allegorical paintings and statuary, illustrating the upward struggle of the masses, to be seen in the buildings of the Voorhuit in Ghent are the result.

The world's great period of art was before art became commercialized. The artists of the Middle Ages excelled because they were made free from the economic struggle. The artist was often subsidized by a wealthy patron, by a noble, or by the state, and was free from the concerns of bread and housing. His living was guaranteed. The beauty of his works augmented his satisfactions.

It should be possible for co-operative democracy to perform this ancient service for art, become its patron, and restore the artist to freedom.

Already co-operation is expressing itself in its standards of architecture. Some of the beautiful buildings in Europe are those of the co-operatives. For dignity and elegance, the central building of the Berlin co-operative society and the office building of the German co-operative wholesale society in Hamburg are noteworthy. The finest business buildings in Glasgow are those of the Scottish co-operative wholesale. The soap factories and the cigar factories of the German wholesale are models of architectural dignity. The store building of the co-operative society of Zurich, Switzerland, is architecturally impressive. The stores of the Stockholm society are models of artistry. In many English towns, the co-operative buildings are the outstanding examples of good architecture. Unfortunately most co-operative societies feel that they cannot yet afford to purchase beauty, the cheapest thing in the world—it pays for itself.

Many co-operative societies employ musicians and maintain orchestras and choirs. The co-operative motion-picture theater is found in many countries. Several large cities now have co-operative theaters. The accomplishments of co-operation up to the present time show the ability of the people in their voluntary societies to build a structure of artistic worth. This structure continues to grow. It expresses beauty wherever the resources of the people can afford it.

In the field of science the British C.W.S. maintains a Research Department in which experts are at work. They make chemical tests, carry on examinations of various products, and experiment upon new devices. This represents science put to social use. An organization capable of using scientists for such purposes is capable of subsidizing scientists to make further discoveries in the interest of humanity. Some co-operative societies have established schools and institutes of science. Many of the wholesales of the European countries maintain chemists and engineers to discover things of advantage to their members. A number of American societies have chemical laboratories and laboratories for research. Consumers Union in the U.S.A. is devoted wholly to testing and to scientific research.

Co-operative societies capable of maintaining medical service are capable of taking the next step and carrying on medical research. Research in the biological sciences, in physics, and mechanics may be carried on in the same way. Just as soon as an organization of people can afford it they can perhaps do nothing better with their surplus than to establish laboratories of research, subsidize scientists, and instruct them to make contributions to scientific knowledge.

Here and there governments have taken a step toward such a program. But the price the governments have exacted has often crushed the spark of freedom. A research chemist in the employ of many a government hazards his job when his discoveries are not favorable to influential business interests. Politics often prostitutes genius. The employee of the political state is not answerable to the people but to the particular party or economic interests which control the government. Still, science is so universal that even under autocratic political regimes, where it is subsidized for the sake of the government, it produces great results for the people.

In the co-operative field, the system of organization is simple and is controlled by the people in whose interest the services are performed. In the co-operative society, the trustees or directors are answerable to the members. The same principles which apply to clerks and manual workers apply also to workers in the field of the sciences and arts. They serve the society of which they are members. The members are close to the control, and are the last and the supreme voice in the judgment of their service.

We may hope for the day when a free society shall embrace so large a proportion of the people, and when their financial resources and vision shall be so great, that the scientist, engineer, inventor, teacher, poet, and artist shall be employed with abundant rewards and guarantees of freedom, to create the things that shall lift mankind to greater heights.

THE HEALTH OF THE PEOPLE

The conquest of disease is one of the marvelous chapters in human history. The bettered conditions of health are due to the advancements of science and to the increasing measure of economic justice which society has yielded to the working people.

Realizing that the maximum of healthfulness has not yet been attained, society should continue to demand a decrease in morbidity. Medical and sanitary measures are bounded on all sides by an economic environment. No disease is purely a medical problem. Poverty is a causative factor in disease more deadly than germs; and money is often a healing balm more sovereign as a remedy than medicines. Both health and disease are contagious. As each individual realizes how his life is influenced by the conduct of others toward him, so must he realize that the fate of others is determined in a reciprocal measure by his conduct toward them.

Health is purchasable. Death comes to those too poor to barter for life. Poverty is the great disease. The poor man is potentially a sick man. The person who eats poor food, lives and works under unhygienic conditions, suffers fatigue, wears inadequate clothing, and is often unemployed, is deprived of life. Hard times increase the death rate as well as the crime rate. The poor man is a dangerous person. He lowers the standard of living of working people.

Health officers once made inspections of foods at the market. This was found to be ineffective. Good results can only be had by going back to the point of production. Now food inspectors go to the dairies and slaughterhouses. But here again it is discovered that the inspections are at a source of profits; and a corrupting hand is apt to blind the eyes. This whole business of trying to regulate somebody else's affairs is difficult and complicated. The only things that people can regulate effectively are their own things. Anything else means complications, political entanglements, corruption, expense, and small results from much effort.

Common sense demands that the knowledge of the sanitary sciences which has been won through the suffering of countless generations shall be neither exclusive nor monopolized. It must be regarded as social knowledge—the heritage of all, its benefits to be accessible freely to the descendants of men, all of whom in due time must contribute their quota to it. To demand that the doctors acquire this helpful knowledge, and then that they enter into competition with one another in selling it, proves good for neither doctor nor patient.

The prevalent organization of society makes the doctor largely a private tradesman. He has advice and services to sell. The more sickness there is, the better he prospers. A society which compels the doctor to be a businessman, to make the lives of the people a part of the business of trade, must take the consequences. Doctors and nurses have useful services to offer, but society causes them often to be hungry when people are healthy and well, and thriving when people are overcome by disaster. This is unsocial and inhuman. Sickness, suffering, and death should be nobody's advantage. Nobody should look to them as the hope of his livelihood. An injury to one should be felt an injury to all. Nobody should be making profits out of the sufferings of others.

In general, the average doctor cannot afford to give the time necessary to do the best for the patient, and the average patient cannot afford to buy all that medical science can do for him.

There is enough medical knowledge for all. To bestow it freely cannot exhaust it. It is infinite. The human channels through which it may flow out to those who need it are all that is required.

Neither doctor nor anyone else should be compelled to have as his life's aim making money—this is deadly. Rather, he should express himself in the performance of that form of human service for which he has aptitude, which satisfies him, and as a reward for which he himself obtains more life.

Health administration presents six possible economic phases: (1) Under individualist economic competition, (2) stateism, (3) labor organization or syndicalism, (4) control by groups of patients, (5) consumer co-operation, and (6) group co-operation.

1. *Health protection under individual economic competition* now approaches the end of its dominance. In some parts of the world it is becoming obsolete. It has denied the doctor the privilege of thinking solely of doing the best possible thing for each patient who comes to his hands, but has compelled him to make this secondary to earning a livelihood and to presenting the appearances of prosperity. The individual doctor no more can possess all medical knowledge. Medicine has become complex and needs the composite practitioner. The individualistic physician should always exist and be welcome, like the profit business; but doctors are steadily being removed from economic competitive

practice. This method of medical business is failing to satisfy society for the same reason that profit business fails to supply other human needs.

2. *The administration of health agencies by the political state* (stateism) has much increased. This is seen in such organizations as municipal and state departments of health, their clinics and hospitals, and state insurance and medical care of the sick. Medical attention is being provided for the civil population, as it is for soldiers. Medical, surgical, and nursing attention by the governments is the system which is being put into practice the world over, and will prevail unless the public, the co-operative movement, or the organized medical profession establish something different. Stateism provides medical care for more people and guarantees salaries for doctors. It offers disadvantages in the form of bureaucracy and political control. It is found to diminish the sense of responsibility and to encourage mediocrity. State medicine is expanding for the same reason that business is becoming socialized, because the competitive profit method fails to serve.

3. *The syndicalist principle in the organization of health agencies* is exemplified in the association of physicians, surgeons, nurses, and other experts into groups to control the administration of their craft and the sale of their labor. The principle is that of the guild. This is the field in which the medical profession can organize itself on the basis of labor and service. There are many such organizations in the United States—doctors' groups and clinics. The national and local medical associations are syndicates, of a sort, and so function in most countries.

4. *Organizations of people,* who may become patients, provide medical service for themselves. Labor and other groups employ physicians, and maintain clinics and hospitals. Most of the hospitals in the United States are owned and controlled by groups of laymen.

5. *The co-operative care of the public health* differs from the above methods in that it approaches the problem from the standpoint of the co-operatively organized consumer—the patient. In this co-operative organization for the care of the people's health, there are certain fundamentals upon which people may insist. The

medical sciences may be lifted out of the field of competitive business. The sick need not be the objects of barter. Patients may organize for their own protection.

Such organization follows the Rochdale principles. Often it is operated in the general co-operative society which conducts stores and other enterprises. Here the society establishes medical service for the members. The medical department is under the control of the board of directors, or of a special board. Some of these societies establish medical service free for all members, financed by the surplus savings of the society. Others establish a separate medical department and require a payment from the member for the service.

In other cases the medical service society is established as an independent organization for that specific purpose. Shares are sold to raise capital. A board of directors is elected. Physicians, chemists, and other experts are employed at a fixed salary. Instead of share-capital, the necessary funds are sometimes raised by a regular assessment. These organizations of potential patients often provide not only medical care, but sickness and death insurance. Their results entitle them to a high place in social esteem.

Denmark, instead of resorting to state medicine as do most European countries, makes use of the co-operative principle in health protection. Sweden does the same. In many countries the co-operative societies are promoting health agencies with noteworthy success. The British co-operative societies have some good examples. In some instances when farms and fine estates have been purchased for agricultural purposes, the mansion or manor house has been converted into a sanatorium. Most of the European countries have many examples of co-operative health institutions. Among these societies we discover the lines of convergence of the scientific and economic side of health conservation. When the co-operative societies, through their economic administration, provide good food and housing for their members, secure pure milk for babies, send children on vacations from the city to the country, provide six weeks rest for parturient women, and secure sick benefits and unemployment pensions for workers, they are doing things for the protection and promotion of health. It is natural that they take the next step and provide medical service.

The possibilities of true co-operative medical service are illustrated by the Volharding society at The Hague, Holland. This is a consumer distributive society, established in 1882. It has a department of insurance against sickness and death. In 1939, before the German invasion, it had 120,000 members connected with its medical section. This organization employs forty doctors, forty-five nurses, and many druggists and technicians. It has a well-equipped hospital clinic, a polyclinic, a dental clinic, and two drugstores. Here are united all the facilities for diagnosis and treatment which make possible the teamwork so necessary for the best results in modern medical science. Experts in the various special fields bring to bear the newest knowledge, supplemented by modern apparatus. Methods for the best treatment of patients are provided. Everything is up-to-date. Each adult member at that time paid $5.20 a year for full medical service of every specialty. Members' wives, who are confined, at childbirth have groceries free for two weeks. The service is superior to that provided by the British government at twice this cost. High-class physicians are employed full time. The salaries paid the doctors are considerably more than the average doctor in Holland earns.

Sickness among working people has always been an expensive matter and fraught with much uncertainty. The worker's family usually goes on from day to day without medical attendance, unless such an organization as the Volharding permits the family to have the best that science provides as its social right. Repeated efforts of the socialists to take this institution out of the hands of the co-operators and put it in the hands of the city authorities have been defeated.

The consumer co-operative society of Paris, L'Union des Coopérateurs, founded in 1919, conducts medical, surgical, and dental clinics, and three drugstores. This is one of the best clinics in Paris. Over 30,000 members of the society use the clinic. In Yugoslavia before World War II there were 120 consumer co-operative health societies in which efficient medical service was supplied at about one-third the usual costs and in which the physicians' incomes were larger. These societies owned hospitals, clinics, pharmacies, baths, lecture halls, and libraries. Prizes were bestowed upon households and societies maintaining themselves in the best state of health.

Co-operative hospitals have been highly successful in Japan especially among the farmers. China has many Cooperative Hygienic Centers organized by industrial workers, with well equipped hospitals. They conduct health improvement education and issue a bimonthly bulletin, *Industrial Hygiene*. The morbidity rate among the members was reduced from 23 per cent in 1942 to 6 per cent in 1946.

Since 1904 the workers of Madrid, Spain, have maintained a health department in their co-operative society, La Mutualidad Obrera. It has several clinic-hospitals. Central and South America have many such co-operative health societies. In Cuba they are not only health but social centers also. The Asturian society, in Havana, has 70,000 members, and many fine buildings including an excellent hospital. The co-operative society in Ghent, Belgium, in its clinic and sickness department, maintains an effective health service. Many other European cities have similar clinics. The Farmers' Union Cooperative Hospital Association, of Elk City, Okla., built its own hospital and began operations in 1931. The size of the hospital was doubled in 1935. This institution is highly successful. Most hospitals in the United States are owned by the laiety organized as consumers.

In the United States, besides the hospitalization plans and group health mutuals involving several million members, co-operative hospitals are developing on a large scale. At the beginning of 1947, fifteen co-operative consumer-owned hospitals were in operation, and fifty were in process of organization. These are mostly west of the Mississippi River. They represent the latest features in hospital construction and equipment.

A group of 150 or 200 families who are of much the same economic status, living in the same neighborhood, may begin in a small way. They organize co-operatively and employ a physician at a beginning salary of $4,000 to $8,000 a year. He is charged with the responsibility of keeping them well. He visits each family once or twice a month. He applies the preventive measures against sickness. He arranges with specialists to care for his group at special rates, and with a near hospital for hospital care. The members pay the hospital at the rate of $10 or $15 a year to be guaranteed three weeks maximum hospitalization. By this means the family physician is preserved—the physician whom the prevalent competitive system is destroying. When enough such local groups exist, they federate and maintain their own central clinic. Preferably an existing hospital is taken over, or they build a hospital. When the association is large enough specialists are employed with salaries, or they may continue to be compensated on a fee basis. The salaries of family physicians should be increased as the association grows and sickness is reduced. It is wise to grade the costs of membership according to income as well as size of family. The credit union, the local co-operative society, or other existing group furnishes a nucleus for such organization. Prevention of disease should be the main object in view.

It is noteworthy that the co-operative societies are carrying on life insurance, the amount of which is steadily increasing. This development of co-operative societies for the care of health and for insurance constitutes a combination of interests with large possibilities. Many societies add burial service and unemployment insurance. The co-operative method needs to combine all these.

The value of co-operative medical service is that the patient is close to the control of the society. In the case of political state service the patient is far away from the control. Co-operation means local autonomy. Responsibility, control, and administration rest with the individual member. He thinks of it as "my society." The state, on the other hand, is so far away that it is not thought of as "my state"—it is the state of the officials, of the politicians. When one is sick he wants to be cared for by something close at home—something that has neighborly significance.

6. *Group co-operation* consists of the organized physicians entering into contract relations with the co-operatively organized consumers. The physicians have control of medical affairs; the consumers control the organization. Under the present competitive business system in medical practice, doctors, like commodities, must be kept scarce in order to keep up prices and make the business succeed. Co-operative organization in all fields makes for abundance. Physicians are employed not only for the 2 per cent of the people who are sick but also for the 98 per cent who think

they are well. The insurance principle is invoked, and everybody in the society makes his annual contribution to the costs. Thus more physicians are employed and preventive medicine is practiced.

Larger health questions, such as have to do with epidemics and contagious diseases, purification of streams, elimination of insects, general community sanitation, international quarantine, and preventive health measures, must fall within the control of political society until co-operative society has developed to the point at which it can administer them; although in India, Yugoslavia, and other countries, co-operative societies for the control of malaria have been successfully operated. These societies are digging ditches for the draining of swamps, killing mosquitoes, and performing other services to protect their members against malaria.

Still, these large functions can be undertaken only by a thorough co-operative organization of society extending over a large area. Co-operation cannot control quarantine and general sanitation for the prevention of the spread of infections until it has pretty generally taken the place of the state. But in these, as in all other social functions, co-operative society ultimately may be able to do everything the state can do. If the former can use force in restraining a diseased or dangerous person, who may inflict damage upon others, co-operative society also can stay the hand that would hurl infection into the community.

In the end, any health organization will be inadequate and inefficient if the people look to the medical sciences alone to solve their health problem. There must be secured, in addition to these, better economic conditions for the people—better housing, food, recreations, and schooling; children freed from labor; war prevented; and industry made safe. These are the aims of the co-operative society. Without these conditions assured, public health measures will continue to be palliative—patching up the wreckage of social and industrial havoc. It is for this reason that the protection of health would seem to be the peculiar province of the co-operative society.[1]

[1] This subject is fully discussed in the Author's book, *The Doctor and the Public*, Harper & Brothers, 1935; and in his pamphlet, *Cooperative Medicine*, published by the Cooperative League, 1946.

Chapter XIX

THE FUTURE

INDUSTRIAL AND SOCIAL POSSIBILITIES

IN 1934, forty countries had a membership in their 250,000 co-operative societies, in the International Cooperative Alliance, of over 100,000,000. This is one person out of every twenty, or one family in every five, in the total population of the world, in membership in a co-operative society affiliated with the Alliance. And in many countries, such as India and the United States, only a small proportion of the societies are in the International Alliance. On the other hand, in some of these countries the majority of the population are embraced in these organizations. On the basis of four people in a family, this means 400,000,000 people in the I.C.A. supplied co-operatively. The total membership in co-operative societies represents about one-fourth the population of the world.

Let us assume an increase of the membership of co-operative societies from a minority to a large majority of the population. Let us assume that the co-operative method of distribution and production has become the prevalent method. This is within the range of possibilities. It already has come to pass in Iceland and in many large districts in other countries. I do not suggest the absolute elimination of the profit motive, because I should regard such an elimination as impractical in the first place and unfortunate in the second. Let us, however, discuss the co-operative organization without reference to the elements outside of co-operative society.

The people would be supplying their wants through their own associations. The service motive would dominate industry. Supply would actually be dominated by demand, rather than demand by supply. A machinery for learning the needs of the people and transmitting that information to the productive centers would exist. The central body which directs production would assemble

288

this information from the statistics of the past year. The surplus necessary to meet contingencies would also be considered.

At present the taste of the public for harmful, unnecessary, and unbeautiful things has been so stimulated by advertising and modified by a hundred years of dominance of the profit motive that at least a generation must pass away before their disappearance might be expected. Even if the co-operative democracy should become a fact tomorrow, one generation at least must die before production becomes anywhere nearly limited to commodities which respond to the practical tests of beauty and utility.

In the present organization of the world, the members of co-operative societies are mostly the employees of profit business. Their relation to the movement is purely that of consumers. In the co-operative democracy they will also be employees of the co-operative societies. Then the completion of the circle will have been attained: production of things to be used by the producers. This will result in the elimination of large-scale investment for the sake of income. With production and distribution for service as the motive of industry, large opportunities for returns from capital in the form of interest, dividends, rent, and speculative profits will have disappeared.

The elimination of opportunities for investment for income would result in people working who now live by income from the labor of others. The increase in the actual number of workers would not be so important, for there would be a decrease in the number of children, women, and invalids now at work, and a decrease of working hours.

Engineers have calculated that, if every able-bodied adult were occupied in useful service, each adult would need work but two hours a day to produce what the world could consume. Or, with an eight-hour day, each would need to work three months a year. The reduction of unnecessary commodities and the increase of laborsaving devices would tend to reduce these hours of labor.

What would the individual who works only two out of the twenty-four hours do with the rest of his time? I leave that to him. The utopians draw pictures of the glorious uses to which he will put his time. He surely will use much of it badly from my point of view. But I shall not impose my preferences upon him if he will not impose his upon me. The main thing is that he shall be free. I shall count on him to make progress. On the whole he will do more to move civilization forward than people who are coerced into doing what some superior intelligence dictates, or more than people who consume their time and exhaust their energy in earning a bare living. I have confidence in the upward movement of free people in a society dominated by the spirit of service.

If the individual wishes to produce something the co-operative society does not produce, if he makes something better and more beautiful, he should be free to do so. He should be free to sell it and accumulate money by its sale. That money he may employ to buy things he needs. And thus he may reduce still more his necessary hours of labor. With little or no opportunity to invest his money for purposes of getting unearned returns, the best thing he can do with it is to spend it. But I feel sure, if he produces something that the people want, or develops a skill to perform service that the co-operative society does not provide, then the next step will be that he will be employed by the society as an expert in his particular art. Should he refuse to bring his service into the society, it behooves the society to induce others to learn to do the thing as well as he, and to make it more available for all.

The freedom of the people to be small capitalists, in a co-operative democracy, we need not fear would make selfish capitalists of them in the sense we fear today. Co-operation, struggling to make headway in a capitalist society, is different from individual capitalism in a co-operative democracy.

The ultimate consumative function is the function of life. It is what one does because it is the thing he likes to do. Labor is compulsory production to get a living. Consumption is the enjoyment of that living. What one does not have to do but does because he likes to do it is leisure-time expression. It is not labor that people want, but leisure and the joys of consumption that go with it. The prevalent cry "We want work" falls short of its meaning unless leisure is the end. Some day smart workers will carry banners demanding "We want leisure." When we see these banners, we shall know that we are on the verge of civilization. When the labor movement gives place to the leisure movement, we shall know that the devices for saving labor are put to social uses. It is not the compulsions of earning a living that we need, but the liberty to live a life.

The purpose of the co-operative way is not to supply people with commodities and services. The purpose is to place the methods of production and distribution upon such a basis that people will get the things they need with less and less effort and thus win more and more leisure. The other name of leisure is freedom—freedom to do what one will with his time. In this free time, he may develop amateurish functions in the arts and sciences. Let there be plenty of amateurs—the product of leisure—and that means plenty of poetry—along with plenty of everything else—plenty of carrots and butter and eggs and houses and gardens. Do not let the farmers—the experts—raise all the food. Let the amateurs have their victory gardens. For every expansion of joyful leisure represents victory. The way to have good poetry and good art of every kind is by having plenty of leisure. The best art is not produced under the compulsion of salesmanship but in the joys of creative leisure. Art must be a product of freedom.

In their co-operative work people are laying the foundation upon which the structure of freedom and leisure may be built. The purpose of the co-operative way is the winning of more leisure for more people, with the ultimate view of perfecting the individual. The futile individual will use leisure to destroy himself. The worth-while individual will employ leisure for his own upbuilding.

As the people become more socially minded, the unfair acquisitive individual should become rare. The natural tendency should be an urge to work in the performance of social service. This is the new patriotism for which we may hope. Patriotism and good citizenship have a natural place in the hearts of men. The same impulse that drives men to kill those who their masters say are enemies of their people should lead men to overcome forces that are hostile to the highest good of their people. It can also bring about the cleansing of pestilential spots and the discovery of cures for disease. It can bring freedom from drudgery, and prompt the invention of laborsaving machinery. It can win liberty from ugliness, and produce beauty. It can secure freedom from much unhappiness, and devise ways to promote human joy. The latent power to do good for mankind needs social appreciation to bring it out. The inventive power of man is a repressed spring. It needs to be freed. There are potential artists today digging coal under the ground, coming out at night tired and discouraged. Potential scientists are standing the day long at whirring machines, their minds benumbed with the monotony and futility of the toil. Inventors are starving in garrets, their inventions not brought to the use of the people.

In the co-operative democracy there should be greater opportunities than ever for the adventures of youth. The struggle against forces of nature which destroy man may take the place of fighting in war. The drama, art, music, invention, discovery—all these offer the spirit of youth not only the qualities of adventure and initiative, but the challenge of competition. Who can do most to make people glad? This question may become as potent to compel youth to action as the old question of battle. Peace is pregnant with adventure. The glorification of war is the monstrous crime with which rulers and ruling classes have deluded youth. War can be abolished only by abolishing its causes. But while these causes are in process of removal, the attention of youth can be directed to the useful services which are capable of providing glory and satisfactions.

Youth must have adventure. It demands the excitements of change. It has ideals which must be fulfilled. Youth craves mass action and comradeship. It wants opportunity for heroism. It covets risks. For this reason it has been led into war. The young launch new enterprises. What is to become of this restlessness of youth? No vision is long enough to peer into the future and see a society without opportunities for adventurous youth. The unbridled sea and winds, the expanses of desert wastes, and the mountain barriers will always summon the adventurous. The untraveled paths of the air lure the fearless. The unfathomed depths of the ocean and the earth hold secrets yet unseen. Science continually beckons youth to come and find new truths in every field. Unconquered nature still challenges youth. The last fact will never be found. The greatest good will never be done. The possibilities for adventure are inexhaustible.

Under the co-operative system there is every inducement to introduce efficiency and laborsaving methods in the interest of the people. The workers who once drudged in industry long years ago rejoiced when they heard of the machine that would do their work and save them drudgery. But many perfections of machinery that were introduced threw workers out of employment and shortened but little the hours of those who still labored. The worker who did not lose his job merely found that he was mated to a bigger and more complex machine than before. Machinery proved a greater blessing to the owner than to the worker. We should expect in the co-operative democracy that every perfection of machinery would shorten hours and lighten labor because the consumer workers would be the owners of the machines. Co-operative democracy would have every urge to set at creative work every man and woman who had creative genius. Their contributions would help free the consumers from toil. The possibilities of the creation and use of laborsaving devices under these circumstances are unlimited. Consider the yet unused electric power, the streams, the tides, the wind, the sun, and atomic energy; add to these a large class of inventors subsidized by the people; and place behind all this the urge of the great mass of society demanding laborsaving devices, and the field of infinite accomplishment is opened.

In the present organization of society, it is but a small minority who seek or reap immediate advantage from laborsaving inventions in industry. Always these new scientific devices are balanced over against man-power costs, and so they are but meagerly employed. The people who own the machines in present-day society are not personally interested in laborsaving devices because they do not perform the labor; while the workers who are concerned have little or no voice in the matter. Different, indeed, would be the situation in co-operative society where the question of profit does not enter and the workers are the owners, and the producers are the consumers.

In addition to laborsaving devices, vocational training and aptitude selection would naturally find a place in the co-operative democracy. Each individual should make himself an expert in some particular function, and his reward would be according to his expertness, his application, and the value of the product of his labor, supplemented by accessory rewards measured by his needs.

The division of labor is a natural matter for co-operation to regulate. The central laundry, the common cooking kitchen, the central heating plant, and such other mutual arrangements as these are not in the field of co-operative dreams; they are already matters of co-operative practice. It is through co-operative societies that people get real experience in these joint enterprises.

The life of the individual is so short that, by the time he has acquired skill and wisdom, his span is done; he becomes incapacitated and dies. Each death takes from the world the skill and experience which life has given. Another individual must begin at the bottom and acquire them all over again, only to die ere he has attained ripeness, or as soon as his hand has gained cunning. The problem is not solved by increasing the length of life of the individual. The co-operative method, on the other hand, has something tangible to offer as a solution. It approaches the problem from the social aspect. In the present organization of society, the individual with skill, genius, or extraordinary talent isolates himself. Society often places him on a pedestal. He reaps the personal rewards of his talent, if he can, and when he dies the world mourns its loss. He leaves paintings, statuary, inventions, discoveries, literature, or works which have value because no one can duplicate them. He is given great praise. If there is no one who can do the things he did, he is acclaimed all the more warmly. He had lived long enough to have attained to a great end; his going left the world poorer.

But the co-operative democracy should not be satisfied to acclaim as the greatest an individual who leaves only works and a memory which none can duplicate. Not the individual who goes off and leaves the world poorer, but the individual who has transmitted his talent to others, should be acclaimed as greatest. Here is the opportunity of the co-operative democracy. When an individual has attained to extraordinary skill or displays unusual talent, society knows that some day he will die. Should the aim be to get as much out of him as possible in the direction of his talent until the end; or should not an effort be made to discover the young who may be placed in his apprenticeship and who may seek to attain to his perfection? I do not mean that the genius should be burdened with the task of teaching apprentices; I mean that apprentices should be burdened with the task of studying the genius. The former would be onerous; the genius should be free to teach or not as he liked. The teaching would be good for both the genius and the apprentice.

The machinery which has to do with vocational selection and vocational training in the co-operative society here comes in operation. Men of a similar heredity and tendency, who conform to the tests to which the expert conforms, may be searched out and their adaptability tested. These may be given the training to lead them in the direction of this expertness. And finally the great expert should feel that society will acclaim him great not to the degree in which he has left works which cannot be duplicated, but to the degree in which he has left successors who are duplicates of himself and who can equal or surpass him in great works. Not the perpetuation of the individual nor of his works, but the perpetuation of the ability to do great things, should be the especial function of the co-operative democracy. The co-operative method of organization is adapted to this end.

Then there is to be solved the uncompleted—the problem of skill which falls short of perfection. This may be approached in the same way. Individuals may work so closely together on these problems, and apprentices may be in such constant training, that as the elder drop out at one end, the work which is moving toward perfection is carried on by the younger. This is accomplished by substituting the co-operative for the individualistic method in the laboratory. The former is more expensive; it requires more people; instead of an individual, it establishes an organism of men, all of whom know what each knows and each of whom knows what all know. This is the co-operative method in science and art.

The individual human being is an association of cells; the old cells die, and are replaced by new. If this replacement could go on indefinitely, the problem would be solved and immortality would be attained. But this cannot be; a time comes when all the cells of the individual man die, and the association of cells is bankrupt—the genius is dead. Although not possible in the individual, immortality is possible in a body of co-operating and co-ordinated workers, all occupied together, supplementing each other, on the same problem. They replenish the units of their social body as fast as loss takes place. And thus knowledge, experience, and skill can be preserved indefinitely in the co-operative organization, while in the individual organism they inevitably come to an end. Co-operation provides in society the scientific principles of working together for all time in close and co-ordinated unison, which nature provides in the individual organism for only a limited period.

Every co-operative society should make use of this principle and have in operation the processes that will discover and train continuously the material for managers and other essential executives, to be always in readiness.

The object of production should become the creation, with the least possible work, of an abundance of the things the people need. What things are to be produced may be determined by the natural demands of the people, by the members in their assemblages, and by boards of experts. These boards may be created for special functions.

A board on household utilities would be composed of experts in the useful things to serve the family group—the construction of beds, bureaus, clothes hangers, bathtubs, and the other things of personal use. A board on foodstuffs would have to do with the study of foods, their sources, values, preparation, and economics. A board on clothing would study the materials, sources, qualities, fabrication, aesthetics, and economics of clothing.

House construction, recreations, drama, music, parks, transportation, communication, health, education, and all the things the people need would naturally be assigned to boards of experts whose functions would be to present recommendations to the co-operative assemblages or to the bodies representing the membership of the co-operative societies. The importance of such organization becomes obvious when one thinks upon the motives which determine production today. These boards would consider the interests of the consumer. How best can he be served and protected? The co-operative organization would not serve and protect the consumer as a paternalistic function; but it would be the consumer, speaking for himself, organizing to have the things he wants and that he has learned are good for him.

Out of this should come not only better and more useful products, but more economic production. One of the great modern expenses is duplication of labor in producing poor things. A pair of shoes that wears out and has to be replaced by the consumer in six months requires about the same labor cost of production as a pair that lasts two years. The profit motive in industry is responsible for an enormous turnover in clothing, furniture, houses, road building, and implements of every kind. This cost to the people is beyond calculation. Labor cost is high when the product soon decays. What is lost by poor material is lost forever, for the same labor that makes poor things could make good things if service of the consumer were the motive.

The co-operative consumers hold in their hands the means to compel the creation of things that will endure. The economic theories of John Ruskin and William Morris miscarried because they tied their idealism to the producers. If the consumer is not the producer, then the shrewdest and often the most unscrupulous producer is the one who survives. While the profit motive favors the production of short-lived goods, the co-operative service motive leads to the production of long-lived goods. And this only is consistent with the advancement of beauty in commercial production. Good things are beautiful.

The problem of eugenics and the breeding of the best human material cannot be discussed here. Suffice it to say: there is little hope for co-operation or for humanity in a society in which the less intelligent and the inefficient breed more children than the highly intelligent and efficient. This is what is going on today, and it spells a decline in the general intelligence and efficiency of the population of the world. A decline of intelligence with an increase of knowledge causes such disasters as the great World Wars. Men have knowledge but not the intelligence to use it wisely. Political government promotes this condition. It wants more taxpayers and soldiers. To solve this problem of eugenics is one of the tasks of co-operation.

INTERNATIONALISM

Co-operative associations had to develop national organizations before they could develop substantial international relations. The movement has now reached a point at which it no longer can be confined within the boundaries of nations. There is the same reason for a union of all of the societies of the world as there is for a national union of societies and for a union of individuals to form the primary society. The principles of the movement, set going by the pioneers, seem to indicate world-encompassing co-operation. Co-operation naturally tends to expand into international fields.

The international organization of co-operation is the International Cooperative Alliance, interrupted only by the wars instigated by political governments as it grows steadily in membership and in influence. For many years the various national co-operative societies in Europe have been trading with one another, and supplying other societies with goods of which they had a surplus. The organization of the International Cooperative Wholesale Society is taking shape under the guidance of the International Alliance. An international wholesale has actually been in existence since 1919. It is the Nordisk Andelsforbund, which is a federation of the national wholesale societies of Norway, Sweden, Denmark, and Finland. It does a large business. The English and Scottish wholesales may also be regarded as an international wholesale because of their large common ownership of property producing raw materials in foreign lands.

The International Alliance is developing various commercial undertakings: international wholesaling, international petroleum supply, international banking, and international insurance. There is no limit to the extent to which international noncompetitive commerce can be carried. As yet it has just begun. The International Wholesale may develop as one of its functions the transmittal of raw materials from agricultural countries to industrial countries and finished products from the latter to the former, as some societies now are doing.

Duties and import tariffs are paid by the consumer. Co-operation stands for free trade. The congress of the Alliance in 1946 passed a resolution favoring the removal of all international tariff trade barriers. The co-operative movement asks no tariff discriminations. The tariff is a tax imposed upon all the consumers in the interest of privileged traders or manufacturers. It is a fruitful source of international hostility, and promotes monopoly and a privileged and a protected class at home. The co-operative movement, not seeking private profit, aims to have free and unobstructed commercial intercourse between all peoples. This idea was expressed by Richard Cobden as follows: "Peace is best secured by the least possible intercourse betwixt governments and the most possible intercourse betwixt peoples."

The congresses of the International Cooperative Alliance are expressions of organized internationalism—perhaps the best the world has yet developed. Also for many years study and recreational groups have been making their international visits from one country to another, to be entertained by fellow co-operators. The International Cooperative School, which was begun at Basel in 1921 and has held sessions each year between wars, promises much for international understanding.

The world is disturbed by racial hostilities, but it is doubtful if the hope of relief resides in any political league or union of nations. International peace can be expected when the commerce of the world is established for purposes of service between co-operatively organized societies, within an international co-operative society. The profit barrier prevents peace.

Cargoes carried by the International Wholesale Society, representing goods from one national society of consumers to another, and within the same society, from one land to another, bespeak a new business era. Such vessels, sailing the seas, with commodities of a single great co-operative international organization, ask for no tariff barriers or navies to enforce discriminations. They are not seeking markets to exploit. They represent a method of commerce free from international commercial rivalry. They are veritable argosies of peace. The vessels sailing on these missions, inconspicuous as they are, are freighted with this principle of international brotherhood for which the world is blindly groping in the uncertain field of politics and sentiment.

THE POSSIBILITIES OF EDUCATION

If co-operation is the common ground upon which all can unite, why do not all unite upon it? If it embraces the principles which make for human brotherhood and a better state of fellowship, why is it not promoted by all those who desire well for mankind? If it can eliminate strife between people and nations, why are not the people more deeply concerned for its advancement? If it makes the necessities and the good things of life more accessible, why has it not the more earnest support of the needy, on the one hand, and of the benevolent, on the other?

The reply to these questions is twofold. Lack of information concerning co-operation is the first answer; and the fact that its principles are opposed to privilege is the second answer. Co-operation has working against it ignorance and avarice.

Those who take the pains to study the possibilities of co-operative democracy become convinced of its power for good. Co-operative education is depended upon to promote it. Two kinds of education are employed: theory and practice. The theory of co-operation, its history, its accomplishments, its possibilities, and its relation to other movements for human betterment are taught. The colleges and universities which give courses on this subject are multiplying. A few have established a professorship of co-operation. Co-operative educators feel that it is not enough that the institutions of higher learning should do this; the plain people, the working people, and above all the young need to be reached.

The schools can teach the children co-operation. As a practical example, little co-operative stores and banks have been organized in some schools to supply the children with the school necessities, and the nonessentials which children usually buy outside. This serves as an object lesson in mutual aid. The French have been particularly successful with this method. Such children's societies give training in business, in parliamentary usage, in administration, and in working together for the common good. Their moral value also is recognized. In the end the children go into life with a practical understanding that there is something besides the profit method in business. Usually children are taught mutual aid and co-operative helpfulness largely as a theory. Practice is found to make a deeper impression.

Experience shows that co-operation can progress no faster than the people can be trained to understand it and administer its business. It cannot be handed to the people ready-made nor can it be administered by others for them. The members themselves have to do it.

Co-operation has two sides: the business administration of economic affairs and the idealistic reorganization of the people. The first requires technical experts who can make business succeed. A successful co-operative society itself is an educational influence in the community. It quietly carries a lesson to all who observe it. The movement has also to develop leaders who can be teachers, advisers, directors, and administrators. Schools for this training are found to be necessary. Already it has such institutions in all countries where co-operation is making noteworthy progress.

The education of apprentices includes the philosophy of co-operation. Upon this as a foundation the students build their technical training. Idealistically this training should inspire the artisan to do good work, to make better things, to take pride in his labor—because the product is for use and not for speculation.

Education of the members in the larger social aspects and in the meaning of co-operation has not advanced commensurately with the growth of its commercial side. For this reason, in many fields co-operation is thought of rather exclusively as a business undertaking. Competitive business has got the people into peculiar habits of thought with regard to their economic relations. That the larger social possibilities of co-operation may be kept before the people so that each co-operative society may be an instrument not only for economic betterment but for enlightenment in the higher social ideals is the dream which co-operative educators cherish.

A most effective form of education is the successful co-operative society itself in action. This is the object lesson method. But it depends in large measure upon education within the society to guarantee its success. When a group of inexperienced people contemplate the establishment of a co-operative business, the best thing they can do is not to go into business, but first to carry on co-operative education among themselves instead. This education is best promoted in small study groups of six to twelve people. A federation of such groups, with occasional joint meetings, ultimately results in action. When an association of people have studied, discussed, and thought about co-operation sufficiently, there comes a time when they can no longer be restrained: they must express themselves in co-operative action. That is the way co-operative business should begin. Co-operative education causes co-operative business, and co-operative business is education in co-operation. Co-operation cannot be handed to people ready made; it must spring from the people themselves—from their own desires and understanding.

Education and more education is the need. Members of co-operative societies themselves need a better and larger understanding of their movement. Co-operative employees need to understand the social significance of the enterprise in which they are engaged. A co-operative undertaking must be a successful business and economically profitable for the members, for with idealism alone there is the danger that the business will suffer from inefficiency. But business success is not enough. Business alone loses sight of the main idea. Co-operation best succeeds when people see in it a great social enterprise, when they are gripped by the desire for justice and better conditions for the whole of mankind, and proceed together through their economic system to attain these ends.

THE ULTIMATE CONSUMER

The Rochdale Pioneers were scarcely conscious of the consumer, but they made a success of consumer business. Much commerce is still carried on in the name of co-operation with little thought of the consumer. Among the farmers, a producer sentiment, to the exclusion of consumer-consciousness, often prevails, even where consumer business is conducted. This confuses co-operative economics and militates against keeping the business straight. Forthright consumer co-operation involves only the ultimate consumer. He is the person who uses up, absorbs into his body, and literally consumes. This applies to food, clothing, housing, recreations, and such co-operative services as health protection, insurance, transportation, and his ultimate disposal in the grave. It means the things that are for his immediate service and which he does not sell again.

Capital goods, or goods which are used to produce other goods for sale for profit, are indirect co-operative factors. Manufacturers who form an organization for the purchase or production of commodities in their industries, as shoe factories co-operatively owning a tannery, are not within the co-operative field, even though they use the name. The Swedish co-operative movement, for example, makes this clear. The national Swedish co-operative league does not admit to its membership farmer purchasing associations. These associations, buying feed, fertilizer, seeds, agricultural machinery, etc., are allied with the farmer marketing associations. They are not for supplying ultimate consumer needs, but for lowering the costs of production, by supplying materials for business in order to increase the difference between the cost and selling price in that business. In the United States the Swedish method is not adopted. Farmer purchasing associations are accepted as consumer co-operatives, which tend to take the next step and establish stores for the supply of consumer goods, or to promote insurance, banking, electric, and other consumer services, or to distribute petroleum products for automobile uses other than commercial. These are moving into consumer co-operation. In this country these farmer organizations are most actively progressing in that direction. They are promoting co-operative education and are penetrating the towns and cities with consumer co-operative organization.

The worker who is a member of a consumer co-operative society is in a peculiar position. He has labor power to sell at the highest price possible. He buys food, housing, and clothing, which constitute his costs, for the production and protection of his energies. The difference between the two prices is the profit of his personal business.

Thus the profit motive does prevail in consumer co-operation. The farmer uses co-operation to reduce the costs of the things he sells, to increase his profits. The individual uses it to reduce the costs of his maintenance, and thus to increase the profit he wins from the sale of his energies or talents. Profit is eliminated from co-operation only when the individual member is employed by his co-operative society, not for a stipulated salary but receives his maintenance in place of salary. Under these circumstances, in place of profit, the individual gets life. This he gets directly instead of buying it with the profit from the sale of his services. In the end, life is the profit he wins by the co-operative method, if an interpretation of profit other than the accepted economic meaning is applied.

However, in evaluating co-operation, ultimate consumption must be the standard. While the use the individual makes of his body is within the consideration of co-operation, it is in the field of ultimate consumption that the philosophical, social, and ethical implications of co-operation largely reside.

These problems are solving themselves in the laboratory of experience. Human beings cannot be wholly classified according to their means of livelihood, segregated into economic compartments, and considered apart from each other. They are all consumers; and harmonizing the interests of all is the function of co-operation.

AFTER WORLD WAR II

The dominance of individualistic competitive profit business is drawing to a close. The rise of stateism threatens. Plans for world-wide reorganization after the war, now developing in the minds of statesmen and economists, look to the re-establishment of political states to solve the problems. These plans would restore political governments in power to exercise authority over the lives of the people, and gradually dominate economic affairs. The expansion of stateism means governments in business to take the place vacated by the fading out of profit business. The efforts of statesmen seem to be to the re-establishment of conditions similar to those which produced the chaos in the world today. This is what the leaders of business are demanding. They want the old conditions back again. The Treaty of Versailles did this twenty-five years ago. The world needs a new deal. However well meant and however efficiently devised, the re-establishment of the profit capitalist dominance of the world's economic affairs can only be viewed, in the light of history and the fundamentals of economy, as moving on toward autocracy and the abnegation of democracy—war and chaos again. On the other hand, the methods of consumer co-operation offer nonprofit private business, democratic freedom in commerce, and control by the people.

Accordingly, the more stable after-war organization in the shattered countries lies in their co-operative societies rather than in their shattered political states and discredited capitalist structures. The co-operatives have proved their ability to produce and distribute. The time has come for the people to turn from their old economic and political ways and to organize their economic affairs in the economic way, leaving to the state those things external to man's capacity to co-operate. This opportunity should be opened to the exploited colonial peoples as well as to the people of other lands. Co-operative democracy is for all.

Chapter XX

GENERAL RÉSUMÉ

ECONOMIC EVOLUTION

THE prevalent economic system is based on the profit motive in production, in distribution, and in the performance of most social services.

As a result of this system the quest for money, in wages, interest, dividends, rent, and other forms of profit, has become a dominating motive in life.

What is called business has as its purpose buying at the lowest price and selling at the highest price, commodities, labor, and the materials necessary to produce things and to maintain labor; and as a result the business of the world takes on the character of speculation or gambling.

The profit system in industry has given rise to production beyond the capacity of the people to purchase; the people who perform service do not receive wages enough to buy the things they produce, because of the increase of price in the interest of profits.

Overproduction in each industrial country demands the seeking of markets in other lands; but the resources of nature have now become so monopolized that the same condition of depreciated purchasing power of the masses of people has become well-nigh universal, and in consequence of this inadequate buying power there exists an economic unbalance which threatens the whole capitalistic economic structure of the world with disorganization.

The profit motive has served as an organizing and constructive force and is the means by which most of the essential commodities are produced and distributed; still its power to create hostilities and antagonisms between peoples constantly threatens the peace of society.

The quest for economic profits is a potent cause of political corruption, poverty, crime, disease, and warfare.

There is always a tendency for things to remain as they are because of social inertia. The masses have little conception of anything better. The prevalent economic system is fixed upon society also because those who believe they profit by it, the people of wealth and influence, are the most powerful social factors; they control largely the governments, the avenues of expression, education, and exchange; they control the means of livelihood of the working masses; and they do not wish the profit system to be replaced by another system.

The discontent that springs from poverty, the intellectual and sentimental revolt at the injustices arising from the profit motive, and the slow processes of education are all tending to prepare the people to seek and accept another purpose in industry.

An increasing number of people are arriving at the conclusion that production, distribution, and administration of economic and social affairs, for purposes of service, offer greater advantages to society than the profit purpose, and that social disorder and injustice will prevail until service becomes the dominant motive.

Voluntary organization of the people in their interest as consumers, to secure larger access to the things of life, is expressed in the co-operative movement.

This is the only nonpolitical organization of the people, effectively in operation, which aims at democratic distribution and production for purposes of service.

Consumer co-operation is a voluntary method whereby the people unite democratically to use their resources to supply their needs. The purpose is to get the largest possible direct access to the things that people want.

Through co-operative societies the consumers perform for themselves the useful functions of supply which are otherwise performed by profit business, by the political state, by charity, or by the unaided individual.

These services are: the retail distribution of commodities, such as food, clothing, personal and household needs; the supplying of services such as banking, insurance, entertainment, recreation, education, news, transportation, communication, housing, and health and property protection; the supply of electricity, gas, heat, water, and other powers; importation and trading; the production, processing, and warehousing of useful commodities; the production and supply of raw materials such as metals, coal, wood, grains, fruits, vegetables, meat, and milk; printing and publishing; the conducting of such useful institutions as restaurants, hotels, laundries, and baths; the promotion of art, science, invention, and research; the adjustment of differences between individuals such as can be effected by arbitration; the provision of useful work for a means of livelihood; and the performance of all other services and the supply of all other commodities which people need.

A co-operative society observes certain definite principles.

Any competent person may be a member of a co-operative society irrespective of race, occupation, religion, politics, or other affiliations, so long as his membership is advantageous and not detrimental to the co-operative society.

Each member puts in a certain amount of money, property, or service to inaugurate the group business. This is a pool of private wealths, to be administered in common for the mutual advantage of the members.

Co-operation stands for private ownership and for private property, as against state ownership; but it practices common administration of the property which each member puts into the society. By this means the amount which each member contributes becomes a concentrated capital which aggregates sums greater than the wealth of the richest individuals and places those of meager circumstances in a superior economic position.

To ensure democracy of control, each member has one vote and no more in the affairs of the society of which he is a member; in the case of the federations of co-operative societies the voting privileges of affiliated organizations may be proportionate to patronage.

The members have direct control of the affairs of their society. They elect a board of directors who find and appoint experts to administer the various types of business for the service of the members. Thus a co-operative society proves the practicability of democracy.

In the interest of expediency it is customary to supply members at the current market price. All that wealth, which is profit in capitalistic business, accumulates as a surplus-saving in the co-operative treasury as the property of the members. After paying overhead costs and setting aside funds for other uses, the balance is returned to the members in proportion to their patronage, thus abolishing the commercial profit and substituting service in its place.

Capital invested in a co-operative society, if it receive interest, is paid a fixed rate which is the minimum current rate of the locality. The purpose is not to give the profits or savings of the business to invested capital but to pay capital only reasonable wages.

A certain amount of the surplus-savings may be used for recreation, art, health, insurance, or other social purposes in the interest of the members as a whole.

Besides the fundamentals of co-operation there are certain expedients which are commonly observed.

Business is done for cash so far as possible. Persons without adequate capital may become members of societies by allowing their capital requirements to accrue from the savings which develop from their patronage. Expansion into new fields of service is the aim. Fair labor conditions and employees' autonomy, compatible with successful competition with profit business, are observed.

Co-operative societies federate nationally. National federations unite internationally in the International Cooperative Alliance. These federations are for purposes of conference, mutual service, protection, and international commerce.

Co-operation begins by performing those services, such as retail supply, which are closest to the people as consumers.

When the successful carrying on of such functions has been mastered, the societies federate to perform larger services.

Thus, co-operative societies move from simple distribution and retailing to wholesaling. The wholesale businesses are owned by the distributive societies, in whose interests they are exclusively conducted. They are administered and controlled by the same methods as their constituent societies.

Wholesaling moves on to buying in large quantities, to importing, warehousing, and finally to manufacturing.

Production is for a known clientele of consumers and is not

subject to the uncertainties of salesmanship and the hazards of over- and underproduction.

Manufacturing moves toward the control of raw material—plantations, fields, mines, and forests.

Thus, beginning with distribution to the consumers, the federations of co-operative societies proceed to ownership of the land and natural resources. This is a gradual progression, and advances only as fast as experience and competence in administrative ability are developed.

Co-operative societies make use of decentralized control, in the interest of democracy, and centralized administration, in the interest of efficiency.

The ultimate destiny of the consumer co-operative movement is to obtain or to produce in factory, shop, mine, sea, air, and land all that the consumers require.

Commercial production that is not owned, controlled, and administered by and for the consumers is profit business. The aim of co-operation is to establish the dominance of service in the place of profit.

In its nature, co-operation trains people as consumers to carry on their affairs independent of profit business and the political state. It does not aim at the confiscation or the abolition of either, but its natural tendency is the creation of the co-operative method in their stead.

This transition takes place only as fast as the co-operative practice makes progress in the presence of competition with profit business and the socialized state. Co-operation grows only by proving its superiority. It has no other method. It must do this against the hostility of the powerful forces of profit business and against the discriminations of political governments which the profit system dominates or governments which would take industries out of the hands of co-operative societies and place them under the ownership and control of the state.

Co-operation is wholly constructive and evolutionary, never destructive or revolutionary. It uses neither force nor coercion, but stands for freedom in commerce. It does not demand the abolition of profit business by edict, law, or confiscation. It keeps itself on the alert and would not deprive itself of the challenge of the competition of profit business.

The expansion of co-operation is never sudden or cataclysmic. Old forms are neither destroyed nor discriminated against. They melt away as new and better forms grow up and prove their value. Co-operation can grow only as it proves its superiority by fair competition.

Unlike profit business, co-operation asks no discriminatory favors of the state; it asks only that it shall not be discriminated against.

As co-operation grows, the need of profit business and of the political state decline. The expansion of co-operation means decrease of the business and regulatory functions of the state.

Co-operation, by its success, demonstrates that consumers organized in co-operative societies can more effectively perform the services otherwise rendered by profit business, and that people organized as members of co-operative societies are fully as intelligent as are the citizens of the state, and more efficient in their own behalf.

Co-operation exemplifies the fact that great social changes which are permanent are those brought about by means similar in character to the end sought. By applying certain methods, in a series of smaller co-operative societies, a great co-operative society, employing these very methods, is ultimately attained.

Co-operation makes use of the principle that like results come from like causes; desirable ends are reached by desirable means. A co-operative democracy is approached by building co-operation from the beginning. This is in contrast with the methods of all other radical and reform movements depending, as they do, upon voting, revolution, the general strike, sabotage, the class struggle, and other divers means.

Consumer co-operation is a structure in process of building, which holds a promise of efficiency for the future. People travel the road, training themselves on the way by doing precisely the things that will be done in a society to come.

Co-operation is evolutionary, friendly, peaceful, undramatic, quiet, and unostentatious.

It is based upon the social morality of the consuming masses, which are interested in the total good of society because they are society. This is different from organization in the exclusive interest of a class—such as the working class or the capitalist class.

Co-operative business is most secure because the patrons are not arrayed against the owners; the patrons of the business are the owners, and thus both patrons and owners are zealous for its success.

Co-operation unites people upon the one common ground on which all people may unite—the fact that they are consumers.

It begins not with the workshop, but with the home and the family and the places where things are consumed and enjoyed. Its primary hypothesis is that the consumers are everybody and that all the machinery of industry and the organization of society should be for them. As this comes to pass the consumers become the producers and the interests of producer and consumer become the same.

In consumer co-operation, sex distinctions are not seen. Co-operation is concerned for all women as well as for all men. Recognizing the family especially, it begins with the existing organization in which the man and the woman are nearest to equality and in which the interest of children is a matter of supreme concern.

The co-operative movement should be allied with no political party, religion, or sect. Where such alliances are formed, a split in the movement inevitably develops, and in the division the neutral body must be regarded as the genuine expression of co-operation.

Co-operative societies desire that the labor which they employ shall be organized in a trade-union for its own protection. The employee also has the right to be a member of the society in which he works. The worker thus has as much voice as any other member of a co-operative society in determining his wages and his conditions of labor.

The co-operative movement is tending toward a co-operative democracy as a substitute for the profit economy and the political state.

Through its local and national organizations of consumers, which meet in congresses to promote their interests, co-operation already has in operation the machinery which is capable of being a substitute for the political machinery of the state. The national union of the consumers, on one hand, and the national union of the employees of co-operative societies, on the other, might constitute the two houses of a parliament which should be capable of serving society more efficiently than do the present systems of political government. This body would not be occupied in making laws, but in devising ways and means of carrying on service for the people. It would not be concerned so much with the governing of people as with the administration of things.

A national central board created by the national co-operative parliament or congress should constitute the executive branch of the co-operative democracy.

In the place of the judiciary, the co-operative movement makes use of boards of arbitration. In the co-operative democracy these would function in the stead of the courts of law of the political state.

Through the federation of all co-operative societies of the world in the International Cooperative Alliance, and through the development of international co-operative wholesaling, production, transportation, banking, and insurance, the world is in process of being welded into an harmonious society from which the main causes of international hostilities are excluded.

Inasmuch as the causes of war rest chiefly upon an economic basis and wars are instigated and promoted most largely by economic forces, co-operation offers hope of world peace and is a potent force making for the abolition of war.

The congresses of the International Cooperative Alliance represent the beginning of a true league of peoples.

Since the consumers are interested for the common welfare of society, co-operation encourages the arts and sciences. It is already subsidizing workers in these fields of culture.

Coincident with the development of co-operative societies goes the movement to release industry from the burdens of taxation and to reclaim the land and the resources of nature from the privileged hands into which much of them has fallen, again to make them the property of mankind, to be employed by co-operative society for purposes of use.

As profit business gives place to politically socialized business and to the expansion of the socialized state, the conflict of economic forces is transferred to the differences between the coercive political state on the one side and the voluntary nonpolitical co-operative movement on the other. This virtually resolves itself into the conflict between regimented society and the free individual.

The movement in the direction of co-operative democracy is naturally prompted by those who suffer from the prevalent politico-economic system, but working with them also are the socially-minded who are drawn to co-operation by intellectual, social, and ethical reasons.

Where co-operative industry becomes dominant, the consumers find work in their own industries and give themselves employment, producing for themselves and serving themselves.

In a co-operative democracy "purchasing power" fades out and gives place to "producing power," and labor becomes the medium with which purchasing is done.

Co-operation elevates service to the position now occupied by money, and, having begun with the consumer, completes the circle and places the working consumer in the position of power.

The worker and the consumer become one in the consumer co-operative democracy; and in this oneness the things called "unearned increment" and "profit" disappear, the worker gets the value of the wealth he produces, and the consumer supplies his needs at cost.

The co-operative movement is based upon a theory of human conduct which is a fundamental part of the biological constitution of mankind; it represents a primitive principle in action which is salutary and upon which the survival of the race depends.

The theory of co-operation has to substantiate it the history of animal kind; not by antagonism and warfare have the best qualities been brought out and preserved, but by mutual aid and service.

The co-operative movement is a growing and demonstrable fact; it is tending in the direction toward which mutual aid points, to save man from the hostilities that would destroy him.

Finally, it is not society but the individual for whom co-operation is concerned. As it moves toward co-operative democracy, it provides access to the materials and opportunities of life, that make for happiness and for the perfecting of men and women. Its aim should be the development of superior individuals, appreciative of cultural values, and with a passion for beauty, truth, and justice.

BIBLIOGRAPHY

Alanne, V. S., *Fundamentals of Consumers Cooperation*. Minneapolis, Northern States Cooperative League, 1935.

———, *Manual for Cooperative Directors*. Coop. Pub. Assoc., 1945.

Bergengren, R. F., *Cooperative Banking*. New York, The Macmillan Company, 1923.

———, *Cuna Emerges—Credit Union Book*. Madison, Wis., Credit Union Nat'l Association, 1935.

———, *Credit Union*. New York, Beekman Hill, 1931.

———, *Credit Union North America*. Southern Publishers, 1940.

Belloc, Hilaire, *The Servile State*. New York, Henry Holt & Co., 1946.

Bogardus, Emory S., *Co-ops on Campus*. The Cooperative League, 1945.

Bolles, Joshua K., *The People's Business*. New York, Harper & Brothers, 1942.

Carr-Saunders, *Consumers Cooperation in Great Britain*. New York, Harper & Brothers, 1938.

Cassau, T. O., *Consumers' Cooperative Movement in Germany*, trans. by J. F. Mills. London, T. F. Unwin, 1935.

Cassier, Ernest, *The Myth of the State*. New Haven, Yale University Press, 1946.

Coady, M. M., *Masters of Their Own Destiny*. New York, Harper & Brothers, 1939.

Cowling, Ellis, *Cooperation in America*. New York, Coward-McCann, 1938.

Daniels, John, *Cooperation—An American Way*. New York, Covici-Friede, 1938.

Faber, Harold, *Cooperation in Danish Agriculture*. London, Longmans, Green and Co., 1931.

Flanagan, James, *Wholesale Cooperation in Scotland*. Glasgow, S. C. W. S., 1920.

Ford, James, *Cooperation in New England*. New York, Survey, 1913.

Fowler, Bertram, *Consumers' Cooperation in America*. New York, Vanguard Press, Inc., 1936.

———, *The Lord Helps Those*. New York, Vanguard Press, 1938.

Gebhard, Hannes, *Cooperation in Finland*. London, Williams & Norgate, 1916.

Gide, Charles, *Consumers' Cooperative Societies*. New York, Knopf, 1922.

Gjoeres, Axel, *Cooperation in Sweden*, trans. by John Downie. Manchester, Eng., Cooperative Union, 1927.

Harris, Emerson P., *Cooperation, the Hope of the Consumer*. New York, The Macmillan Company, 1918.

Herrick and Ingalls, *Rural Credits*. New York, D. Appleton & Co., 1914.

Hirsch, Max, *Democracy Versus Socialism*. Henry George School, 1939.

Holyoake, George Jacob, *History of Cooperation*. New York, E.P. Dutton & Co., Inc., 1906.

———, *Rochdale Pioneers*. Manchester, Eng., Cooperative Union, 1892.

Hough, E. M., *Cooperative Movement in India*. London, P. S. King & Son, 1932.

Hunter, Robert, *Revolution*. New York, Harper & Brothers, 1940.

Johns Hopkins University Studies, *History of Cooperation in the United States*, 1888.

Kallen, Horace M., *Decline and Rise of the Consumer*. New York, Appleton-Century Co., 1936.

Kayden, E. M., and Antsiferov, A. N., *Cooperative Movement in Russia During the War*. New Haven, Yale University Press, 1929.

Kress, A. J., *Capitalism, Cooperation, Communism*. Washington, D. C., Ransdell, 1932.

———, *Introduction to the Cooperative Movement*. New York, Harper & Brothers, 1941.

Kropotkin, Peter, *Mutual Aid*. New York, Knopf, 1925.

———, *The Conquest of Bread*. New York, G. P. Putnam's Sons, 1906.

Lersch, Heinrich, *Die Pioniere Von Eulenburg*. Gutenberg, 1934.

Lucas, James, *Cooperative Movement in Scotland*. Manchester, Eng., Cooperative Union, 1920.

Mead, M., *Cooperation and Competition Among Primitive Peoples*. McGraw-Hill, 1937.

Mercer, T. W., *Dr. William King and the Cooperator*. Manchester, Eng., Cooperative Union, 1922.

Nock, A. J., *Our Enemy the State*. New York, W. Morrow & Co., 1935.

Odhe, Thorsten, *Finland, A Nation of Cooperators*, trans. by John Downie. London, Williams & Norgate, 1931.

Oerne, A. E., *Cooperative Ideals and Problems,* trans. by John Downie. Manchester, Eng., Cooperative Union, 1926.

Ogata, Kiyoshi, *Cooperative Movement in Japan*. London, P. S. King & Son, 1923.

Oppenheimer, Franz, *The State*. New York, Vanguard Press, 1920.

Paul, L. A., *Cooperation in U. S. S. R.* London, V. Gollancz, 1934.

People's Year Book, Manchester, Eng., C. W. S., Annual.

Popper-Lynkens, Josef, *Die Allgemeine Naehrpflicht*. Rikola Verlag, 1923.

Randall and Daggett, *Consumers' Cooperative Adventures*. Whitewater Press, 1937.

Redfern, Percy, *The Consumer's Place in Society*. Manchester, Eng., Cooperative Union, 1920.

——, *John T. W. Mitchell*. Manchester, Eng., Cooperative Union, 1924.

——, *Story of the C. W. S., 1863–1913*. Manchester, Eng., Cooperative Wholesale Society, 1913.

Rocker, Rudolph, *Nationalism and Culture*. New York, Covici-Friede, 1937.

Shadid, M., *A Doctor for the People*. New York, Vanguard Press, 1940.

——, *Principles of Cooperative Medicine*. Elk City, Okla., Communicy Hospital, 1939.

Sonnichsen, Albert, *Consumers Cooperation*. New York, The Macmillan Company, 1919.

Spencer, Herbert, *The Man Versus the State*. Mitchell Kennerly, 1916.

Tucker, D. S., *Evolution of People's Banks.* New York, Columbia University Press, 1922.

Turner, H. H., *Case Studies of Consumers' Cooperatives.* Columbia University Press, 1941.

U. S. Department of Labor, *Organization and Management of Consumers Cooperative Associations and Clubs* (Bulletin No. 665). Washington, Government Printing Office, 1941.

——, *Organization and Management of Cooperative Gasoline and Oil Associations* (Bulletin No. 606). Washington, Government Printing Office, 1934.

——, *Organization and Management of Cooperative Housing Associations* (Bulletin No. 608). Washington, Government Printing Office, 1934.

Voorhis, Jerry, *The Morale of Democracy.* Georgetown Press, 1941.

Walter, Karl, *Cooperation and Charles Gide.* London, P. S. King & Son, 1933.

——, *Cooperation in Changing Italy.* London, P. S. King & Son, 1934.

Warbasse, J. P. See page ii.

Ward, Leo C., *Ourselves Incorporated.* New York, Harper & Brothers, 1945.

Wolff, Henry W., *People's Banks.* London, P. S. King & Son, 1919.

Woolf, Leonard, *Cooperation and the Future of Industry.* London, Allen & Unwin, 1918.

PERIODICALS

Review of International Cooperation. London, Eng., International Cooperative Alliance.

Consumers' Cooperation. New York, The Cooperative League of the U. S. A. 1914 to 1943, indexed.

Co-op. Chicago, National Cooperatives, Inc.

(See *People's Year Book* for other periodicals.)

INDEX

320

30130

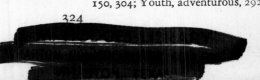

DATE DUE

GAYLORD			PRINTED IN U.S.A.